JOURNEY TO PSYCHOLOGY

College Admissions & Profiles

Rachel A. Winston, Ph.D.

Lizard Publishing is not sponsored by any college. While data was derived by school, state, or nationally published sources, some statistics may be out of date as published sources vary widely based upon the date of submission and currency of numbers. Attempts were made to obtain the best information during the writing of this book from, NCES, U.S. Census Bureau, U.S. Department of Education, Common Data Set, College Board, U.S. News & World Report, college, and organizational sites. Descriptions of colleges are a compilation of college website information as well as student, faculty, and staff interviews with individuals and often from unique experiences and impressions. Attempts were made to triangulate multiple points of light. If you would like to share program information, data, or an impression of a specific college, please write to Lizard Publishing at the address below or at the e-mail address: *collegeguide@yahoo.com*

Lizard Publishing, 7700 Irvine Center Drive, Suite 800, Irvine, CA 92618 *www.lizard-publishing.com*

Lizard Publishing creates, designs, produces, and distributes books and resources to provide academic, admissions, and career information. Our mental process is fueled by three tenets:

- Ignite the hunger to learn and the passion to make a difference

- Illuminate the expanse of knowledge by sharing cutting edge thinking

- Innovate to create a world that makes the transition from dreams to reality

We work with academic leaders who transform the educational landscape to publish relevant content and advise students of their educational and professional options, with the aim of developing 21st-century learners and leaders. We also work with students to publish their books and present widely diverse ideas to the college/graduate school-bound community. With headquarters in Irvine, California, Lizard Publishing works virtually with authors to edit, publish, and distribute both hard copy and paperback books.

This book was published in the U.S.A. Lizard Publishing is a premium quality provider of educational reference, career guidance, and motivational publications/merchandise for global learners, educators, and stakeholders in education.

Book design by Michelle Tahan *www.michelletahan.com*

Book formatting by Obinna Chinemerem Ozuo

Book website: *www.collegelizard.com*

LIZARD PUBLISHING

This book is dedicated to Caley Lynch, Hannah Karabian, and David Shapiro who epitomize empathy, support, wisdom, and professionalism.

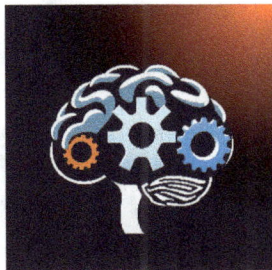

ACKNOWLEDGMENTS

There is never enough room to acknowledge every person. Numerous people contributed to my perspective regarding psychology, neuroscience, medicine, innovation, and education. Students, faculty, counselors, and researchers added to my knowledge base or taught me indelible lessons. Over a lifetime of experiences working with students, I am wiser and more worldly.

I gratefully acknowledge Michelle Tahan, Jasmine Jhunjhnuwala, E. Liz Kim, Jacqueline Xu, and Chenoa Robbins as well as my family, friends, colleagues, and professors. With profound gratitude, I also acknowledge those I have known in the universes of medicine, psychology, counseling, and education.

As a faculty member in the UCLA College Counseling Certificate Program, I met many dedicated counselors who devote their lives to serving and supporting students. Meaningful contributions to this book have also been made indirectly by admissions representatives, college counselors, and faculty members who took a special interest in its success.

I would also like to thank the thousands of students I have taught, counseled, or supported in my nearly four decades of service.

"If I see so far, it is because I stand on the shoulders of giants."
Isaac Newton

Isaac Newton once said, "If I see so far, it is because I stand on the shoulders of giants." A few of those giants whose broad shoulders lift ed me higher and helped teach invaluable lessons include Shauna Bahri, George Barsoom, Dania Baseel, Lauren Bayeh, Lisa Blair, Pria & Ria Chawla, Lana Debboneh, Peter Liang, Allie Maloney, Dario Mena, Hana Moradi, Ara Moran, Nickon Sabahi, Tala Salman, Max Sheng, Ava Tazerouni, Michelle Temby, Natalie, Jayden Villegas, and Nick Wei

Finally, there would be no book covering university psychology programs and no career in college admissions counseling without the support of Robert Helmer, whose tireless efforts support me every single day.

ABOUT THE AUTHOR

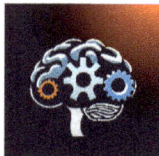

D r. Rachel A. Winston is a tireless student advocate. She has served the educational community as a university professor, college advisor, statistician, researcher, author, cryptanalyst, motivational speaker, publishing executive, and lifelong student. As one of the leading experts in college counseling and an award-winning faculty member, Dr. Winston has spent her lifetime learning, teaching, mentoring, and coaching students. Her counseling practice centers around college admissions, college essays, portfolios, and intellectual conversations about life and career pursuits.

She started college at thirteen and graduated from college programs in such widely ranging disciplines as chemistry, mathematics, computers, liberal arts, international relations, negotiation, conflict resolution, peacebuilding, business administration, higher education leadership, interpreting, college counseling, and publishing. Throughout her education, she attended and graduated from Harvard, University of Chicago, University of Texas, GWU, UCLA, Syracuse, CSUF, CSUDH, Pepperdine, Claremont Graduate University, and Gallaudet University.

Her position working in Washington, D.C. on Capitol Hill and with the White House in the 1980s took her to approximately a hundred universities training campaign managers at colleges from Colorado to California, thoroughly dotting the western states. Later, she led college tours with students and their families on road trips throughout the United States. She has taught or counseled thousands of students over her career and speaks at conferences and academic programs throughout the world.

As a professor and avid writer for numerous publications, she won the 2012 McFarland Literary Achievement Award, Bletchley Park Cryptanalyst Award, and numerous other awards, including Faculty Member of the Year, Leadership Tomorrow Leader of the Year, and college service and leadership awards. While studying Human Capital at Claremont Graduate University, she was a scholarship recipient at the Drucker School of Management. She was also elected to the statewide Board of Governors for the Faculty Association for California Community Colleges, where she served on their executive committee.

She also served as a faculty member for the UCLA College Counselor Certificate Program and the Director of Mathematics at Brandman University. She taught at Embry Riddle Aeronautical University, Chapman University, Cal State Fullerton, and a handful of California Community Colleges, including Cerro Coso College where she represented the entire faculty as the Academic Senate President and retired in 2016. Over her career, she taught mathematics on television, in small and large lecture halls, online, and via live interactive satellite and telecourses.

AUTHOR'S NOTE

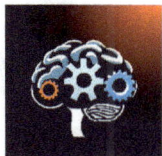

You are reading this book because you are considering admission to colleges where you open the doors to the worlds of psychology and cognitive science. Whatever route you took to get to this point, you are in the right place. Right now, you need to gather information to make informed decisions.

While many people offer advice, suggestions differ. Friends will tell you the 'right' way or the way their neighbor was accepted. Graciously accept this anecdotal information, pursuing photography with your heart and mind as you commit to learning more.

Dig deeper to consider both expert and current information from counselors who have worked with hundreds of students. Changes in programs, curricula, requirements, and links happen each year.

Doublecheck each program's specifics yourself. Each school's profile information is current as of March 2025. However, since researching this book, changes may have taken place. There are other college guidebooks written by talented and experienced counselors, though none like this book on psychology. Nevertheless, I admire and cheer on their efforts.

> "We are what we think. All that we are arises with our thoughts. With our thoughts, we make the world."
> — Buddha

This book, providing lists of colleges, admissions information, and profiles, is different in that it also offers unique tidbits. I hope you find the information valuable. Your job is to begin early by assembling lists of possible schools to consider. Create a road map and set yourself on a clear path.

If you see an error in this book or even a suggestion for a future edition, please write to Dr. Rachel A. Winston at collegeguide@yahoo.com. We will fix the entry with the next printed version. All of that said, this book was written with you in mind.

This book contains a wealth of information. Meanwhile, there are also Internet sites that contain free downloads, FAQs, testimonials, and offers to help you with your applications. Some of these advisors are knowledgeable and provide valuable assistance. Unfortunately, students and parents often hunt around the web, searching for a tremendous number of hours to seek the information they need. This book aims to resolve this problem with college admissions data and profiles to make your search easier.

For now, though, I will assume you want to attend college to study psychology and are reading this book to find programs that will get you on your way toward your goal. As a talented, education focused candidate who is willing to work very hard, you are in the right place. In these programs, you will explore your creative mental capabilities while collaborating in hands-on projects. To begin, mastery of biology, psychology, and statistics are requirements for success.

As you investigate colleges, you will find differences in programs, equipment, methods, priorities, or first-year requirements. At some schools, you will not declare a major until your second year. Either way, this book will help you reach your goal. Applying to and writing essays for each application will require research. Discover why each program you are considering may be right for you and determine the specific reasons why you are a good fit.

While you might believe that colleges are relatively similar, each program's nuances make them unique. These small differences may seem confusing. My goal is to demystify the information and process.

CONTENTS

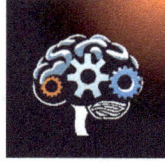

CHAPTER 1
PAST, PRESENT, & FUTURE OF PSYCHOLOGY

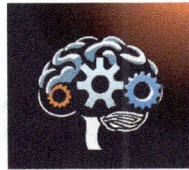

"The goal of education is not to increase the amount of knowledge but to create the possibilities for a child to invent and discover, to create individuals who are capable of doing new things."

– Jean Piaget

E very aspect of psychology is undergoing a revolution. Artificial intelligence is leading the way to advanced discoveries in how and why we think and behave, deepening our understanding of the human mind. With each new discovery, researchers are uncovering insights that could redefine cognition, behavior, human interaction, and mental health. Whether you are fascinated by the mysteries of consciousness, eager to contribute to mental healthcare advancements, or intrigued by the psychology of decision-making, there has never been a better time to study psychology. With the field rapidly evolving, students today have the unique opportunity to be at the forefront of discoveries that will shape the future.

College research centers are exploring human interaction and brain behavior on multiple levels. The field is data-driven. Today, we not only have access to volumes of statistical information that can be accessed from the Internet, calculations can also be performed instantaneously with software that can provide insights into the choices people make in foods, activities, and connections. Abnormal psychology is undergoing a transformation, too, with our deeper understandings of electrochemical and biochemical processes. Inspiration to study this field is a great starting point. However, a thorough grounding in statistics, biology, and even basic computer programming will be a plus on your quest to understand choices, actions, and ruminations.

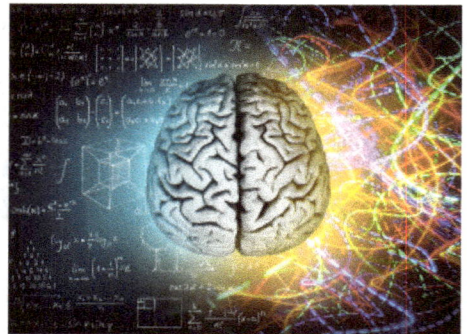

FUTURISTIC PSYCHOLOGY IS NO LONGER SCIENCE FICTION: NEUROPSYCHOLOGY AND BRAIN MAPPING

One of the most exciting frontiers in psychology is neuroscience, the study of how brain function impacts cognition and behavior. Advancements in brain imaging technology, such as functional MRI and magnetoencephalography, allow scientists to study real-time neural activity in a way that was never before possible. Imagine watching your brain activity with enhanced fMRI video in real time. It's all too exciting. While opportunities abound, dangers lurk. Nevertheless, progress is moving more swiftly than you might think.

Artificial intelligence, quantum chips, and innovative inspiration are converging in a symphony of activity. New technologies allow researchers to gain insights from multiple points of light and integrate findings from a wide array of data and observations. Researchers at institutions such as Harvard University, Stanford University, and Johns Hopkins University are exploring how specific brain regions are involved in learning, memory, emotion, and mental health.

This field is particularly intriguing for those interested in understanding conditions such as Alzheimer's disease, ADHD, or traumatic brain injuries. Imagine being part of a team developing early detection methods for dementia or helping patients with brain injuries regain cognitive functions. Insights from neuropsychology are bridging the gap between neuroscience and psychology, offering unparalleled avenues for exploration.

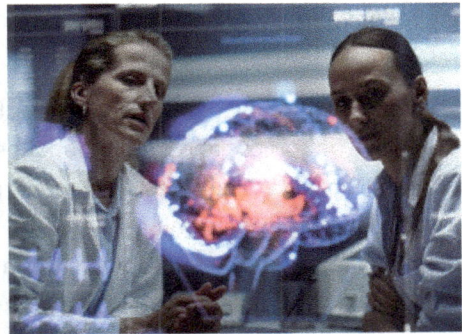

ARTIFICIAL INTELLIGENCE, ROBOTICS AND PSYCHOLOGY

The intersection of artificial intelligence and psychology is opening new dimensions in understanding human behavior. AI is now being used to analyze patterns of thought and action. The next steps include predicting and preventing mental health crises. Additionally, advancements in robotics are inspiring personalized digital therapists to analyze brain activity and support human efficiencies. At institutions like MIT, the University of California, Berkeley, and Carnegie Mellon, researchers are using machine learning to detect early signs of depression, anxiety, and schizophrenia based on speech patterns, facial expressions, and social media activity.

One of the most fascinating projects in this space is the development of AI-driven mental health applications. These virtual psychologists are designed to provide immediate support and even adjust their approach based on individual user needs. This area of exploration present opportunities to shape the future of mental health care through AI innovations.

THE SCIENCE OF HAPPINESS AND POSITIVE PSYCHOLOGY

While psychology has historically focused on mental illness, there is a growing movement regarding positive psychology. This field emphasizes gratitude, engagement, accomplishment, positive emotions, and the overall science of well-being. This research area was advanced by psychology professors Martin Seligman, who began his work at Cornell and continued at the University of Pennsylvania, and Mihaly Csikszentmihalyi, who significantly advanced this area of study at the University of Chicago and Claremont Graduate University. Researchers at Yale, Harvard, Michigan, and UT Austin are also at the forefront of studying what makes life meaningful, how to cultivate happiness, and the best methods for fostering resilience.

Imagine helping people live more fulfilling lives by investigating the factors that drive happiness and motivation. Research in positive psychology is shaping policies, workplace cultures, and educational systems. Corporations and academic institutions are transforming environments into hubs where people feel engaged, connected, and respected. Universities are now offering entire courses and research labs dedicated to understanding happiness, emotional intelligence, and life satisfaction. Thus, with numerous possibilities to examine data, you might consider focusing on personal and societal well-being.

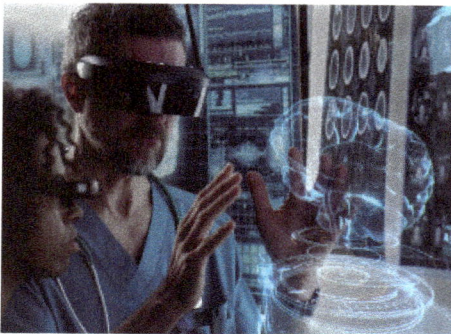

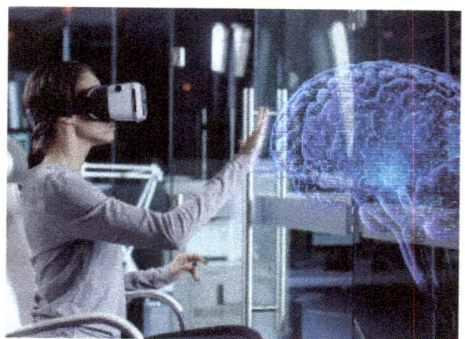

THE PSYCHOLOGY OF VIRTUAL REALITY
AND HUMAN PERCEPTION

Virtual reality is no longer just for gaming. Scientists are using VR to help open the doors to recuperative environments and futuristic spaces, helping individuals with therapy, adaptation, and engagement in the transformative worlds of tomorrow. This advancing topic, combining technology with perception, is wide open. Researchers at Stanford and the University of Southern California are using VR to study phobias, PTSD, and cognitive rehabilitation. By creating immersive environments, these scientists simulate anxiety-inducing situations and help patients overcome fears in controlled settings.

Technology and robotics are taking the lead. If you are fascinated by perception and cognition, this field offers an exciting blend of digital spaces and psychology. The implications extend beyond therapy. Researchers are exploring how VR can train astronauts for space missions, assist in stroke recovery, and enhance empathy by allowing users to experience life from different perspectives. VR can take people to locations in the world they may not otherwise have the opportunity to visit where they can experience euphoria, serve on an investigative archeological team, or perceive love and companionship.

SOCIAL MEDIA AND MENTAL HEALTH

The impact of social media on mental health is one of the most hotly debated topics in psychology today. Universities such Columbia, Princeton, and UCLA are conducting groundbreaking research on how platforms like TikTok, Instagram, Facebook, and X influence self-esteem, anxiety, and social interactions.

Students entering these areas of study consider how rapid scrolling of random inputs influence behavior. Questions abound. How does screen time affect brain development? Can social media be designed to promote psychological well-being instead of addiction? Researchers are even collaborating with tech companies to create healthier digital environments. While most researchers believe social media does impact mental health, questions remain as to what, how, and why. Psychology researchers are entertaining possibilities about the real-world impacts of cell phones and potentially future implanted devices.

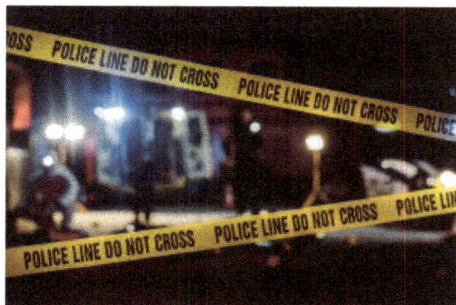

FORENSIC PSYCHOLOGY AND CRIMINAL BEHAVIOR

Crime dramas often depict forensic psychologists profiling serial killers, but the real work of forensic psychology is even more intriguing. Universities such as John Jay College of Criminal Justice, UCI, and the University of Florida conduct research on delinquincy, lie detection, and eyewitness testimony. Especially with the advanced capabilities of artificial intelligence, new possibilities open the doors to understanding the psychology of criminal behavior.

Forensic science is closely related, though more science-oriented. Still, there is a need to understand the psychology of unsubs, a term used by law enforcement to describe unknown subjects, particularly in criminal profiling and investigations.

Students interested in psychology and law will find this field particularly exciting. Recent studies challenge the reliability of memory in courtroom testimony, and psychologists are working with legal professionals to develop better interrogation methods that reduce false confessions. Forensic psychology is an electrifying path if you seek to combine psychology with justice.

THE FUTURE OF CLINICAL PSYCHOLOGY AND PSYCHEDELIC RESEARCH

Perhaps one of the most controversial but promising areas of psychology is psychedelic research. Scientists at Johns Hopkins, NYU, and UCSF are studying the use of psychedelic-assisted therapy to treat depression, PTSD, and addiction.

Recent clinical trials have shown that substances like psilocybin (found in magic mushrooms) can have profound, long-lasting effects on mental health when administered in therapeutic settings. The results are so promising that the FDA has granted breakthrough designation to some psychedelic treatments. If you are fascinated by novel approaches to mental health care, this is an intriguing field to explore.

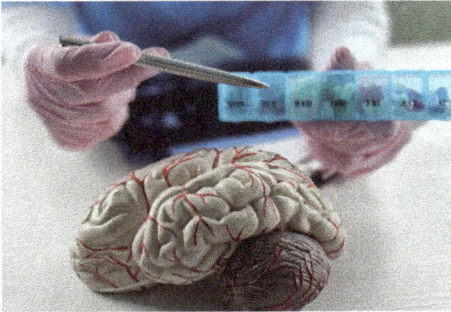

WHY STUDY PSYCHOLOGY NOW

With so many groundbreaking discoveries happening in psychology, there has never been a more exciting time to enter the field. The demand for psychologists is growing, particularly in mental health, AI-human interaction, and criminology. Whether you dream of working in cutting-edge research, clinical practice, or even tech industries, a psychology degree provides versatile career options.

Moreover, psychology is at the heart of understanding humanity. By studying psychology, you will gain critical thinking skills, a deep understanding of human behavior, and the ability to make meaningful contributions to society. Whether you want to improve mental health care, innovate in AI, or revolutionize education, psychology is the gateway to a future filled with possibility.

The real problem is not whether machines think but whether men do.
— B.F. Skinner

THE EVOLUTION OF PSYCHOLOGY

Psychology has undergone numerous changes over the centuries. Conceptualizations of human perception, cognition, behavior, and mental illness have evolved from philosophical speculation to a rigorous empirical science. Each historical period has been built upon the foundations of the past, refining theories, methodologies, and applications. Transformations in the study and applications of psychology can be traced through five major periods:

1. Ancient and Pre-Modern Foundations
2. The Birth of Modern Psychology
3. The Rise of Schools of Thought
4. The Expansion of Psychological Theories
5. Contemporary Advancements in Understanding Cognition & Neuroscience

The ancient and pre-modern foundations of psychology laid the groundwork for later scientific exploration. Thinkers such as Plato and Aristotle debated the nature of knowledge and the human mind, setting the stage for future inquiries into cognition and behavior. Philosophers like René Descartes and John Locke expanded on these ideas, introducing concepts of dualism and empiricism, which later influenced experimental psychology. The shift toward a systematic study of human thought became possible as these early theorists questioned how the mind and body interact.

The birth of modern psychology in the late 19th century marked a significant turning point. Wilhelm Wundt established the first psychology laboratory, focusing on introspection and structuralism, while William James emphasized functionalism, shaping psychology as a distinct field of study. The emergence of psychoanalysis, spearheaded by Sigmund Freud, introduced the importance of the unconscious mind, childhood experiences, and personality development. These contributions led to new frameworks that examined the mind beyond mere philosophy, incorporating scientific observation.

The early 20th century saw the rise of major schools of thought, including behaviorism, psychoanalysis, and cognitive psychology. John B. Watson and B.F. Skinner shifted the focus to observable behavior, leading to advances in learning theories. Meanwhile, Carl Jung and Alfred Adler refined Freud's ideas, contributing to personality and counseling psychology. Jean Piaget and Lev Vygotsky pioneered research in cognitive development, demonstrating the active role of experience and social interaction in shaping intelligence. These varied perspectives broadened psychology's scope, influencing education, therapy, and research methodologies.

The mid-20th century brought further expansion with humanistic psychology and social psychology. Figures such as Carl Rogers and Abraham Maslow emphasized self-actualization and personal growth, shifting attention toward individual agency. Simultaneously, psychologists like Solomon Asch and Stanley Milgram investigated social influence and obedience, highlighting the impact of societal factors on human behavior. The growth of cognitive psychology, led by Noam Chomsky and Daniel Kahneman, refined our understanding of perception, memory, and decision-making, further bridging psychology with neuroscience.

Advances in technology and neuroscience have revolutionized contemporary psychology. Researchers such as Elizabeth Loftus and Steven Pinker explore memory and language, while Martin Seligman's positive psychology movement promoted well-being and resilience. Mihály Csíkszentmihályi, known for his work on flow theory, added to conceptual foundations in positive psychology. Neuroscientific imagery and study allow for deeper investigations into brain function, consciousness, and emotional processing. These modern developments continue to build upon historical theories, making psychology a dynamic and ever-evolving discipline that integrates past wisdom with cutting-edge discoveries.

The world needs psychologists now more than ever. As technology reshapes our lives and mental health challenges increase globally, those with expertise in psychology will play a pivotal role in shaping the future. The advancements happening today in neuroscience, AI, mental health, and forensic psychology are paving the way for a new era in psychological science. If you are eager to explore the depths of the human mind and contribute to transformative change, the time to start your journey in psychology is now.

CHAPTER 2

COLLEGES & CAREERS IN PSYCHOLOGY

"Limitations live only in our minds. But if we use our imaginations, our possibilities become limitless."

– Jamie Paolinetti

Psychology, the scientific study of human behavior and mental processes, offers numerous avenues of pursuit. You will never be bored with the expanding number of directions you can take. If you are intrigued by understanding people, improving communication, and solving real-world problems, psychology is a rewarding field.

Learning the art and science of psychology will help you develop critical thinking, problem-solving, and analytical skills. You will gain expertise in conducting research, interpreting psychological studies, and using statistics. Furthermore, you will become a more confident interpersonal speaker by understanding human interactions, emotions, and behaviors.

The pandemic taught society to consider outcomes when people are confined and have limited freedom. Without the socialization of school, sports, and group environments, people needed to be industrious in finding new hobbies, pursuits, and ways to connect. As life and the world around us changed in 2020, people wondered about how to improve mental health, well-being, cognitive development, and emotional regulation.

With a broad perspective on mental health's importance in society, psychology opens doors to fields of interest such as healthcare, business, education, human resources, social services, and research. Studying psychology offers numerous opportunities, allowing individuals to work in healthcare, education, business, criminal justice, and research, with career options depending on the level of education pursued. Some areas only require a bachelor's degree, while others require a graduate degree for specialization.

Career Options with a BA/BS (entry-level assistant/technical positions)

Behavioral Health Technician – Assist therapists in mental health facilities.
Career Counselor Assistant – Assist in career planning and job placement.
Case Manager – Support individuals in healthcare or social services.

Human Resources Specialist – Recruit, train, and support employees.
Market Research Analyst – Study consumer behavior and trends.
Psychiatric Technician – Support patients with mental health conditions.
Rehabilitation Specialist – Help individuals with disabilities or injuries.
Sales & Marketing Representative – Utilize psychology in consumer behavior.
Social Services Coordinator – Work in non-profits or community outreach.
Substance Abuse Counselor (w/Certification) – Assist individuals in recovery programs.

Careers Requiring a Master's or Doctorate (counseling/clinical practice/research/education)

Clinical Psychologist (Ph.D./Psy.D.) – Diagnose/treat mental disorders.
Counseling Psychologist (MA, MS, Ph.D.) – Provide therapy for individuals and families.
Forensic Psychologist (Ph.D./Psy.D.) – Apply psychology in legal and criminal justice settings.
Industrial-Organizational Psychologist (MA, MS, Ph.D.) – Apply psychological principles to workplace productivity and organizational behavior.
Marriage & Family Therapist (MA, MS) – Counsel couples and families.
Neuropsychologist (Ph.D.) – Study brain-behavior relationships.
Psychiatrist (M.D.) – Serve as a medical doctor specializing in mental health treatment.
Research Scientist (Ph.D.) – Conduct psychological studies in universities or research institutions.
School Psychologist (MA, MS, Ed.S.) – Work with students on academic and emotional well-being.
University Professor (Ph.D.) – Teach and conduct research in higher education.

UNIVERSITY PSYCHOLOGY RESEARCH

With technology's progress in analyzing images and data, numerous innovative areas of research are gaining prominence. Here are a few subspecialties in psychology for you to consider, along with universities that lead the way in new discoveries.

Addiction Neuroscience & Behavioral Pharmacology: Study brain mechanisms behind addiction and substance abuse treatment.
Leading Universities: Colorado-Denver, Columbia, Emory, Florida, Harvard, Johns Hopkins, Michigan, Pitt, South Carolina, UCLA, UCSD, UCSF, UNC Chapel Hill, UPenn, UT Austin, Wash U in St. Louis, Washington, and Yale

Artificial Intelligence & Machine Learning in Cognitive Science: Apply AI to model and understand cognitive functions.
Leading Universities: Carnegie Mellon, Cornell, Georgia Tech, Harvard, Maryland, Michigan, MIT, Stanford, Michigan, Princeton, Stanford, UC Berkeley, UCLA, UCSD, UIUC, UNC Chapel Hill, UPenn, UT Austin, Washington, and Yale

Behavioral Neuroscience: Examine the biological bases of behavior.
Leading Universities: Arizona, Boston U, Colorado, Emory, Florida, Harvard, Johns Hopkins, IU Bloomington, Iowa, Michigan, Minnesota, Northeastern, Northwestern, NYU, Pitt, Princeton, Rice, UChicago, UCLA, UCSD, UNC Chapel Hill, UPenn, Vanderbilt, and Wisconsin-Madison

Brain-Computer Interfaces: Technological development that enables direct communication between the brain and external devices.
Leading Universities: Brown, Carnegie Mellon, Columbia, Duke, Florida, Georgia Tech, Johns Hopkins, Maryland, Michigan, Minnesota, MIT, Pitt, Rice, Stanford, UC Berkeley, UCSD, UIUC, UPenn, USC, UT Austin, Washington, and Wisconsin-Madison

Cognitive Neuroscience: Neural mechanisms underlying cognitive processes.
Leading Universities: Brown, Columbia, Duke, Emory, Florida, Harvard, Johns Hopkins, Michigan, MIT, Northwestern, NYU, Pitt, Princeton, Rice, Stanford, UChicago, UC Berkeley, UCLA, UCSD, UIUC, UNC Chapel Hill, UPenn, UT Dallas, Vanderbilt, Wash U in St. Louis, Washington, Wisconsin-Madison, and Yale

Cognitive Rehabilitation & Neuropsychology: Design interventions to improve cognitive functions after injury.
Leading Universities: Arizona, Brown, Boston U, Emory, Florida, Harvard, Johns Hopkins, Michigan, Northwestern, Pitt, UCLA, UCSD, UPenn, UT Dallas, Washington, and Wisconsin-Madison

Computational Neuroscience: Math models used to understand brain function.
Leading Universities: Brown, CalTech, Carnegie Mellon, Columbia, Duke, Emory, Georgia Tech, Harvard, Johns Hopkins, MIT, Northwestern, NYU, Princeton, Rice, Stanford, UChicago, UC Berkeley, UCSD, UPenn, Washington, and Yale

Computational Psychiatry & Mental Health Diagnostics: AI and computational models used to advance mental health diagnosis and treatment.
Leading Universities: Brown, Carnegie Mellon, Columbia, Duke, Harvard, Johns Hopkins, Michigan, MIT, NYU, Pitt, Princeton, Stanford, UChicago, UC Berkeley, UCLA, UCSD, UNC Chapel Hill, UPenn, UT Austin, Washington, and Yale

Consciousness & the Mind-Body Problem: The neural basis of consciousness.
Leading Universities: Arizona, Brown, CalTech, Carnegie Mellon, Columbia, Duke, Emory, Harvard, Johns Hopkins, MIT, NYU, Northwestern, Princeton, Rice, Stanford, UChicago, UC Berkeley, UCLA, UCSD, UPenn, and Yale

Developmental Psychology and Neuroscience: Brain development and socialization from infancy through adulthood.
Leading Universities: Duke, Emory, Harvard, Johns Hopkins, Michigan, Minnesota, MIT, NYU, Northwestern, Princeton, Rice, Stanford, UChicago, UC Berkeley, UCLA, UCSD, UNC Chapel Hill, UPenn, Virginia, Wash U in St. Louis, Washington, & Yale

Neurodegenerative Diseases: Alzheimer's and Parkinson's and the development of therapeutic interventions.
Leading Universities: Brown, Columbia, Duke, Emory, Harvard, Johns Hopkins, Mayo Clinic, Michigan, MIT, Northwestern, Stanford, UChicago, UC Berkeley, UCLA, UCSD, UCSF, UPenn, UT Dallas, Vanderbilt, Wash U in St. Louis, Washington, & Yale

Neuroeconomics: Economics and psychology in the study of decision-making.
Leading Universities: CalTech, Carnegie Mellon, Columbia, Duke, Harvard, Johns Hopkins, Michigan, MIT, Northwestern, NYU, Princeton, Stanford, UChicago, UC Berkeley, UCLA, UCSD, UPenn, USC, Virginia, Wash U in St. Louis, & Yale

Neuroethics: Ethical issues related to neuroscience research and applications.
Leading Universities: Brown, Columbia, Duke, Emory, Harvard, Johns Hopkins, Michigan, Minnesota, MIT, Pitt, Princeton, Stanford, UChicago, UC Berkeley, UCLA, UCSD, UPenn, UT Austin, Vanderbilt, Virginia, Wash U, St. Louis, Washington, & Yale

Neurogenetics & Psychiatric Genetics: The genetic basis of neurological and psychiatric disorders.
Leading Universities: Arizona, CalTech, Colby, Colorado, Columbia, Georgia State, Harvard, Harvey Mudd, IU Bloomington, Johns Hopkins, Knox College, Lehigh, MIT, New Mexico State, Purdue, Stanford, UChicago, UCLA, UCSF, UPenn, Wash U in St. Louis, & Yale

Neuroimaging & Brain Mapping: Techniques to visualize brain structures and functions.
Leading Universities: CalTech, Carnegie Mellon, Columbia, Duke, Emory, Harvard, Johns Hopkins, Minnesota, MIT, Pitt, Princeton, Stanford, UChicago, UC Berkeley, UCLA, UCSD, UCSF, UPenn, USC, UT Austin, Wash U in St. Louis, & Washington

Neuroplasticity & Brain Adaptation: The brain's ability to reorganize itself by forming new neural connections.
Leading Universities: Boston U, CalTech, Columbia, Duke, Emory, Harvard, Johns Hopkins, Michigan, MIT, Pitt, Princeton, Stanford, UChicago, UC Berkeley, UCLA, UCSD, UCSF, UPenn, USC, UT Austin, Wash U in St. Louis, & Washington

Psychopharmacology: The effects of drugs on the mind and behavior.
Leading Universities: Columbia, Duke, Emory, Florida, Harvard, Johns Hopkins, Michigan, MIT, Northwestern, Pitt, Princeton, Stanford, UChicago, UC Berkeley, UCLA, UCSD, UCSF, UNC Chapel Hill, UPenn, UT Southwestern, Washington, & Yale

Sensory Analysis & Perception: Brain processing of sensory information.
Leading Universities: Brandeis, CalTech, Carnegie Mellon, Columbia, Duke, Emory, Harvard, Johns Hopkins, Minnesota, MIT, NYU, Pitt, Princeton, Stanford, UChicago, UC Berkeley, UCLA, UCSD, UPenn, UT Austin, Washington, Wisconsin, & Yale

Sleep & Circadian Rhythms: The brain's regulation of sleep & biological rhythms. *Leading Universities:* Brown, Arizona, Columbia, Harvard, Johns Hopkins, Miami, Michigan, Northwestern, Princeton, Stanford, UC Berkeley, UCLA, UPenn, & Washington

Social & Affective Psychology: Neural mechanisms of social behavior & emotion. *Leading Universities:* Dartmouth, Emory, Harvard, Johns Hopkins, Maryland, Michigan, NYU, Princeton, Stanford, UChicago, UC Berkeley, UCLA, UIUC, UNC Chapel Hill, UPenn, UT Austin, Virginia, Wash U in St. Louis, Wisconsin-Madison, & Yale

These fields offer cutting-edge research. The universities listed are among the leaders in these fields. Many of these schools appear repeatedly in different lists. Just know that psychology is a hotly researched topic at most universities. Numerous universities provide specialized opportunities for investigation, innovation and discovery. For example, the following liberal arts colleges also have excellent student-centered research programs focused on psychology.

Amherst College	Lafayette College
Barnard College	Mount Holyoke College
Bates College	Rhodes College
Bryn Mawr College	Scripps College
Colby College	Skidmore College
Connecticut College	Smith College
Dickinson College	St. Olaf College
Franklin & Marshall College	Trinity College
Gettysburg College	Union College
Kenyon College	Wheaton College

UNDERSTANDING THE MIND & TRANSFORMING LIVES

Psychology is the key to understanding the complexities of the human experience. Researchers in the field unravel the mysteries of thoughts, emotions, and behaviors, offering insights that shape our relationships, communities, and societies. To study psychology is to embark on a journey of deep inquiry that not only transforms the way we perceive the world but also empowers individuals to effectuate change. A career in psychology is more than a profession. For most students, psychology is a calling, a purpose-driven path with the goal to heal, innovate, and uplift lives.

PSYCHOLOGY TOUCHES EVERY LIFE

Psychology plays a role in every stage of life, from childhood to old age, from moments of joy to the depths of suffering. Understanding psychological principles helps us grasp why people think and act the way they do, shedding light on everything from personal relationships to workplace dynamics and from education to criminal justice. Psychology fuels progress in fields such as medicine, artificial intelligence, and human-computer interaction. The science of the mind influences thoughts and behaviors from marketing strategies to public policy and from designing learning environments to shaping rehabilitation programs.

Yet, at its core, psychology is about the human connection. Whether in a therapist's office, a research lab, or a classroom, psychology allows us to engage with people in profound ways. The underlying principles offer tools to help individuals struggling with anxiety, trauma, addiction, and relationships. The framework and therapeutic interventions help people heal, grow, and thrive.

HOPE IN A COMPLEX WORLD

We live in a world where mental health crises are at an all-time high. Stress, depression, and anxiety affect millions of people globally. The need for psychological insight has never been more urgent in the wake of the pandemic, rapid technological advancements, and shifting societal norms. Psychology stands at the forefront of mental health advocacy, offering solutions that reduce suffering and promote well-being.

Imagine being the person who helps a child overcome a crippling phobia, who gives a war veteran the tools to manage PTSD, or who guides a struggling student toward confidence and self-belief. Counseling can profoundly support individuals through life events while helping to cultivate stronger, healthier communities. In our complex world, where social issues such as homelessness, crime, and systemic inequality impact families, psychologists can make a positive impact. Every major challenge in society, from addiction to political divisiveness, benefits from psychological research and intervention.

UNLOCKING THE HUMAN MIND

What could be more fascinating than exploring the mind? Psychology invites us to investigate the hidden depths of human cognition, memory, and behavior. Why do people fall in love? What causes someone to act heroically or cruelly? What triggers happiness, creativity, or resilience in the face of adversity?

The study of psychology provides endless opportunities for curiosity and discovery. Whether you are exploring how the brain rewires itself after trauma, studying the impact of culture on personality, or diving into the science of decision-making, psychology is an intellectual adventure that never ceases to inspire.

A CAREER OF MEANING AND PURPOSE

A career in psychology is more than a way to earn a living. The field of study offers avenues to change lives and make a difference. Whether as a clinical psychologist, researcher, counselor, forensic psychologist, or organizational consultant, psychology offers a path of purpose where every insight gained can improve lives.

If you are drawn to understanding the human experience, find meaning in helping others, and are captivated by the mysteries of the mind, then psychology offers a beacon for your life's purpose. By studying psychology, you will embrace the curiosity for lifelong learning, discovery, and transformation, both for yourself and for those lives you will touch.

CHAPTER 3

SPORT PSYCHOLOGY, KINESIOLOGY, & THE PURSUIT OF ATHLETES' MENTAL HEALTH

"What you are thinking, what shape your mind is in, is what makes the biggest difference of all."

– Willie Mays

The dynamic and fast-growing field of sports and exercise psychology is transforming how we understand human potential. Once centered primarily in kinesiology programs, many psychology departments across the nation are adding classes in sports psychology, reflecting a deeper awareness of the powerful connection between the mind and body. As society embraces the value of fitness not just for athletes, but for everyone, people now also recognize that mental strength is as vital as physical training. For athletes aiming to reach the highest levels of performance, sports psychology is essential. An athlete's mental edge fuels resilience, focus, and the persistent pursuit of excellence.

Advancements in sports psychology have shed light on the relationship between emotional regulation and athletic performance. Athletic greats like Jim Abbott, Andre Agassi, Simone Biles, Tom Brady, Bethany Hamilton, LeBron James, Virat Kohli, Kylian Mbappé, Lionel Messi, Alex Morgan, Michael Phelps, Derrick Rose, Mohamed Salah, Monica Seles, and Kurt Warner exemplify remarkable determination. Kobe Bryant once explained that the path to greatness does not come without roadblocks so, "Be sad. Be mad. Be frustrated. Scream. Cry. Sulk."

Meanwhile, although Muhammad Ali, Usain Bolt, Michael Jordan, John McEnroe, Conor McGregor, Rafael Nadal, Cristiano Ronaldo, and Serena Williams used passion-filled intensity to fuel success, this technique is the exception rather than the norm. Research studies reveal that extreme emotion regulation and impulsivity are linked to decreased performance, emphasizing the importance of composure and psychological maturity for successful athletic performance.

The convergence of AI and medicine has revolutionized sports psychology. Today, performance-driven analysis is data-driven and preventive rather than reactive. Exercise routines are tailored to each athlete's cognitive and emotional profile. The technology-driven science of personalized psychology allows athletes to perform better and stay mentally healthy, confident, and balanced.

ARTIFICIAL INTELLIGENCE & PERSONALIZED MENTAL PERFORMANCE

Artificial intelligence is revolutionizing sports psychology by enabling real-time monitoring of an athlete's cognitive and emotional states. Advanced tools powered by machine learning algorithms such as BERT and neural networks can now analyze a wide array of data, including facial expressions, vocal tone, heart rate variability, and sleep-recovery metrics. A novel system that integrates BERT with XGBoost has emerged to predict psychological states with high precision, offering adaptive, personalized interventions that support peak performance. These technologies assist sports psychologists in proactively identifying early signs of stress, anxiety, burnout, or loss of focus, enabling timely and individualized mental coaching before issues escalate.

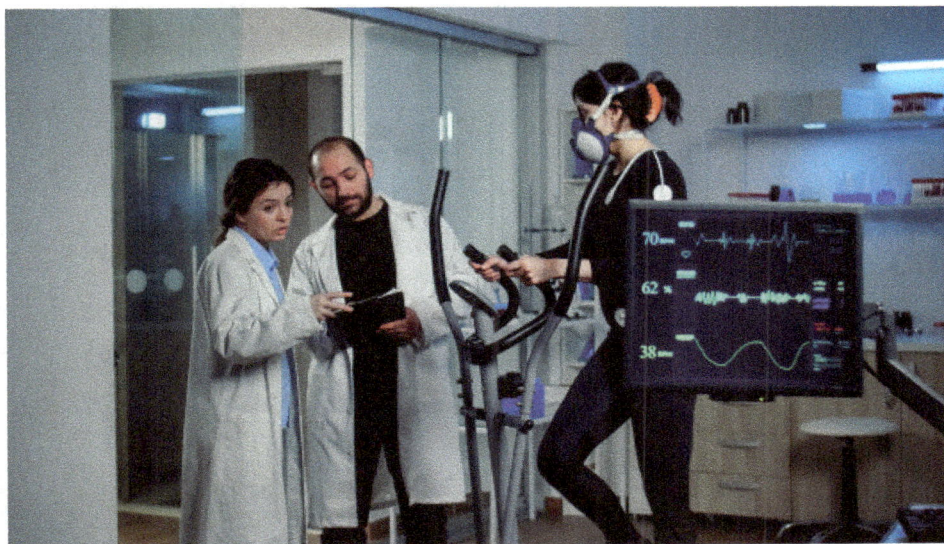

NEUROFEEDBACK & BRAIN-COMPUTER INTERFACES

Neurofeedback is a key tool in sports medicine. Medical technology offers systems where athletes can "train" their brain to stay calm, focused, or motivated during high-pressure moments. These systems track alpha and beta brain waves to provide feedback. Effective optimization is essential in split-second decision-making. Mechanisms in sports psychology allow for focus under stress, emotional regulation, and quicker reaction times.

INJURY RECOVERY & PSYCHOLOGICAL RESILIENCE

Increasingly, modern medicine focuses on physical as well as mental recovery. Physiological and psychological readiness are equally important. Novel AI tools and virtual teletherapy platforms can now monitor mood, motivation, and mental fatigue throughout the rehabilitation process. For example, athletes recovering from ACL tears may use VR and AI-guided biofeedback to overcome the fear of reinjury. Cognitive behavioral therapy apps powered by AI offer on-demand mental health support, while also improving resilience.

PREDICTIVE ANALYTICS & MENTAL FATIGUE MANAGEMENT

Artificial intelligence can process vast amounts of performance data to predict cognitive overload. By integrating training volume, travel schedules, and biometric data, coaches and psychologists can detect early signs of mental fatigue, adjust training loads, prevent psychological burnout, and optimize peak performance.

VIRTUAL REALITY AND SIMULATED PRESSURE SCENARIOS

The power of virtual reality in sports is clearly demonstrated in simulated scenarios. Virtual reality is being used to replicate high-pressure game situations in a controlled, repeatable environment. Athletes can mentally rehearse free throws, penalty kicks, or crowd pressure with full immersion, allowing sports psychologists to teach mental visualization, access self-regulation techniques, build emotional resilience, and induce muscle memory under pressure.

PROCESSING SETBACKS & FAILURE

Addressing the psychological aftermath of failure is another critical area of focus. Especially, when athletes are injured and can no longer play a sport they have competed in for a decade, they often undergo a rollercoaster of emotion and a sense of being lost in their life pursuit. Sports psychologists can made a significant difference in the lives of these individuals who need to find a new direction for their energy and commitments.

Experts advocate for systematic psychological support to help athletes cope with setbacks, emphasizing that confronting and processing failure can lead to resilience and future success. This approach includes regular psychological assessments and the development of dual-career plans to provide athletes with a broader life perspective beyond sports.

Furthermore, the transition from athletic careers to post-sport life presents unique psychological challenges. Research indicates that many former collegiate athletes experience emotional difficulties during this period, highlighting the need for effective career transition programs. Implementing psychoeducational initiatives can better prepare athletes for life after sports, addressing issues such as identity loss and coping strategies.

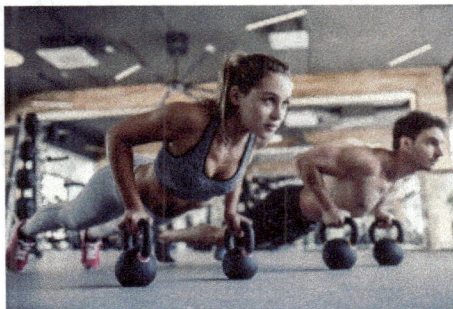

TEN UNDERGRADUATE PROGRAMS W/STRONG PROGRAMS FOCUSED ON SPORT PSYCHOLOGY

(See Chapter 18 for A List of More than 50 Universities)

Adams State University (Alamosa, CO)
Program:
BA & minor in Sport Psychology
Highlights:
Collaborative program between the Departments of Psychology & Kinesiology
Prepares students for graduate studies in sport psychology
Human Performance Lab w/treadmills, bikes, and computers

Research Focus:
Psychological principles in health, physical activity, and sports performance

Arcadia University (Glenside, PA)

Program:
BA Sport Psychology
Highlights:
Mandatory study abroad at UK universities (e.g., University of Stirling, St. Mary's University College)
Senior year includes thesis projects and internships
Coursework in behavioral neuroscience, health psychology, and statistics
Research Focus:
Cross-cultural sport psychology, athlete behavior, and psychological assessments

Barry University (Miami Shores, FL)

Program:
BS Applied Sport & Exercise Sciences w/concentration in Sport, Exercise, & Performance Psychology
Highlights:
Faculty are Certified Mental Performance Consultants
Real-world projects and community service integrated
Performance Behavior Lab w/observation & video analysis rooms
Research Focus:
Performance enhancement, mental skills training, psychological interventions in sport

California State University, Long Beach (Long Beach, CA)

Program:
BS Kinesiology w/option in Sport Psychology
Highlights:
Options include sport psychology and leadership
Prerequisites in Anatomy, Physiology, and Introductory Psychology
Multiple research labs, including one focused on sport psychology
Research Focus:
Motivation, anxiety, and psychological performance in athletes

Kent State University (Kent, OH)

Program:
BS Sport, Exercise, & Performance Psychology (also online)
Highlights:
Motivation, mental training, and stress management
Prepares students for advanced study and applied careers
Research methodology and evaluation
Research Focus:
Psychological mechanisms in sports and performance

National University (San Diego, CA)

Program:
BA Sport Psychology (also online)
Highlights:
Courses pre-reviewed for CMPC certification eligibility
Center for Performance Psychology
Publishes the *Journal on Performance Psychology*
Research Focus:
Applied performance psychology, cognitive-behavioral strategies, peak performance research

Robert Morris University (Moon Township, PA)

Program:
BS Psychology w/concentration in Sport Psychology
Highlights:
General and specialized sport psychology courses
Senior thesis and practicum
Real-world sport psychology integration
Research Focus:
Team dynamics, mental resilience, and athlete-focused interventions

Texas A&M University – Kingsville (Kingsville, TX)

Program:
BS Kinesiology w/concentration in Sport Psychology; minor in Psychology required
Highlights:
Courses include Applied Sport Psychology, Biomechanics, and Sport Economics
Human Performance Lab research and assessment
Research Focus:
Interdisciplinary research on physical performance and mental preparedness

Texas Christian University (Fort Worth, TX)

Program:
BS Kinesiology w/concentration in Sport Psychology
Highlights:
Courses include Sport Psychology, Social Psychology, Statistics, & Abnormal Psychology
Student-led research and required internships
Sport Psychology Lab
Research Focus:
Mental toughness, performance anxiety, and psychological resilience

West Virginia University (Morgantown, WV)

Program:
BS Sport & Exercise Psychology
Highlights:
Courses include Social Psychology of Sport & Psychology of Injury

Internship and practicum opportunities
Preparation for graduate programs
Research Focus:
Athlete mental health, injury recovery, and performance enhancement

INTERNATIONAL SPORTS COMPETITION:
A MULTI-BILLION-DOLLAR INDUSTRY

Athletics is a global cultural force that brings together people of all ages, backgrounds, and abilities. Sports crosses language and cultural barriers, bringing people together in a way that even diplomacy cannot. Thousands of amazing athletes compete worldwide in diverse sports. The Olympics is an excellent example of the drive and determination required to master a sport and reach the highest levels of competition with athletes from countries across the planet.

2026 WINTER OLYMPIC SPORTS – MILANO CORTINA

Alpine Skiing
Biathlon
Bobsleigh
Cross-Country Skiing
Curling
Figure Skating
Freestyle Skiing
Ice Hockey

Luge
Nordic Combined
Short Track Speed Skating
Skeleton
Ski Jumping
Ski Mountaineering
Snowboarding
Speed Skating

2028 SUMMER OLYMPIC SPORTS – LOS ANGELES

Archery	Gymnastics – Artistic
Artistic Swimming	Gymnastics – Rhythmic
Athletics (Track & Field)	Gymnastics – Trampoline
Badminton	Handball
Baseball/Softball	Judo
Basketball	Lacrosse
Beach Volleyball	Modern Pentathlon
Boxing	Rowing
Breaking	Rugby
Canoe Slalom	Sailing
Canoe Sprint	Shooting
Cricket	Skateboarding
Cycling – BMX Freestyle	Sport Climbing
Cycling – BMX Racing	Squash
Cycling – Mountain Biking	Surfing
Cycling – Road	Swimming
Cycling – Track	Table Tennis
Diving	Taekwondo
Equestrian – Dressage	Tennis
Equestrian – Eventing	Triathlon
Equestrian – Jumping	Volleyball (Indoor)
Fencing	Water Polo
Field Hockey	Weightlifting
Flag Football	Wrestling – Freestyle
Football (Soccer)	Wrestling – Greco-Roman
Golf	

Behind the roar of the stadiums and the passionate pursuit of elite athletes lies a world of professionals whose expertise makes performance possible and sustainable. Studying fields like kinesiology, sport psychology, exercise science, and sports studies offers a glimpse into the human body and mind at their peak.

Sports competition requires a team of individuals who work tirelessly in the background of this multibillion-dollar industry. These individuals support athlete's health, wellness, and education while also influencing the media and global economics. For students who are passionate about sports, movement, and human potential, these fields offer a rigorous and dynamic journey that unites science, strategy, and social impact. You could have a front row seat to a lifetime of thrilling events.

What makes the pursuit of sports business, psychology, training, medicine, and law particularly inspiring is the opportunity to stand at the intersection of biology, psychology, and performance. In kinesiology and exercise science, students explore the mechanics of motion, injury prevention, and rehabilitation, while gaining hands-on experience in laboratories, athletic settings, and clinical environments.

In sport psychology, practitioners dive deep into the mental health game of understanding motivation, resilience, team dynamics, and performance anxiety. These disciplines empower students to improve both individual lives and team outcomes. Whether the professional behind the scenes is helping an athlete overcome fear, supporting a veteran's recovery, or working on mental conditioning programs for Olympians, the career can be supremely satisfying.

Studying the realm of courses surrounding these fields offers an intellectually diverse set of topics. Furthermore, for many who are former athletes themselves, the opportunities are also deeply motivational. Imagine being the one who identifies how a change in mindset can transform an underdog into a champion or how a new strength training approach reduces injury across an entire team.

These disciplines give students a front-row seat to personal breakthroughs, collective victories, and lifelong change. The ability to use knowledge to inspire others, optimize potential, and elevate human performance makes this field uniquely fulfilling. There is something profoundly human about helping someone return to the sport they love, find purpose through movement, or tap into inner strength in the face of adversity.

Moreover, these disciplines offer students a passport into some of the most exciting sectors in today's world: professional sports, public health, education, media, and entrepreneurship. The skills students acquire in biomechanics, coaching, communication, counseling, data analysis, and leadership are transferable and in high demand.

Whether you are working with world-class athletes or designing community fitness programs, graduates in sports psychology, kinesiology, and exercise science play vital roles in shaping the present and future of sports and human well-being. And, in an era increasingly focused on mental health, equity in sports, and sustainable athletic practices, the need for skilled and ethical professionals has never been greater.

Pursuing a career in the sports industry offers a lifetime of passion, persistence, and purpose. For those who are energized by challenge, inspired by movement, and committed to improving lives, this journey offers endless avenues for discovery and contribution.

Below is a list of potential careers available to students pursuing degrees in kinesiology, sport psychology, exercise science, or sports studies:

POTENTIAL CAREERS

- Academic Researcher
- Athletic Coach
- Athletic Director
- Biomechanist
- Cardiac Rehabilitation Specialist
- Chiropractor
- Clinical Exercise Physiologist
- Community Health Coordinator
- Corporate Wellness Consultant
- Ergonomics Specialist
- Exercise Physiologist
- Fitness Director
- Health Coach
- Kinesiologist
- Massage Therapist
- Motor Behavior Specialist
- Occupational Therapist
- Orthopedic Technician
- Personal Trainer
- Physical Education Teacher
- Physical Therapist
- Recreational Therapist
- Rehabilitation Specialist
- Research Coordinator (Sports or Health Sciences)
- Sport Agent
- Sport and Performance Psychologist
- Sport Analyst or Commentator
- Sport Lawyer (with law degree)
- Sport Marketing Manager
- Sport Medicine Technician
- Sport Psychometrist
- Sports Data Analyst
- Sports Event Manager
- Strength and Conditioning Coach
- University Professor
- Wellness Program Director

"Champions aren't made in the gyms. Champions are made from something they have deep inside them – a desire, a dream, a vision."

– Muhammad Ali

CHAPTER 4

ADVANCES, COLLEGES, & CAREERS IN NEUROSCIENCE

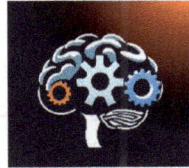

"With confidence, you have won before you have started."

– Marcus Garvey

Neuroscience is one of the most fascinating and rapidly evolving fields of study. If you choose this direction, you will leap into an exploration of the most complex and mysterious organs in the human body. Engaging in cutting-edge research will offer you endless wonder. From the moment you begin your upper-division coursework, you will explore how humans think, feel, learn, and remember. Whether you are captivated by understanding how memories are formed or how diseases like Alzheimer's ravage the mind, neuroscience is the gateway to unraveling these mysteries. Neuroscience combines cutting-edge technology with diverse fields like biology, psychology, engineering, and computer science, making the adventure dynamic, innovative, and remarkably enticing all at the same time.

Accelerating innovations in brain and nervous system science are spurred by the race to slow the neurological aging processes, cure diseases, and resolve crises in alcohol and drug addiction. Colleges, private research institutions, and medically related industries are actively exploring potential breakthroughs in this thoroughly exciting and multidisciplinary field of modern science. At the undergraduate level, neuroscience students typically engage in courses covering molecular biology, cognitive science, neuroanatomy, and neurophysiology, with opportunities for laboratory work, internships, and independent research.

As a student potentially interested in neuroscience, your path ahead is packed with endless possibilities. Top universities, such as Harvard, Stanford, and the University of Pennsylvania, are just a few of the major institutions providing world-class programs in fields from neurobiology and neuropsychology to disease progression and neuropharmacology. Your university education will offer a mix of classroom learning and hands-on research, giving you the chance to work with experts and utilize cutting-edge tools like brain imaging and neural simulation. Whether you are observing brain activity through advanced scanning techniques or studying the molecular structure of neurons, every day will bring a new discovery and precipitate novel approaches.

In MS, Ph.D., MD, or MD/Ph.D. programs, you will dive even deeper, exploring neural engineering, cognitive neuroscience, or brain-computer interfaces. These programs will push you to more fully understand the brain and embark on self-designed projects, potentially leading to transformative discoveries that change lives. Your breakthroughs may cure neurological disorders or develop technologies that allow humans to communicate directly with machines. Whether you are studying at MIT, Yale, UCLA, CalTech, Georgia Tech, the University of Rochester or another cutting-edge university, your education will empower you to think critically, creatively, and practically about how neuroscience intersects with healthcare, technology, and society.

Your pursuit of neuroscience will open the door to exciting and impactful career possibilities. You might decide to work in clinical neuroscience, helping patients with conditions like Alzheimer's, Parkinson's, or epilepsy. Alternatively, you could channel your talents into the tech industry, where your expertise in neural networks could help revolutionize artificial intelligence. Neuroscientists also work in research labs like the BRAIN Initiative, government agencies like NIH, or innovative biotech startups, developing new treatments, devices, and therapies that change the way we understand and support healthy brain functioning.

Ultimately, neuroscience is an adventure into the very core of what makes us human. Whether you seek to delve into groundbreaking research, impact the future of technology, or improve the lives of those suffering from neurological conditions, neuroscience offers you the chance to make your mark. As a student embarking on this path, you will be equipped with the tools to understand the brain's mysteries and contribute to shaping the future of medicine, technology, and human potential.

Whether you pursue behavioral psychology, biopsychology, cognitive psychology, neural imaging, or neuroscience, the journey may take you beyond your comfort zone. However, the rewards are immense and the possibilities and boundless.

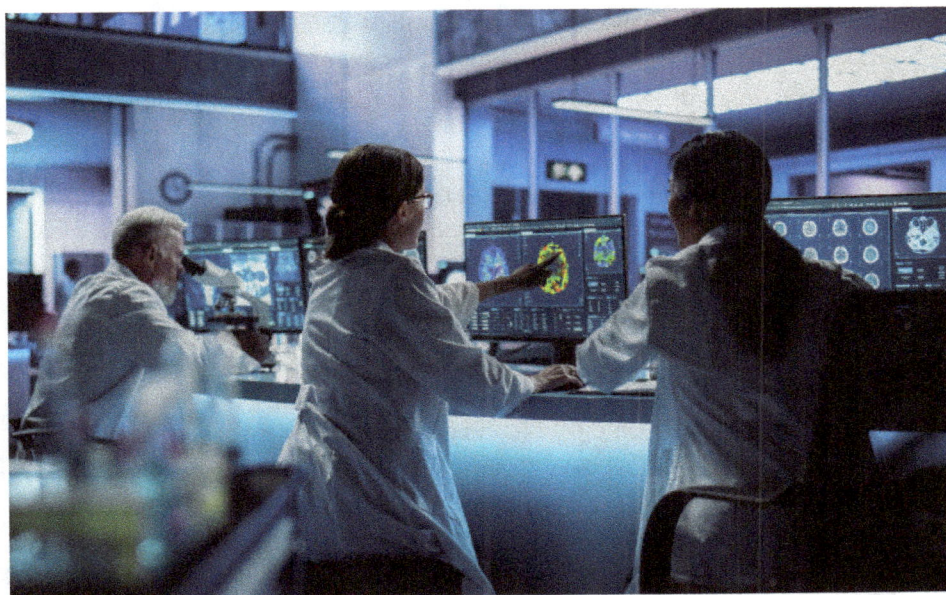

RESEARCH INSTITUTIONS/CENTERS AT THE FOREFRONT OF NEUROSCIENCE

Allen Institute for Brain Science (Seattle, WA):
- *Research Focus:* Mapping the brain's intricate wiring and clarifying cellular composition with detailed 3D images of mouse brains that capture the shapes of neurons and their synapses.
- *Impact:* These comprehensive maps serve as invaluable resources for researchers, facilitating studies on brain function, development, and diseases.

BRAIN Initiative (Nationwide, Coordinated by NIH):
- *Research Focus:* Mapping neural circuits, measuring patterns of neural activity, and understanding the interplay between brain function and behavior.
- *Impact:* The discovery of previously unknown brain regions advances the science of neural dynamics, exploring treatments for neurological and psychiatric disorders.

Harvard University (Cambridge, MA):
- *Research Focus:* Advanced imaging software and computational methods to analyze, characterize, and map activity onto the brain.
- *Impact:* Understanding of how humans observe and organize objects, actions, and scenes in the brain have the potential to inform treatment possibilities for cognitive disorders.

Human Connectome Project (Washington University, St. Louis):
- *Research Focus:* Analyzing how each brain region interacts and how these connections relate to behavior and mental health.
- *Impact:* Relating connectivity to brain disorders may lead to improved diagnostics and treatments.

Johns Hopkins Brain Science Institute (Baltimore, MD):
- *Research Focus:* Mapping neural circuits involved in sensory processing and developing interventions for mood disorders.
- *Impact:* Uncovering the neural basis of sensory experiences allows researchers to consider novel treatments for conditions like depression and anxiety.

MIT Picower Institute (Cambridge, MA):
- *Research Focus:* The molecular and cellular mechanisms underlying learning and memory, including synaptic plasticity and neural circuits.
- *Impact:* Knowing these cellular mechanisms may lead to interventions for memory-related disorders.

Stanford University (Stanford, CA):

- Research Focus: Neuron-glial interactions within the nervous system focused on oncological diseases.
- Impact: These insights are poised to produce novel treatments for brain cancers along with insights into how neural activity influences tumor growth.

University of California, San Francisco (San Francisco, CA):
- Research Focus: Neurodegenerative diseases.
- Impact: Slowing the course of diseases offers new avenues for treatment.

PROMINENT FOCUS AREAS OF NEUROSCIENCE

Affective Neuroscience

Behavioral Neuroscience

Cellular/Molecular Neuroscience

Clinical Neuroscience

Cognitive Neuroscience

Computational Neuroscience

Developmental Neuroscience

Neurodegenerative Diseases

Neurodevelopmental Disorders

Neuroeconomics

Neuroengineering

Neuroethology

Neurogenetics

Neuroimaging

Neuroinformatics

Neuropharmacology

Neurophysiology

Neuroplasticity

Social Neuroscience

Systems Neuroscience

In Order of Most Actively Researched:

1. **Neurodegenerative Diseases Research**
   (Alzheimer's, Parkinson's, ALS)

2. **Cognitive Neuroscience**
   (Memory, attention, and language)

3. **Neurodevelopmental Disorders Research**
   (Autism, ADHD)

4. **Clinical Neuroscience**
   (Bridges research with treatment for neurological and psychiatric disorders)

5. **Neuroplasticity**
   (Crucial for learning, recovery, and adaptability)

6. **Behavioral Neuroscience**
   (Understanding behavior interdisciplinary appeal)

7. **Neuroimaging**
   (Advances in imaging are critical for diagnosis & additional research)

8. **Cellular/Molecular Neuroscience**
   (Foundation for neuron-level processes)

9. **Computational Neuroscience**
   (Modeling/understanding neural dynamics)

10. **Social Neuroscience**
    (Important for understanding human interactions)

11. **Systems Neuroscience**
    (Insights into neural circuit functions)

12. **Developmental Neuroscience**
    (Key for understanding critical life-stage changes)

13. **Neuropharmacology**
    (Drug development in neurological disorders)

14. **Neurophysiology**
    (Understanding electrical/chemical neural activities)

15. **Neurogenetics**
    (Genetic testing and therapy advancements)

16. **Neuroinformatics**
    (Accelerates data analysis and collaboration)

17. **Neuroengineering**
    (Rapid growth in prosthetics and brain-machine interfaces)

18. **Affective Neuroscience**
    (Focus on emotions, mental health, and well-being)

19. **Neuroeconomics**
    (Gaining traction with decision-making and risk evaluation)

20. **Neuroethology**
    (Niche but impactful for evolutionary insights)

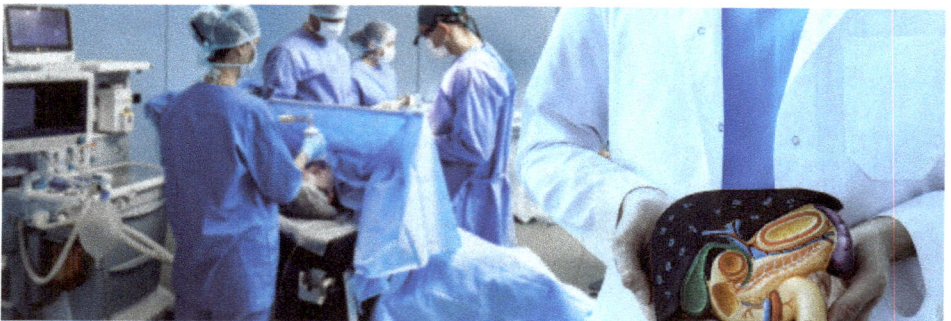

BRAIN DISORDERS & ASSOCIATED
UNIVERSITIES WITH THE TOP RESEARCH CENTERS

Alzheimer's Disease
- ☐ **Description**: A progressive neurodegenerative disorder leading to memory loss, cognitive decline, and behavioral changes.
- ☐ **Prevalence:** Most common cause of dementia, affecting millions worldwide.
- ☐ **Key Symptoms**: Memory impairment, confusion, disorientation, difficulty with daily tasks.

Top U.S. Colleges: Brown, Harvard, Indiana U, Johns Hopkins, Mayo Clinic, MIT, NYU, Stanford, UCI, UCLA, UCSF, U of Miami, UPenn, Wake Forest, WVU

Notable Colleges Abroad: German Center for Neurodegenerative Diseases, University College London, University of Melbourne, University of Oxford

Amyotrophic Lateral Sclerosis (ALS)
- ☐ **Description:** A progressive neurological disease affecting motor neurons, leading to muscle weakness and atrophy.
- ☐ **Prevalence:** Rare but well-known due to figures like Stephen Hawking and awareness campaigns.
- ☐ **Key Symptoms:** Weakness, difficulty speaking, swallowing, and breathing.

Top U.S. Colleges: Columbia, Duke, Emory, Harvard, Johns Hopkins, MIT, Northwestern, Stanford, UCSD, UCSF, U of Florida, U of Miami, U of Michigan

Notable Colleges Abroad: KU Leuven (Belgium), University of Melbourne, University of Oxford, Western University (Canada)

Autism Spectrum Disorder (ASD)
- ☐ **Description**: A neurodevelopmental condition affecting social interaction, communication, and behavior.
- ☐ **Prevalence**: Increasingly diagnosed; affects children and persists into adulthood.
- ☐ **Key Symptoms**: Difficulty with social interaction, restricted interests, repetitive behaviors.

Top U.S. Colleges: ASU, Drexel, Harvard, Northwestern, St. Joseph's, Stanford, UC Davis, UCLA, UCSD, UNC Chapel Hill, U of Washington, Yale

Notable Colleges Abroad: La Trobe University (Australia), University of Cambridge, University of Oxford, University of Toronto

Epilepsy
- ☐ **Description**: A neurological disorder characterized by recurrent seizures due to abnormal brain activity.
- ☐ **Prevalence**: Affects people of all ages; highly treatable in many cases.
- ☐ **Key Symptoms**: Seizures, temporary confusion, loss of consciousness, and uncontrolled movements.

Top U.S. Colleges: Augusta, Emory, Northwestern, NYU, Stanford, UCI, UCSF, UChicago, U of Colorado, U of Florida, UPenn, UT Health Sciences, Yale
Notable Colleges Abroad: Oxford, UCL (UK), U of Melbourne, U of Toronto

Huntington's Disease
- **Description**: A genetic disorder causing the progressive breakdown of nerve cells in the brain.
- **Prevalence**: Rare but devastating; affects individuals in mid-adulthood.
- **Key Symptoms**: Uncontrolled movements, cognitive decline, and psychiatric issues.

Top Colleges in U.S.: Columbia, Florida Atlantic, Johns Hopkins, Ohio State, Stanford, UCI, UCSD, UCSF, U of Arkansas, U of Iowa, U of Michigan, UPenn
Notable Colleges Abroad: Cardiff University (UK), Monash University (Australia), Univ. College London (UK), Univ. of British Columbia (Canada)

Migraine
- **Description**: A neurological condition characterized by severe headaches often accompanied by nausea and sensitivity to light and sound.
- **Prevalence**: Affects a significant portion of the population, especially women.
- **Key Symptoms**: Intense, throbbing headaches, visual disturbances, and sensitivity to light or sound.

Top U.S. Colleges: Albert Einstein, Harvard, Mayo Clinic, NYU, Stanford, UCI, UCSD, UCSF, U of Colorado, U of Rochester, U of Virginia, WashU in St. Louis
Notable Colleges Abroad: King's College (UK), Norwegian University of Science & Technology, University of Copenhagen, University of Melbourne

Multiple Sclerosis (MS)
- **Description**: An autoimmune disorder where the immune system attacks the myelin sheath covering nerve fibers.
- **Prevalence**: More common in young to middle-aged adults, especially women.
- **Key Symptoms**: Fatigue, difficulty walking, vision problems, and muscle weakness.

Top U.S. Colleges: Columbia, Harvard, Johns Hopkins, Mayo Clinic, NYU, Pitt, Stanford, UCLA, UCSF, U of Colorado, U of Miami, U of Michigan, WashU
Notable Colleges Abroad: Karolinska Institute (Sweden), University College London, University of Melbourne, University of Toronto

Parkinson's Disease
- **Description**: A neurodegenerative disorder affecting movement due to the loss of dopamine-producing neurons.
- **Prevalence**: Second most common neurodegenerative disease, especially in older adults.
- **Key Symptoms**: Tremors, rigidity, bradykinesia (slowness of movement), postural instability.

Top U.S. Colleges: Boston U, Emory, Northwestern, Oregon H&S U, Pitt, Rush,

UCSD, UCSF, USC, U of Colorado, U of Miami, UConn, UPenn, Wash U, Yale

Notable Colleges Abroad: École Polytechnique Fédérale de Lausanne (Switzerland), Univ. of Cambridge, Univ. of Oxford, Univ. of Plymouth

Stroke

- ☐ **Description**: A condition caused by interrupted blood flow to the brain, leading to tissue damage.
- ☐ **Prevalence**: Major cause of disability and death globally.
- ☐ **Key Symptoms**: Sudden numbness, weakness, confusion, vision problems, and difficulty speaking.

Top U.S. Colleges: Duke, Johns Hopkins, Stanford, UCLA, UCSF, U of Cincinnati, U of Miami, U of Michigan, U of South Carolina, UT Southwestern

Notable Colleges Abroad: Capital Medical University (China), University of Tasmania, University of Queensland

Traumatic Brain Injury (TBI)

- ☐ **Description**: Brain dysfunction caused by an external mechanical force, such as a blow to the head.
- ☐ **Prevalence**: Common among individuals involved in accidents, sports, or falls.
- ☐ **Key Symptoms**: Headaches, confusion, memory problems, mood changes, and loss of consciousness.

Top U.S. Colleges: Baylor, Boston U, Icahn, Indiana U, Mount Sinai, OSU, Pitt, NYU, Stanford, UCLA, UCSF, UPenn, U of Florida, U of Washington, WashU

Notable Colleges Abroad: University of Cambridge, University of Gothenburg (Sweden), University of Melbourne, University of Toronto

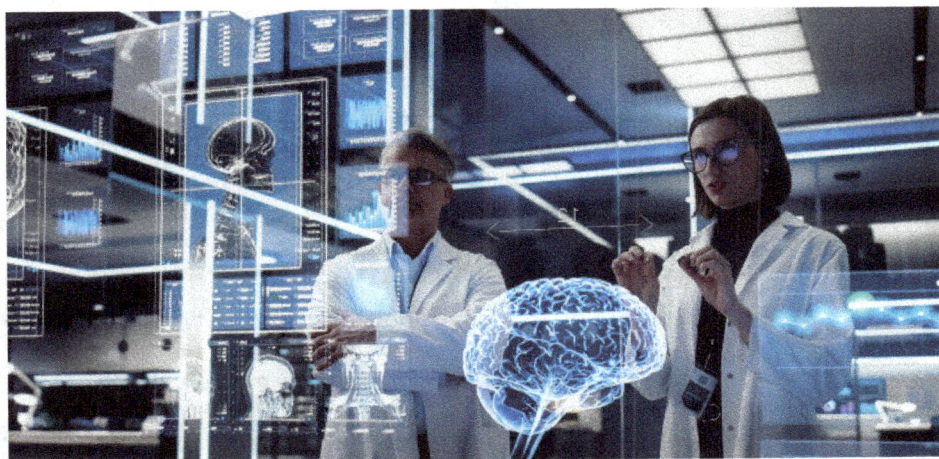

THE HORIZON OF BRAIN SCIENCE:
WHAT TO EXPECT BY 2035

Curing Alzheimer's and Reversing Neurodegeneration

Gene-editing tools like CRISPR and therapies targeting misfolded proteins are advancing rapidly. Researchers at MIT and UCSF are also exploring synaptic regeneration to restore lost cognitive function. Recent experiments involving cerebrospinal fluid infusions and young blood plasma suggest the potential reversal of the brain's aging, delaying dementia and Parkinson's progression. With these advances, Alzheimer's may no longer be a terminal disease but a treatable condition.

AI-Powered Mind Reading and Thought-to-Text Communication

Advancements in artificial intelligence and brain-computer interfaces will allow real-time decoding of thoughts into text or speech. Neural implants and non-invasive BCIs will translate brain signals into words, helping paralyzed individuals communicate directly from their thoughts. Early versions of this technology are underway. Next-generation AI models will refine their accuracy. Beyond medical applications, thought-controlled smart devices will allow typing and speaking to become obsolete. Users will think; their devices will respond.

Quantum Computing's Acceleration of AI Advances

Quantum computing and AI will redefine how we understand and model the brain. Classical computers struggle with the immense complexity of brain networks using only ones and zeros. Yet, quantum algorithms will allow for precise real-time simulations of neural activity since they have infinite capabilities, breaking down the continuum of possibilities between 0 and 1. Researchers at IBM and Google's Quantum AI Lab predict that by 2035, we will be able to fully simulate micro-scale brain circuits, revealing insights into consciousness, emotions, and mental disorders. Artificial intelligence, powered by deep learning and large-scale neuroimaging, will be able to detect brain diseases years before symptoms appear, enabling preventative treatment strategies that could stop disorders like ALS, schizophrenia, and bipolar disorder before they manifest.

Brain Augmentation and Memory Enhancement

Memory prosthetics inserted into the brain to improve functionality will become a reality. Researchers will enhance human cognition using implantable brain chips. Early trials in epilepsy patients show significantly improved memory recall using deep brain stimulation. By 2035, these implants could significantly boost learning speeds, prevent memory loss, and even allow individuals to store and retrieve information like a hard drive. Students could upload new knowledge instantly. People suffering from amnesia or brain injury might fully recover their lost memories. The implications include educational access, slowed aging, and even intelligence augmentation.

Eradicating Mental Illness and Unlocking Consciousness

Neuroscience will potentially cure depression, PTSD, and anxiety disorders through neural modulation and AI-driven therapy. Real-time brain rewiring will repair trauma-related neural pathways. Additionally, advancements in integrated information theory and global workspace theory suggest that by 2035, we will be able to map and transfer human consciousness into digital form and induce states of creativity, relaxation, or hyper-focus on demand. AI, neuroscience, and quantum computing will converge, allowing scientists to decipher the human mind.

YOUR CAREER & FUTURE IN NEUROSCIENCE

Neuroscience offers numerous impactful career opportunities. Whether you are fascinated by the mysteries of the human brain, passionate about mental health, or eager to develop cutting-edge technology, a neuroscience degree opens doors to exciting possibilities. Advancements in artificial intelligence, neuro-engineering, and brain-computer interfaces offer a wide range of possibilities for those eager to invent the future. The beauty of neuroscience is that the field bridges multiple disciplines, allowing you to carve out careers that align with your interests in medicine, research, business, and technology.

Medical school is a potential career option. If you are drawn to healthcare, a neuroscience degree provides a strong foundation for becoming a neurologist, neurosurgeon, or psychiatrist. There are many paths to medical school (MD or

DO). However, most involve research and clinical experiences. In your science labs and research positions, you are likely to delve deeply into the intricacies of neuroscience. In addition to taking the MCAT and completing prerequisites, graduate school, post-baccalaureate programs, or advanced science certification may serve as precursors on the road to your medical school degree.

A neuroscience degree also paves the way for careers in neuropharmacology, where scientists develop treatments for conditions such as Alzheimer's, Parkinson's, and epilepsy. You might apply for positions in pharmaceutical companies or continue to graduate school and earn a PharmD. If you are interested in mental health, you might consider pursuing neuropsychology, and earning an MS, PsyD, or Ph.D. to help patients recover from brain injuries or cognitive disorders.

Neuroscience graduates are making waves in public health, policy, and advocacy, shaping the way societies approach brain-related issues such as addiction, mental illness, and neurodegenerative diseases. You might consider addiction therapy, mental illness treatment, or personalized medicine for schizophrenia, bipolar disorder, or ADHD.

Beyond clinical applications, quantum computing technology will revolutionize neuroscience. Careers that combine neuroengineering and artificial intelligence allow graduates to design brain-computer interfaces, prosthetic limbs controlled by thought, and neuroenhancement tools that improve cognition. Startups and biotech firms are racing to develop next-generation treatments using CRISPR gene editing and personalized medicine. Opportunities also exist in human-computer interaction, virtual reality, and neurogaming, where neuroscience principles enhance user experiences and cognitive performance. As companies invest in neurotechnology, the demand for skilled neuroscientists in technology industries continue to soar.

Neuroscience graduates are not confined to traditional career paths. With the field's interdisciplinary nature, graduates can become corporate consultants, launch a neuro-focused startup, conduct research for pharmaceutical companies, or educate the public on groundbreaking discoveries. You might even go to law school to pursue neuroethics or intellectual property. Alternatively, you might consider graduate school in forensic science to provide expert analysis in criminal cases.

Whether you are exploring the depths of consciousness, improving mental health treatments, or innovating the next generation of brain-computer interfaces, your degree in neuroscience will put you at the forefront of opportunities to change the world. Use your inspiration and perspiration to passionately pursue your neuroscience-focused career as you shape the future of brain science.

Neuroscience is by far the most exciting branch of science because the brain is the most fascinating object in the universe. Every human brain is different - the brain makes each human unique and defines who he or she is.

- Stanley B. Prusiner

CHAPTER 5

ACADEMIC PREPARATION & COMPETITIONS

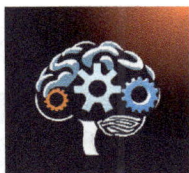

"Don't compare yourself with other people; compare yourself with who you were yesterday."

– Jordan Peterson

Student-centered competitions inspire a sense of purpose. With each round, a student continues to grow, learn, and improve. As the level increases, races, games, or problems get harder and competitors become even more formidable opponents. Resilience and persistence are essential qualities. The lessons learned in competition remain throughout life, helping individuals continue when they want to quit, work harder at improving themselves, and staying true to themselves even when challenges are not always fair.

Whether embarking on competitions involving speed cubing, chess, Scrabble, poetry, art, debate, or Science Olympiad, the lessons are valuable. Academic competitions test knowledge, but they also serve as powerful platforms for growth, discovery, and inspiration. High school students participating in these competitions ignite their innate curiosity and push self-imposed boundaries. Students practice, organize, and regroup, going beyond textbooks to apply what they have learned in exciting, real-world contexts. These events stretch thinking and resolve problems, allowing students to explore their passions in ways that are deeply rewarding and personally transformative.

Beyond academics and social assimilation, competitions build confidence and character. They teach perseverance in the face of setbacks, while cultivating discipline, fostering collaboration, and developing communication skills. When students prepare for and compete with their peers, they learn how to handle pressure, speak with conviction, and adapt quickly. Win or lose, every participant walks away with something valuable: a sharper mind, a stronger spirit, and a deeper understanding of what it means to challenge themselves.

Most importantly, students connect to a broader community of thinkers, dreamers, and doers who share their excitement for and interests in international affairs, law, science, robotics, or rocketry. In these vibrant, competitive environments, students discover their willingness to spend sleepless nights on the floor of a massive hackathon or in conference center halls reciting information for a debate. These experiences spark lifelong interests. For any student looking to grow intellectually and personally, stepping into the world of student-centered competitions is one of the most empowering and enriching choices of their four years of high school.

COMPETITIONS AND PRIZES

Consider participating in these competitions. This alphabetized list is a start.

3M Young Scientist Challenge – Sponsored by 3M and administered by Discovery Education, this competition for middle school students has been in existence since 1999. Students create an innovation to improve people's lives. Ten finalists are chosen based on communication, creativity, originality, potential, and a short video explaining their project. Finalists are paired with 3M scientists who mentor them through the development process. One national winner is selected.

American Rocketry Challenge – This competition is the world's largest student rocket contest. In 2002, the Aerospace Industries Association and the National Association of Rocketry first sponsored this Design, Build, Fly rocketry contest for middle and high school students is designed to increase interest in STEM subjects. Typically, the top 100 teams are invited to the National Finals where prizes are awarded in different categories. The American Institute of Aeronautics & Astronautics holds Design-Build-Fly contests on the collegiate level.

American Society of Human Genetics Essay Contest – This high school competition considers topics related to human genetics. Students write no more than 750 words. The Annual DNA Essay Contest's 2024 question asked, "Provide an example of how the interplay of genetics and environment can shape human health."

Bioethics Essay Contest – This STEM writing competition allows high school students to explore ethical issues in science and technology.

BioGENEius Challenge – This internationally recognized high school competition students started in the early 1990s to focus on STEM solutions to biotechnology problems. Categories include Healthcare, Agriculture-Biotechnology, and Industrial-Environmental Biotechnology. Winners are chosen in each category.

Breakthrough Junior Challenge – This science video competition encourages students 13 to 18 to create short videos that explain complex scientific ideas in engaging ways. Participants compete for prizes, including a $250,000 college scholarship, a $50,000 award for their teacher, and a $100,000 school science lab.

Broadcom MASTERS (Math, Applied Science, Technology, and Engineering for Rising Stars) – Since 2011, this prestigious middle school science and engineering competition awards students for innovative STEM projects and teamwork. Thirty finalists are selected to participate in a team-based, hands-on STEM competition which showcases the most practical and extraordinary science fair projects.

Conrad Challenge – This competition, started in 2008, continues the legacy of astronaut Charles "Pete" Conrad Jr. (the third to walk on the Moon). This multi-phase competition focuses on innovation and entrepreneurship. Teams of 2-5 high school students pitch ideas to solve global challenges. Winners present their ideas to judges at the Innovation Summit. Winners who develop a viable, scalable, solution with real-world impact span a range of discoveries.

eCYBERMISSION – In 2002, the U.S. Army Educational Outreach Program began sponsoring this online STEM competition for middle school students. Student teams propose a solution to a real-world challenge. Along with regional winners in each grade level – 6,7,8, and 9 – with one national winner.

Engineer Girl Writing Contest – This writing contest, sponsored by the National Academy of Engineering focuses on how engineering impacts the world.

ExploraVision Science Competition (Toshiba & the National Science Teaching Association) – Started in 1992, this is one of the world's largest K-12 science competitions. Students use futuristic thinking and innovative solutions to develop and explore technology that may exist in 20 years. National, regional, and honorable mention winners are selected each year in four grade-level categories.

FIRST Robotics Competition (FRC) – FIRST (For Inspiration and Recognition of Science & Technology) sponsors the international high school FRC, which started in 1992. Student teams design, build, and program robots for competitions, promoting education, teamwork, and innovation at different levels.

Genius Olympiad – This high school competition, coordinated by the Terra Science Education Foundation, focuses on environmental issues. Based in New York, students compete worldwide in the areas of science, visual and performing arts, writing, business, and robotics. Awards are given in each category.

Google Science Fair – First launched in 2011, this online science and engineering competition is open to students 13 to 18 who pose a question, develop a hypothesis, and conduct research. Regional finalists compete to be global finalists. These students are invited to Google's headquarters for the final round. Prizes are given in different age-specific and thematic categories.

International Biology Olympiad (IBO) – Started in 1990, more than a million students have competed in preliminary competitions. On the international level, this prestigious event includes up to four of the top competitors selected from their National Biology Olympiad's local, regional, and national competition rounds.

Students from more than 75 countries come together each year to compete for the world prize.

International Chemistry Olympiad (IChO) - This annual high school competition started in 1968 with three European teams and now represents 90+ countries. Each participating country selects its national team and two team leaders through its internal competition process. Team selection process varies by country. The IChO includes a 5-hour laboratory practical exam and a 5-hour written theoretical and experimental exam. Individual and team awards are presented.

International Olympiad on Astronomy & Astrophysics (IOAA) – The annual IOAA international high school competition started in 2007. Recently, 52 countries competed. National teams of up to five members (two team leaders) are selected by the participating country, typically from its national competition. The IOAA includes theoretical, observational, and practical exams. Individual and team awards are presented.

International Physics Olympiad (IPhO) – This high school competition, started in 1967, recently hosted students from 90 countries. Each participating country selects its national team and two team leaders through its internal competitions. The team selection process varies by country. The IPhO tests knowledge and problem-solving in theoretical and experimental exams. Individual and team awards are presented.

Junior Science and Humanities Symposia (JSHS) – Established in 1958 by the U.S. Army, Navy, & Air Force, this program challenges high school students to conduct STEM research in regional events. Winners advance to the national competition. Students present original research. The winners receive scholarships.

Lexus Eco Challenge – Started in 2007, this competition is for middle and high school students. The goal of the Land & Water Challenge and Air & Climate Challenge is to develop and implement programs that provide real-world environmental solutions to communities. Sixteen winning teams – eight from middle and high school – are awarded prizes and given the opportunity to participate in the Final Challenge, where the grand prize winners are selected.

Living Rainforest International Schools Essay Competition – This essay contest challenges students to write about a topic involving sustainable living and human's relationship with nature.

MATE ROV (Remotely Operated Vehicle) - This event brings students, educators, and professionals globally to compete in underwater robotics (categories for different skill/age groups). Participants designed and built ROVs to complete mission tasks that simulated real-world scenarios, emphasizing problem-solving in marine technology.

Microsoft Imagine Cup Junior – Introduced in 2020, this high school technology and innovation competition was created as part of Microsoft's broader Imagine Cup for university students. The junior level seeks to encourage students to pursue technology and computer science by developing global solutions for social impact. Winners are selected by their participation and development of technology like machine learning, virtual reality, artificial intelligence, and augmented reality.

Moody's Mega Math (M3) Challenge – M3, started in 2005, is a mathematics competition for high school students. Over a 14-hours, teams use models to solve real-world challenges. The top four to six teams are awarded scholarships.

NASA Competitions - Cube Quest, Break the Ice, Deep Space Food, and Watts on the Moon – These offer prizes totaling $5,000,000 to teams.

NASA Scientist for a Day Essay Contest – Students are challenged to write an essay about a topic related to space and planetary science. The 2025 Power to Explore topic was, "If you could plan an RPS-powered mission to any moon in our solar system, which moon would you choose to unravel its mysteries?"

National Bioethics Bowl – In this U.S. intercollegiate competition, students debate ethical issues in medicine, biotechnology, and healthcare. In each round, teams are given a case and present arguments to the other team and judges.

Ocean Awareness Contest (Bow Seat Ocean Awareness Program) – This high school art, writing, and advocacy competition invites students to present their art, research, and essays to win awards.

Regeneron ISEF - International Science & Engineering Fair – Started in 1950, this competition is one of the largest high school science events. Students present their research and discoveries and win one of hundreds of prizes in multiple categories. Grand Awards – 17 ISEF categories; each has first, second, third, and fourth place. There are also special awards given by public and private organizations.

Regeneron Science Talent Search – Started in 1942 by Westinghouse and Intel, this is the oldest U.S. science talent competition. From 300 scholar semifinalists, 40 finalists are chosen to present their research in D.C. and compete for awards

RoboCup –This is the world's largest international robotics/AI competitions. The long-term goal is to create a fully autonomous humanoid robot capable of winning in soccer against the reigning human World Cup champions.

Samsung Solve for Tomorrow – In this middle and high school student contest, participants use STEM solutions to address real-world issues. State winners are selected. National finalists are chosen to receive prizes, technology, and resources.

Science Olympiad - This STEM competition engages students from middle and high schools across the country. Teams participate in various events that involve building devices, experimenting, solving problems, and answering written tests.

Shell Science Lab Challenge – In 2010, the Shell Oil Company began sponsoring this contest, administered by the National Science Teaching Association for middle and high school science teachers who approach science in an innovative way. Approximately 18 winners receive a lab makeover with equipment and resources.

Society for Technical Communication High School Writing Contest – This contest challenges students to write essays on topics regarding science and technology.

Wiki Science Competition: – This photo contest encourages the creation of science imagery. Categories include People in Science, Microscopy, Non-Photographic Media, Image Sets, and Wildlife & Nature, Astronomy. November/December every two years. National and International levels – winning national-level images go on to the international level; unaffiliated countries are considered "other".

Young Naturalist Awards (American Museum of Natural History) – This essay competition is for middle and high school students with scientific research/writing.

21 PROGRAMMING CONTESTS

Good Luck!!! "May the force be with you!"

ACM International Collegiate Programming Contest (ICPC)

The ICPC is a prestigious, worldwide programming competition with 3-member teams that solve algorithmic problems, showcasing programming skills. The ICPC holds regional contests over six continents.

Notes: Teams have three students and one coach. Over 50,000 students, 3,000 universities, 110 countries; about 140 teams compete in the World Finals. The fee is about $100/team. The prizes may include trophies, medals, or cash prizes.

AtCoder Grand Contest (AGC)

AGC is a programming contest organized by AtCoder, a Japanese platform. The contest tests skills in data structures, algorithms, and problem-solving.

Notes: All age groups, from beginner to expert, can participate. Most of the 2,000 to 3,000 participants are advanced high school or college students – no entry fee - participants register on the AtCoder website. Winners receive cash prizes and/or certificates. The finals are held online.

Baidu Star

Baidu Star is a Chinese programming contest organized by Baidu and open to students and professionals.

Notes: College students or professionals enter at no cost. The contest, which draws thousands of participants, is open to anyone with knowledge of algorithms and data structures. The winners receive cash prizes, job offers, or internships.

CodeChef Long Challenge

CodeChef's Long Challenge is a 10-day online programming contest. Participants have ample time to solve a series of problems.

Notes: All ages are invited, though most of the 20,000 – 25,000 participants are advanced high school and college students. Some are hobbyists seek to sharpen their skills. Register on CodeChef. Winners receive cash prizes, merchandise, or certificates.

Codeforces Contest

Codeforces, known for its dynamic ranking system and large global community, hosts programming contests. Participants solve problems under a time constraint.

Notes: All ages are invited to compete with 5,000 and 10,000 participants. Register at Codeforces for free. Participants win certificates, t-shirts, or cash prizes.

Codeforces Global Rounds: These free events have more challenging problems. Fierce competition attracts 10,000-15,000 top coders from around the world.

CyberPatriot (National Youth Cyber Defense Competition)

CyberPatriot is a U.S. cybersecurity competition for middle/high school students. Teams compete to secure computer systems and networks in simulated environments.

Notes: Teams of 2-6 students and a coach, take part in rounds. National winners receive scholarships, trophies, or recognition. Cost: about $200/team; over 6,000 teams participate.

Educational Computing Organization of Ontario (ECOO) Contest

ECOO hosts a programming contest for high school students in Ontario, Canada, focused on algorithmic problem-solving.

Notes: Hundreds of teams enter (~$100) with a coach. Winners receive medals, trophies, or recognition.

Facebook Hacker Cup

This annual competition challenges participants to solve algorithmic problems in multiple rounds; the top coders advance to the finals.

Notes: All ages are invited. Free. Individual registration (about 20,000 participate). Cash prizes, t-shirts, or plaques for winners.

Google Code Jam

This annual coding competition invites programmers globally to solve algorithmic problems in several rounds, culminating in a world final.

Notes: All ages are invited. Free. Individual registration (about 50,000 participants). Cash prizes up to $15,000, t-shirts, or plaques.

Google Hash Code

In this team-based programming competition coders work together to solve a real-world engineering problem within a fixed time frame.

Notes: All ages are invited. Free. Register in 2-4 person teams. With over 100,000 participants, Google offers winning teams cash, t-shirts, or plaques.

Hackerrank Contests

Regular timed programming contests, including algorithms, data structures, and AI, help to improve coding skills.

Notes: All ages are invited. Free. Individual registration on Hackerrank. Prizes include cash, swag, or job opportunities.

ICPC for Women (ICPCW)

This programming contest encourages women to compete in programming.

Notes: Female college students compete in teams of 3 students and one coach. Prizes can include trophies, medals, and cash.

International Olympiad in Informatics (IOI)

This is one of the most prestigious computer science competitions for secondary school students testing skills in algorithmic problem-solving, programming, and informatics.

Notes: About 400 high school students worldwide compete in individual contests for medals, certificates or scholarships.

Kaggle Competitions

This data science and machine learning competition includes real-world predictive modeling problems with prizes and recognition within the data science community.

Notes: Individual or team - varies based on the contest. Thousands compete for cash prices up to $100,000, along with job opportunities and recognition.

Kick Start (Google's coding competition)

These online coding competitions feature algorithmic challenges help participants improve their coding skills and prepare for technical interviews.

Notes: All ages are invited. Free. Individual competition with 10,000-15,000 participants. Prizes include recognition and t-shirts.

Microsoft Imagine Cup

This global competition is for student technologists, developers, and entrepreneurs. Participants create innovative solutions to real-world problems using Microsoft technology.

Notes: Students 16+ compete in teams of 1-3 members for cash, mentorship, and project funding up to $100,000. Thousands compete annually.

NASA Space Apps Challenge

In this global hackathon, participants develop solutions to challenges related to space exploration, Earth science, and technology.

Notes: Teams of all ages compete for free in coding, design, and engineering. Over 40,000 participants compete for recognition, NASA items, and invites to NASA events.

PICOCTF

Middle/high school students, participate in fun, game-like cybersecurity challenges.

Notes: Free event with 1-4 student teams. Over 20,000 students compete for scholarships, cash, and recognition.

TopCoder Open (TCO)

In this international annual programming/algorithm competition, participants compete in coding challenges, including algorithms, data science, and marathon matches.

Notes: All ages can join this free individual event. Register on TopCoder. Prizes up to $15,000, merchandise, and recognition.

USACO (USA Computing Olympiad)

U.S. high school students compete in progressively challenging algorithmic problems.

Notes: Free for enrolled HS students in this individual event with 5,000-7,000 participants. Prizes include medals, certificates, and qualification for the IOI.

Yandex Algorithm

This annual competition challenges participants with difficult algorithmic problems.

Notes: Popular among Russian-speaking programmers in this free individual event. All ages are welcome. Register on Yandex. Prizes include cash, merchandise, and certificates.

11 POPULAR CAPTURE THE FLAG COMPETITIONS

ASIS CTF - One of the largest and most popular online CTF competitions, this worldwide event is known for its difficult and creative challenges.

> **Location:** Online

Boston Key Party (BKP) CTF - Boston Key Party is a large, well-known, and highly regarded online CTF competition with innovative challenges and participation from top teams globally.

> **Location:** Online

DEF CON CTF - The most famous CTF competitions worldwide, held annually at the DEF CON hacker conference. Elite teams come from around the globe and feature highly complex challenges. Winning this competition is considered a major accomplishment.

> **Location:** Las Vegas, NV

Facebook CTF - In this cybersecurity competition, participants solve security challenges, including cryptography, reverse engineering, and web security. All ages are invited. Free. Register in teams (hundreds compete). Cash prizes and recognition in the cybersecurity community.

> **Location:** Online

Google CTF - This global competition offers both beginner and advanced challenges, drawing thousands worldwide. Cybersecurity topics include reverse engineering, cryptography, and web exploitation.

> **Location:** Online

Hack-A-Sat CTF – This space-focused competition is hosted by the U.S. Air Force and Space Force. This major event involves hacking satellite systems and defending against cyberattacks.

> **Location:** Online and DEF CON Las Vegas, NV

HITB CTF – The Hack In The Box CTF security competition draws global participants, featuring advanced challenges and attracting top teams.

> **Location:** HTB conferences in Amsterdam, Dubai, Singapore, etc.

PlaidCTF - Plaid Parliament of Pwning CTF, centered at Carnegie Mellon University, is one of the most competitive and well-regarded CTF events globally, attracting teams worldwide with challenging cybersecurity problems covering areas such as web hacking, reverse engineering, exploitation, forensics, and cryptography.

> **Location:** Online

RuCTF - This major CTF competition is known for its unique challenges and high level of difficulty. Universities and companies compete.

> **Location:** Yekaterinburg, Russia

UCSB iCTF (International CTF) - The UCSB iCTF is one of the longest-running academic CTF competitions, with offensive/defensive challenges and attracting students/professionals from around the world.

> **Location:** University of California, Santa Barbara and online

VolgaCTF - This international competition attracts high-level teams from various countries in high-impact challenges.

> **Location:** Russia

25 TOP HACKATHONS

AngelHack – This online hackathon series fosters entrepreneurship, encouraging participants 18 and older to turn their ideas into startups.

Cal Hacks - UC Berkeley hosts Cal Hacks, one of the largest college hackathons in the world for about 2,000 students, fostering innovation in various fields.

Dragon Hacks - Drexel's hackathon, with about 300 college students, focuses on innovation and technology development.

DubHacks – In Seattle, U-Dub hosts the largest Pacific Northwest event for college students, with about 800 students.

ETHDenver – This free event is a leading blockchain hackathon and conference focusing on decentralized applications and Web3 technologies for about 2,000 participants ages 18 and up.

Hack the North – In Canada's largest hackathon, hosted at the University of Waterloo, college students focus on building innovative tech solutions. The event is free and hosts about 1,500 participants.

Hack the Planet – Planet Labs, a company specializing in satellite imagery and Earth data, hosts this free event for about 1,000 entrants on climate change and environmental sustainability challenges using satellite data and geospatial analysis.

HackDuke - Known as "Code for Good", HackDuke focuses on social innovation and using technology to solve societal problems with about 600 college students.

HackGT - Georgia Tech's fall hackathon attracts about 1,500 college students to work on tech-driven projects.

HackIllinois - Hosted at the University of Illinois with tracks for software development, hardware, design, and data science, about 1,000 students create innovative solutions to real-world problems – prizes and networking.

HackKU – This University of Kansas-sponsored event brings about 200 students together to create innovative projects in 36 hours.

HackMIT – Hosted by MIT, this is one of the largest free undergraduate hackathons, attracting around 1,000 students globally to solve real-world challenges.

HackNY – This free NYC-based college student hackathon with about 300 participants promotes creativity and innovation in technology.

HackNYU - NYU's global hackathon is held simultaneously in New York, Abu Dhabi, and Shanghai, focusing on innovative tech solutions. The spring event is free for the 500 college students who attend.

HackRU - Rutgers offers about 600 college students a chance to work on exciting tech projects over 24 hours.

HackUMass – Held at UMass, this free event for college students brings 1,000 students together to create tech solutions in a collaborative environment.

HackZurich – At Europe's largest free hackathon, more than 500 participants 18 and up focus on creating innovative and impactful digital solutions.

Junction - Europe's leading hackathon with about 1,300 participants, hosted in Finland, focuses on building digital and hardware projects.

LA Hacks – In the largest hackathon in Southern California, UCLA hosts this free event for about 1,500 college students focusing on creating impactful tech solutions.

Major League Hacking (MLH) Hackathons – MLH organizes a series of free hackathons primarily for 200-500 college students worldwide. This competition is known for promoting student innovation and learning.

MHacks – The University of Michigan hosts one of the largest and most influential student hackathons in the U.S. for college students.

PennApps – This was one of the first hackathons. PennApps' competitive environment brings about 1,500 college students to this free event.

TechCrunch Disrupt Hackathon – This free popular hackathon for about 1,000 participants 18 and up focuses on innovative tech solutions.

TreeHacks – Stanford hosts its premier hackathon in the winter for about 1,000 participants. College students solve pressing societal challenges.

Yale Hack – Yale's hackathon encourages around 300 college students to create innovative solutions in various fields.

ARTISTIC, WRITING, AND PHILOSOPHY COMPETITIONS

Adroit Journal - Gregory Djanikian Scholarships (Poetry and Short Story)
- Eligibility: Emerging writers who have not published full-length collections or novels, regardless of age, geographic location, or educational status
- Prizes: $100-$200 and publication of their portfolios of poems or short stories in a future issue of the _Adroit Journal._

American Foreign Service Association (AFSA) High School Essay Contest
- Topic: Changes annually, with the 2024 topic focusing on how U.S. diplomats can adapt and mitigate global challenges
- Eligibility: High school students
- Prizes: $2,500, an all-expense-paid trip to Washington, D.C., a voyage on Semester at Sea, and the winner's school receives 10 copies of an AFSA publication on diplomacy

American Legion Oratorical Contest
- Topic: U.S. Constitution (varies annually)
- Format: 8-10 minute speech delivered without technology
- Eligibility: High school students
- Prizes: Travel and lodging expenses covered for department winners and their chaperones

American Philosophical Association
- Topics: Various (bioethics, climate, democracy, film, health, law, policy, race, etc.)
- Eligibility: High school, college, and graduate students
- Prizes: Vary by submission type

Ayn Rand Essay Contests
- Books: _Anthem, The Fountainhead, and Atlas Shrugged_
- Eligibility: Students in grades 8-12 and, for _Atlas Shrugged_, also college students
- Prizes: Up to $25,000

Bennington Young Writers Awards

- Categories: Poetry, Fiction, Nonfiction
- Eligibility: High school students in grades 9-12
- Prizes: $250, $500, $1,000

Bill of Rights Institute – We the Students Essay Contest

- Topic: Natural rights
- Eligibility: High school students
- Prizes: $500-$7,500

Bow Seat Ocean Awareness Art, Poetry, and Writing Contest

- Categories: Art, Poetry, Writing
- Eligibility: Students aged 11-18 worldwide
- Prizes: $100-$1,500

Columbia Scholastic Press Association (CSPA) Contests

- Categories: Six categories, four award categories (Gold Circles)
- Eligibility: High school and college students

Concord Review

- Focus: Academic research papers on history
- Eligibility: High school students
- Prizes: Emerson Prize

Daughters of the American Revolution (DAR) Essay Contests

- Middle School: American History Essay Contest
- High School: Patriots of the American Revolution Contest
- Prizes: Certificates, medals, monetary awards

David McCullough Essay Prize

- Topics: American history
- Eligibility: High school students
- Prizes: $10,000, $5,000, $1,000

Elie Wiesel Prize in Ethics Essay Contest

- Topic (2025): "What challenges awaken your consciousness?"
- Eligibility: College students
- Prizes: $10,000, $5,000, $3,000, and $1,000

EngineerGirl Writing Contest

- Topics: Engineering and global impact
- Eligibility: Students in grades 3-12
- Prizes: $100-$500

Girls State, Girls Nation, Boys State, Boys Nation – American Legion & Auxiliary

- Focus: Leadership, government learning
- Eligibility: Top high school students in each state
- Prizes: Varies by event

Great History Challenge

- Focus: History passion and interest
- Eligibility: Middle school students
- Prizes: National championship qualification

Holocaust Art & Writing Contest

- Categories: Art, film, poetry, prose
- Eligibility: High school students
- Prizes: 1st, 2nd, and 3rd place awards

International History Olympiad

- Qualification: National History Bee & Bowl Tournaments, U.S. History Bee, Qualifying Exam
- Divisions: Varsity, JV, Middle School, Intermediate, Elementary
- Prizes: Varies by event

Jane Austen Society of North America Essay Contest

- Categories: High school, college/university, graduate school
- Prizes: $1,000, $500, $250

John F. Kennedy Center for the Performing Arts VSA Playwright Discovery Program

- Eligibility: Students ages 14-19 with disabilities
- Prizes: Playwrights program participation at the Kennedy Center

John Locke Global Essay Competition

- Categories: Philosophy, Politics, Economics, History, Psychology, Theology, Law
- Eligibility: Students
- Prizes: Varies by category

Nancy Thorp Poetry Contest

- Eligibility: Female high school and college students
- Prizes: $350, publication, scholarships

National Council of Teachers of English (NCTE) Contests

- Achievement Awards in Writing: Sophomores and juniors
- The Humanities and a Freer Tomorrow: Juniors and seniors
- Prizes: Certificates, $500-$1,000

National History, Geography, Science, Political Science Bee

- Eligibility: Individual students
- Prizes: National and international competition qualification

National History Day Contest

- Focus: Historical events or figures
- Eligibility: Students
- Prizes: National Contest participation at the University of Maryland

National History Bowl – International Academic Competitions (IAC)

- Focus: Global history quiz competition
- Eligibility: Teams of up to four students
- Prizes: National championship qualification

National Society of High School Scholars Creative Writing Scholarship

- Categories: Poetry, Fiction
- Eligibility: High school students
- Prizes: $2,000

New York Public Library Young Lions Fiction Award

- Eligibility: Writers younger than 35.
- Prizes: $10,000.

Princeton's Lewis Center of the Arts – Leonard Milberg HS Poetry Prize

- Eligibility: 11th-grade students
- Prizes: $1,500, $750, $500

Princeton University's Lewis Center of the Arts – 10-minute Play Contest

- Eligibility: 11th-grade students
- Prizes: $100-$500

Profiles in Courage Essay Contest

- Eligibility: U.S. students in grades 9-12
- Prizes: $100-$10,000

Rachel Carson Landmark Alliance – Sense of Wonder/ Sense of the Wild Contest

- Eligibility: Teams of two or more people of different generations
- Prizes: Varies by submission

Saint Mary's College of California River of Words Contest

- Focus: Natural world topics
- Eligibility: Students aged 5-19
- Prizes: More than 100 prizes

Scholastic Art and Writing Competition – Alliance for Young Artists & Writers

- Categories: Various art and writing categories
- Eligibility: Teens in grades 7-12
- Prizes: Scholarships up to $12,500

Society of Prof. Journalists/Journalism Education Assn. HS Essay Contest

- Focus: Journalism and societal issues
- Eligibility: Students in grades 9-12
- Prizes: $1,000, $500, $300

Sons of the American Revolution (SAR) Contests

- Categories: Writing, Oration, Poster, Eagle Scout
- Prizes: Cash prizes

Veterans of Foreign Wars – Voice of Democracy Youth Scholarship Essay

- Eligibility: Middle and high school students
- Prizes: $1,000-$35,000

World Historian Student Essay Competition

- Eligibility: K-12 students
- Prizes: $500

Writopia Lab Worldwide Play Festival
- Eligibility: Playwrights aged 6-18
- Prizes: Prizes for performed plays

YoungArts National Writing Competition – The National Foundation for the Advancement of Artists
- Categories: Visual, literary, performing arts
- Eligibility: High school students
- Prizes: Varies by category

Young Playwright's Festival - The Blank Theatre
- Eligibility: Students aged 9-19
- Prizes: Professional production of plays

Young Writers' Annual Showcase
- Eligibility: Students aged 4-18
- Prizes: $100, trophy, publication

BUSINESS COMPETITIONS

Blue Ocean High School Entrepreneurship Competition – Business pitch competition based on the Blue Ocean Strategy.

DECA – Events Competitive events in business, marketing, finance, and entrepreneurship.

Diamond Challenge for High School Entrepreneurs – Global entrepreneurship competition.

Enactus World Cup (High School Division) – Social entrepreneurship.

FBLA (Future Business Leaders of America) – Business and leadership.

High School Fed Challenge – A competition by the Federal Reserve focused on monetary policy and economics.

Junior Achievement National Student Leadership Summit (JA NSLS) – Business and entrepreneurship pitch competition.

MIT Launch X – Business and entrepreneurship competition.

National Economics Challenge – Tests economic knowledge in micro, macro, and international economics.

Wharton Global High School Investment Competition – Stock market simulation and investment challenge.

HISTORY COMPETITIONS

American Foreign Service National High School Essay Contest – A diplomatic history and foreign policy essay competition hosted by the U.S. Foreign Service.

Concord Review – A prestigious competition where students submit high-quality research papers for publication on historical topics.

Davidson Fellows Scholarship (History Category) – A prestigious award for students who complete an advanced historical research project.

International History Olympiad – A global history competition featuring quiz-style events, exams, and simulation-based challenges.

John Locke Institute History Essay Competition – A high-level history essay competition where students write essays on major historical themes.

Gilder Lehrman Lincoln Essay Competition – Students write essays about Abraham Lincoln's legacy and impact on American history.

National History Day (NHD) – A nationwide research-based competition where students create papers, exhibits, documentaries, performances, and websites.

National History Bowl – A team-based history competition with buzzer-style quiz rounds on a wide range of historical topics.

SPJ/JEA High School Essay Contest (Journalism History Focus) – A competition where students analyze the historical role of journalism in society.

World Scholar's Cup (History Section) – An academic competition that includes a history category in its Team Debate and Scholar's Challenge events.

PSYCHOLOGY COMPETITIONS

American Psychological Association (APA) TOPSS Essay Competition – High school students write essays on psychology topics.

Behavioral Economics Challenge – Psychology/economics decisions.

Brain Bee at the Regional and National Levels – Tests knowledge in neuroscience and psychology.

CogSci High School Research Competition – Cognitive science research.

International Brain Bee – Neuroscience competition for HS students.

Psi Chi National Honor Society in Psychology High School Research Competition – Psychology research awards.

Psychology Science Fair (Regeneron ISEF, Google Science Fair, etc.) – Conduct research in psychology and behavioral sciences.

Society for Neuroscience (SfN) Next Generation Award – Recognizes high school students for outreach in neuroscience.

The Brain Awareness Video Contest – Students create videos about neuroscience topics.

The Neuroscience Research Prize – Sponsored by the American Academy of Neurology for outstanding research in neuroscience.

POLITICAL SCIENCE COMPETITIONS

American Legion Oratorical Contest – Constitutional speech contest.

Constitutional Rights Foundation's Mock Trial Competition – Simulated court trials for aspiring lawyers and policymakers.

Harvard Model Congress – A government simulation for students interested in politics.

International Public Policy Forum (IPPF) – Global debate competition focused on public policy issues.

Junior Statesmen of America (JSA) Debate Competitions – Public policy and government debate contests.

Model United Nations (MUN) – International relations, diplomacy, and debate competitions.

National Speech & Debate Association (NSDA) – Includes policy debate, public forum, and congressional debate.

Princeton Moot Court – Legal and policy debate competition.

We the People: The Citizen and the Constitution – A civics and constitutional law competition.

Yale Model Congress – Government simulation where students take on roles in a mock legislature.

FILM & VIDEO COMPETITIONS

All American High School Film Festival - The largest scholarship-granting high school film festival globally, featuring screenings in NYC.

Austin Film Festival (Young Filmmakers Competition) - A free contest for high school students, showcasing films during the festival.

C-SPAN's StudentCam - A national documentary competition inviting students to explore issues of national importance.

Meridian Stories - Offers digital storytelling competitions across various subjects, encouraging creativity and collaboration.

One Earth Young Filmmakers Contest - An international contest focusing on environmental themes (students up to age 25).

OUR PRIDE Education & Film Competition - Young filmmakers create stories documenting LGBTQ+ people, places, & events.

Student Television Network (STN) Contests - Hosts competitions in broadcast journalism, video production, & filmmaking.

Very Short Film Festival - Encourages students to create short films, offering awards, mentoring, & prizes.

YoungArts (Film Discipline) - A national competition for excellence in narrative, documentary, experimental, & animation.

JOURNALISM & WRITING CONTESTS

JEA Journalist of the Year Scholarships - Recognizes outstanding high school journalists with scholarships & national recognition.

NSPA Individual Awards – Honors excellent journalism (writing, design, & photography).

Quill & Scroll Contests - Offers competitions for student journalists, including writing, photography, & design.

Pulitzer Center Student Contests - Invites students to engage with global issues through writing and multimedia projects.

New York Post Scholars Contest - A writing competition for New York high school students (winners published in the *New York Post*).

IMPORTANCE & VALUE OF COMPETITIONS

Competitions not only inspire new ideas, but they also develop skills in adaptability, creativity, and teamwork. Students must start by understanding the rules and stepping back to figure out what tools, skills, and unique approaches they might take to separate themselves from the pack. Winners display motivation, inspiration, and perseverance.

In the process of diving into the project or building the skills necessary to be the best, students typically learn how to devise a plan, organize a set of procedures, and implement whatever is required to succeed. In math and science knowledge-based competitions, students acquire vast amounts of information.

Similarly, neuroscientists must incorporate diverse topics and consider mitigating circumstances that may confound or alter a plan or solution. New tools and techniques are imagined, helping to develop scientifically sound, repeatedly tested, and effective methods and outcomes. Whether you are competing individually or in a group, you will grow and gain valuable skills. In groups, you will implement unique project designs, programming strategies, management methods, and evaluation processes. The point is not to copy previous teams but to build upon the seeds of success.

CHAPTER 6
SUMMER PROGRAMS & INTERNSHIPS

"In order to succeed, people need a sense of self-efficacy, to struggle together with resilience to meet the inevitable obstacles and inequities of life."

– Albert Bandura

Start early to gain software, design, business, and engineering experiences. Internships and summer programs are as important in your educational pathway as coursework. The lessons you learn from working collaboratively with mentors is equally important. Historian and scholar, W.E.B. DuBois (1868-1963), a founding member of the NAACP and the first Black American to earn a Ph.D. at Harvard said, "Education must not simply teach work - it must teach life." Your college, experiential, and life education go hand-in-hand, driven by purpose and foresight since life truly is a journey, not a destination.

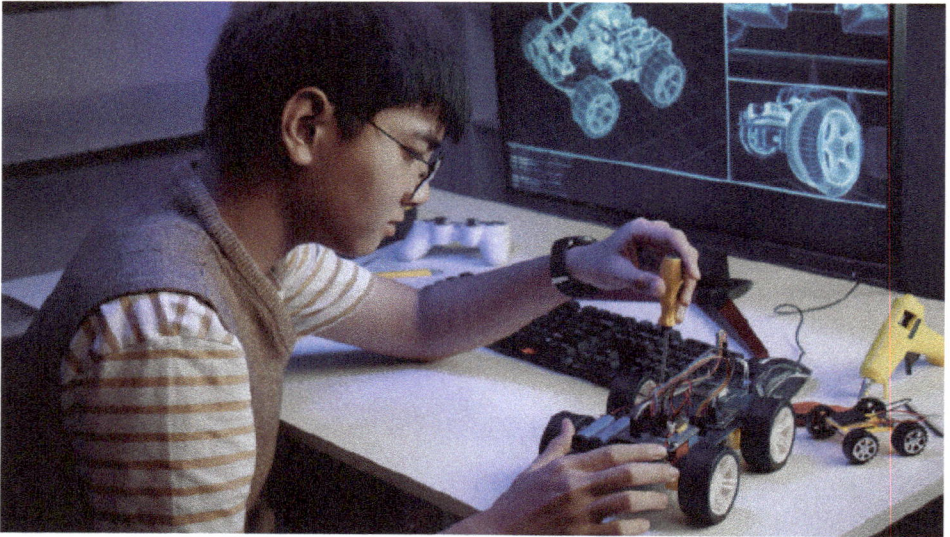

WHY PARTICIPATE IN SUMMER PROGRAMS/INTERNSHIPS?

Although some students participate to look good and show dedication, the real reason should be to develop skills with feedback from specialists. Discussions, seminars, and portfolio development are immensely valuable for any future pursuit. However, merely living on a campus and getting a feel for what college is like cannot be understated. Some immersions like Girls Who Code, Code Connects, Veritas AI Scholars, NextGen Boot Camp are completely online. Other programs like the iD Tech camps offer robotics, AI, and tech programs at 65 locations. You might intern with the National Parks Service, NASA, Depts of Defense, Energy, Labor, or Treasury.

Consider attending MIT's Splash November weekend event, where high school students choose from 250+ hands-on classes. The cost was $50 in 2025.

Note: The following list is not exhaustive nor an endorsement of any program. Dates, camps, internships, descriptions, and length may change yearly.

SUMMER CAMPS & PROGRAMS FOR ART, ARCHITECTURE, COMPUTER SCIENCE, ENGINEERING, & SUSTAINABILITY

Alabama

Auburn University – Engineering Camps - STEM - Architecture Camp – Creative Writing – Industrial Design - Multiple Sessions/Scholarships Available

Work w/professors. Counselors support/supervise students. Engineering Summer Expo (9th-11th); Senior Engineering Expo (12th); Computing/ Robotics for All (7th-8th) Minority Intro to Engineering (11th- 12th); Paper & Bioresource Engineering Camp (12th); Computer Science, AI, Cybersecurity (9th-12th)

Cyberpatriot - Air Force Assn National Youth Cyber Education Program - 1 Week

HS Students - Multiple camp locations, incl Calhoun CC & the Univ. of Alabama

Defense Intelligence Agency Summer College Internship-Engineering/Technology

10-14 Week Summer Internship Program Intelligence/Tech Apply in Feb Huntsville, AL - College Jr/Sr or Grad Student

GenCyber – 5-day Nat Security Agency-Sponsored Cybersecurity Camp for HS Students - Univ. of Alabama, Huntsville - Taught by Cyber Industry Professionals

Engaging & Dynamic - Role-playing, visual aids, activities, discussions: Computer networking, systems security, cyber operations, defense, AI, virtual reality

Tuskegee University Taylor School of Architecture & Construction Science

Virtual Preview of Architecture and Construction at Tuskegee (V-PACT) 3-hour Virtual Program. Preview Architecture & Construction Science 2-Week Program

Alaska

GenCyber – 5-day Nat Security Agency-Sponsored Cybersecurity Camp for HS Students - Univ. of Alaska, Anchorage – Taught by Cyber Industry Professionals

Engaging & Dynamic - Role-playing, visual aids, activities, discussions: Computer networking, systems security, cyber operations, defense, AI, virtual reality

Arizona

Arcosanti – Re-Imagined Urbanism – 6-week discussion-based classes - AZ

Architecture & ecology (arcology). Learn in the World's First Prototype Arcology. Core values: (1) Frugality & Resourcefulness, (2) Ecological Accountability, (3) Experiential Learning, (4) Leaving a Limited Footprint, Arcosanti is juxtaposed to mass consumerism, urban sprawl, unchecked consumption, & social isolation.

Bank of America Student Leaders Program - 3+ AZ Cities - HS Students - 8 Wks

Paid internships with nonprofits. Work experience & leadership development. Week long all-expense-paid Student Leaders Summit in Washington, DC in July. Submit application essays, recommendations, and resume in January.

Cyberpatriot - Air Force Assn National Youth Cyber Education Program - 1 Week

HS Students - Multiple camp locations, incl Cochise CC & the Univ. of Arizona

Earthwatch Teen Expeditions - 15-18 year olds - Portal, AZ - 8 days

Following Forest Owls in the Western U.S. - Learn how climate change threatens the routine of species as tree cavities and food sources disappear. study habitats

Engineering Education Outreach - at ASU - 1-wk day camp for 11th/12th Graders

Train, collaborate, & compete in the National Underwater Robotics Competition
Fun, hands-on training ground in buoyancy, electricity, & autonomy. No Exp Nec.

GenCyber – 5-day Nat Security Agency-Sponsored Cybersecurity Camp for HS Students - Grand Canyon University – Taught by Cyber Industry Professionals

Engaging & Dynamic - Role-playing, visual aids, activities, discussions: Computer networking, systems security, cyber operations, defense, AI, virtual reality

National Institute of Health – 8-week Paid Internship Program – Phoenix, AZ

Biomedical research internship for students 17 years or older by June.
HS-SIP for high school juniors & seniors June to August hands-on research.

Science and Engineering Apprenticeship Program (SEAP) – US Navy - Flagstaff

8-weeks, 300 openings, 30 research labs nationwide, $4,000-$4,500 salary. HS students must be 16+ years old. Apply starting in August for following summer.

University of Arizona Summer Engineering Academy - HS Students - Hands-on

3-day and week-long residential camps; ChallENGe Accepted, Engineer Society
Apply Feb-March; projects, mentorship, networking, engineering exploration

Arkansas

Bank of America Student Leaders Program - Pulaski - HS Students - 8 Wks

Paid internships with nonprofits. Work experience & leadership development.
Week long all-expense-paid Student Leaders Summit in Washington, DC in July.
Submit application essays, recommendations, and resume in January.

University of Arkansas – In Person & Virtual Design Camp – Fayetteville, AK

Grades 9-12 - design projects, studio gps, tours, & meetings w/local designers.
No fee; design camp; students are paired w/faculty member in a studio group.
Advanced Design Camp for students in Grades 11-12, 2 weeks in Fayetteville.

California

Academy of Art University – 4-6 Week Pre-College Art/Design/Fashion/Film - SF

Advertising, Animation/VFX, Architecture, Fashion, Game Devt, Graphic Design. Illustration, Ind Design, Motion Pictures, Music Prod, Photo, Writing for Film/TV

Bank of America Student Leaders Program - 25+ CA Cities - HS Students - 8 Wks

Paid internships with nonprofits. Work experience & leadership development. Week long all-expense-paid Student Leaders Summit in Washington, DC in July. Submit application essays, recommendations, and resume in in January.

Boeing Summer Internship – High School & College – Seal Beach & Palmdale, CA

Hands-on Industry Experience - Aviation and Engineering Internships

California State Summer School of the Arts (CSSSA) Sacramento - Grades 9–12

Rigorous 4-week, visual/ perf arts - 2D & 3D, painting, printmaking, sculpture, ceramics, digital media, & photography; scholarship opp for CA residents.

Cal Poly Pomona Engineering Summer Program - On-Campus, Hands-On

Workshops, labs, team projects, lectures & speakers - mechanical, civil, electrical

Canon Insights Summer Internship – Canon USA – Irvine, CA

Computer Science Major – 2nd or 3rd year; Position: Computer Vision Tech Assist with Quality Assurance Engineers; Digital Imaging Solution Division

COPE Scholars Program – Healthcare Internship – 280 Training/Experience Hrs

Locations: Anaheim/Orange, Bakersfield, Covina/Glendora, Hanford, Irvine, L.A., Mendocino County, Mission Viejo, Newport Beach, Oxnard, Riverside, Simi Valley, Tulare, Woodland Hills

Health Scholars must be 18+. Students assist w/basic healthcare for medical or nursing school, etc. Certificate of Completion - Keck Graduate Institute.

COSMOS – UC - California State Summer School for Math & Science – 4 weeks

Hands-on research program for California high school students (9-12) pursuing STEM fields; students live on campus and work with UC researchers. Application opens in January and closes in Feb. Topics from biomedical to space science.

Cyberpatriot - Air Force Assn National Youth Cyber Education Program - 1 Week

HS Students - Multiple camp locations, including Consumnes River Col & LBCC

Edwards Air Force Base - Lancaster, CA - Air Force Research Labs - 8-12 Weeks

Students participate in mentored ongoing research. Paid internship: comp sci, physics, materials science, & aerospace. Workshops, seminars, presentations.

Edwards Lifesciences Summer Internship Program – BS, MS, Ph.D., MBA - Irvine, CA

Currently enrolled in college - Interested in healthcare related programs Proficient in engineering drafting software, writing, or business/leadership

GenCyber – 5-day Nat Security Agency-Sponsored Cybersecurity Camp for HS Students at CSU Bakersfield & CSU San Bernardino – Taught by Cyber Industry

Engaging/Dynamic: Role-playing, visual aids, activities, & discussions: Computer networking, systems security, cyber operations, defense, AI, & virtual reality

Getty Museum – Paid Student Gallery Guide – Los Angeles, CA

Paid summer internship for teens ($2,400 in 2022). Learn the fundamentals of museums and public speaking while leading visitors around the grounds.

Also available – Open Call for teen photographers to share images, 8-week paid STEAM internship, and Summer Latin Academy at the Getty Villa to learn Latin.

Great Books Summer Program - Stanford University - Grades 6-8 and 9-12

Great Books & Big Ideas, Writer's Workshops, and Literary Travel Programs Read, Write, & Discuss Big Ideas in Literature and Philosophy with scholars

Golden Gate National Parks Conservancy - Linking Individuals to their Natural Community (LINC) 6-Week Summer Program for HS Students - San Francisco, CA

Trail work, habitat restoration, community clean up, wildlife monitoring, outdoor fun

Harvey Mudd Annual Future Achievers in Science & Technology (FAST) Program

All-expenses paid fly-in program for high-achieving college-bound HS seniors September or October weekend. Apply in August - speakers, presentations

Keck Graduate Institute (KGI) - 3-Week High School Summer STEM Program & Summer Undergrad Research Experience (SURE) - Claremont, CA - 16+ yrs old

Hands-on research experience w/KGI faculty mentor; seminars & workshops

Laguna College of Art & Design Pre-College Program – Laguna Beach, CA

Animation, Sculpture, Drawing Fundamentals, Figure Drawing, Graphic Design

Los Angeles Air Force Base - L.A., CA - Air Force Research Labs - 8-12 Weeks

Students participate in mentored ongoing research. Paid internship: comp sci, physics, materials science, & aerospace. Workshops, seminars, presentations.

Los Angeles County Office of Education's Career Technical Education Internships

This 6-8 week summer internship is for HS students to gain real-world experience and technical training in 15 industry sectors.

NASA Jet Propulsion Laboratory – Pasadena, CA (Apply by March 31)

Paid Internship - Must be in an undergraduate in a STEM subject

NatureBridge Summer Programs - Yosemite National Park - 1-2 weeks

Environmental science education, & hands-on fieldwork while backpacking for students in 7th - 12th grades. Connect to nature with trail building, habitat restoration, and wilderness exploration.

Otis College of Art and Design Summer of Art Intensive - 4 Weeks– Los Angeles
Portfolio/studio training for students 15+ - art, architecture, design, digital and printmaking; lectures and critiques. Merit/ need-based scholarships available.

Parker Hannifin Corporation – Paid Summer Internship – Irvine, CA
Mechanical or Industrial Engineering Major – Flight Control, Aircraft Systems

Pathway Summer Program Dept of Energy RENEW Initiative-HS/College Students
Mentorship, hands-on engineering/technology - Lawrence Berkeley National Lab

Rady Children's Hospital - Summer Medical Academy - San Diego, CA
Students 15-19 years old can apply to attend this 2-week medical training camp.

Rosetta Institute for Biomedical Research - 2-Week Middle/High School - Alameda
Molecular Biology of Aging, Cancer, Immunology, Neuroscience, Medicinal Chemistry, Bioinformatics of Cancer, Intro to Cellular & Molecular Medicine

Salk Institute - Heithoff-Brody HS Summer Scholars Program - San Diego Schools
8-Week hands-on biological research/paid internship in La Jolla - Mentorship Seminars, workshops, biotech site visits, research, presentations. Apply Dec-March

Sandia National Labs - Livermore, CA - Engineering/Tech Internship - HS/College
* Ages 16+ - FT HS Student - Work on STEM Projects with mentors
* 10-12 Week College Summer Internship, Year-Round Internship, & Co-Ops

Santa Clara University Summer Engineering Seminar (SES) – 10th and 11th Grade
4-day program introduces students to engineering practice, research, and education

School of Creative & Performing Arts (SOCAPA)–Occidental College (13-18-yr-olds)
2-week, 3-week - learn Filmmaking, Screenwriting, Dance, Music, Photography

SCI-Arc (Southern California Institute of Architecture) Immersive 4-week Summer Program (Design Immersion Days) – Los Angeles
Introduction to the academic and professional world of architecture – Grades 9-12

Science and Engineering Apprenticeship Program (SEAP) – US Navy Camp Pendleton, Port Hueneme, Pt. Mugu, San Diego, Monterey, Corona
8-weeks, 300 openings, 30 research labs nationwide, $4,000-$4,500 salary. HS students must be 16+ years old. Apply starting in August for following summer.

Sierra Club's Summer Outings - Channel Islands
Kayaking and hiking - families can go together to explore scenic areas

SpaceX – Summer Engineering/Co-op – Hawthorne, Irvine, & Vandenberg AFB
Paid Internship - Must be in an undergraduate in a STEM subject.

Stanford University Summer Programs for HS Students - Apply by March

Art & Architecture Exploration Program - 3 Weeks - Architecture, Art, Drawing, Dance, Creative Writing, Music, and Photography

Earth & Environmental Sciences - HS research program w/labs, tours, field trips, discussions, speakers, & research methodology at the Doerr School of Sustainability.

Humanities Institute - 3-Weeks On-Campus, 11th & 12th Grade - Explore politics, literature, and philosophy with Stanford professors and graduate students.

ID Tech (on-campus, not sponsored by S.U.) - Courses in coding, Minecraft game design, and other aspects of computer, VR, AR, & AI technology.

Math Circle - 10-Week Accelerated Math Program - Online w/groups for advanced students in grade levels from 1st to 12th grade - year round.

Middle School Scholars Program (SMSSP) - Free - Low-Income Students Grades 6 & 7 - Selective & rigorous for exceptional students - 3 Weeks

Psychology & Neuroscience Pre-College Summer Institute - 2-3 Weeks Intensive study in psychology and neuroscience with lectures, discussions, and hands on activities.

Stanford Anesthesia Summer Institute (SASI) - 2 Week medical internship for HS students & pre-med undergrads seeking careers in clinical medicine.

Stanford Institutes of Medicine Summer Research Program (SIMR) 8-Week internship for HS juniors/seniors interested in biomedical research (Bioeng, Cancer, Cardiovascular, Genetics, Immunology, Neurobiology) Apply Dec - Feb.

Stanford Medical Youth Science Program (SMYSP) 5-Week Medical Research Program for Juniors & Seniors (US Citizens or Permanent Res) - Highly competitive

Stanford Summer Engineering Academy (SSEA) - 4 weeks - Fully Funded Exceptional students engage in hands-on engineering - highly competitive

SUMaC – Stanford University Mathematics Camp - Highly selective & intensive program in advanced mathematics & problem solving.

TeenNat - Grades 10-12, 6-Week, Hands-On Research - Pepperwood Preserve

Scientific inquiry, data collection, & statistical analysis. The program develops a sense of stewardship and appreciation for the natural environment.

Tesla Internships – Average $33/hour – Dozens of Positions Throughout CA

Full-Time Automotive Design, Engineering Technologies, Vehicle Service Research/Training

University of California, Berkeley Summer Programs for HS Students

Academic Talent Development Program (ATDP) & Explorations - Students can take 2 Berkeley courses w/small classes & hands-on activities.

AI4ALL @ UC Berkeley - 9th & 10th Grade Underrepresented Students - Learn about computer programming & artificial intelligence - Free, On Campus

Computer Science Academy - 2 Weeks - Rigorous immersion into coding, & problem-solving. Intense exploration of "big ideas". Apply by March.

Environmental Design (CED) Program - Students pursue environmental studies hands-on, immersive experiences in urban planning & sustainable design.

ID Tech (on-campus, not sponsored by UCB - Courses in coding, Minecraft game design, and other aspects of computer, VR, AR, & AI technology

Psychology Pre-College Summer Institute - 3-6 Weeks Students take college-level psychology courses and engage in discussions and activites related to cognitive science, neuroscience, and social psychology.

University of California, Davis - Young Scholars Program (YSP) - Apply in March

6-week STEM Summer Research Program - Rising juniors and seniors

University of California, Irvine Engineering Summer Academy &AI Camp

The on-campus engineering academy includes guest speakers, holds interactive workshops in robotics, computer science, mechanical engineering.

AI Camp 1-wk - NSF funded "Privacy IoT and AI" - Create Alexa-like assistants using Raspberry Pi, Python, and OpenAI interfaces.

UCLA Computer Science Intro Track - 6 Week Boot Camp - Apply by June 1

This coding boot camp includes college-level classes & labs in computer science, design, coding, and computational techniques (strings, lists, structures, and functional decomposition). No experience necessary.

UCLA SummerJumpstart Summer Art Inst, Digital Media Arts Inst, Digital Filmmaking Institute, Game Lab Institute. Computer Science Summer Institute

2-week program - Portfolio development– college credit available
Drawing, Painting, Photography, Sculpture, Video Art, Animation, and Game Design

University of California, San Diego - Academic Connections - HS Students

Lab and academic programs/projects in STEM subjects - 3-week program

University of California, Santa Barbara - Research Mentorship Program

6-week STEM Summer Research Program - Rising juniors and seniors

University of California, Santa Cruz HS Student Science Internship Program

10-week research internship for high school students in STEM fields. Conduct research with a faculty/doctoral student mentor. Apply in March.

USC Psychological Science & Society - 4 Weeks - June/July Los Angeles

This summer program for HS students explores classic and contemporary psychological theories with real-world hands-on activities.

University of Southern California Viterbi Discover Engineering - HS Students

Hands-on program in designing, 3D printing, building, & testing projects, Field trips to JPL, Hyperion Treatment Plant. Topics include aerospace, biomedical, chemical, computer science, electrical, environmental, industrial, and mechanical engineering. Also, the SHINE Program (biomedical/robotics)

USC Summer Film, Writing, Drama, and Architecture Programs – 2-4 Weeks
Creative Writing Workshop, Comedy Performance, Exploring Architecture

Colorado

Bank of America Student Leaders Program - 10+ CO Cities - HS Students - 8 Wks
Paid internships with nonprofits. Work experience & leadership development. Week long all-expense-paid Student Leaders Summit in Washington, DC in July. Submit application essays, recommendations, and resume in January.

Catalyst Campus - Colorado Springs, CO - Air Force Research Labs - 8-12 Weeks
Students participate in mentored ongoing research. Paid internship: comp sci, physics, materials science, & aerospace. Workshops, seminars, presentations.

Colorado School of Mines Summer Programs for HS Students - Golden, CO
Engineering Design Camp - 10th - 12th - Real world problem solving and engineering design while living on the Mines campus.

SUMMET (Summer Multicultural Engineering Training) - 11th & 12th - Program for ethnic/racial minorities, women, and first-gen college students.

Cyberpatriot - Air Force Assn National Youth Cyber Education Program - 1 Week
HS Students - Training at the National Cybersecurity Center, Colorado Springs.

Defense Intelligence Agency Summer College Internship- Engineering/Technology
10-14 Week Summer Internship Program Intelligence/Tech Apply in Feb Colorado Springs, CO - College Jr/Sr or Grad Student

GenCyber – 5-day Nat Security Agency-Sponsored Cybersecurity Camp for HS Students - Univ. of CO Denver & Colorado Springs – Taught by Cyber Industry
Engaging & Dynamic - Role-playing, visual aids, activities, & discussions. Computer networking, systems security, cyber operations, defense, AI, & virtual reality

Mentorship for Environmental Scholars (MES) Program - 10 Wk Paid - HS/College
Grand Junction Dept of Energy Site - Research in Environmental Science & STEM

National Security Agency (NSA) – Paid Computer Internship – Aurora
Students must be at least a junior in high school with interest in business, engineering, or computer science. Apply between September 1 and October 31.

University of Colorado, Boulder - Summer STEM Program - K-12 Options
STEM programs for all age levels - topics include AI, computer science, DNA, biomedical engineering, biotechnology, geology, technology design, LEGOs, math, medicine, programming, rockets. microbes, and video games.

University of Colorado Summer Science Program Intensive - HS Students 5-6 Wks
Biochemistry and molecular biology research - experimental design/synthesis; advanced lab techniques, lectures, collaborative workshops - highly competitive

Connecticut

Bank of America Student Leaders Program - 3+ CT Cities - HS Students - 8 Wks

Paid internships with nonprofits. Work experience & leadership development.
Week long all-expense-paid Student Leaders Summit in Washington, DC in July.
Submit application essays, recommendations, and resume in January.

GenCyber – 5-day Nat Security Agency-Sponsored Cybersecurity Camp for HS Students - Univ. of New Haven – Taught by Cyber Industry Professionals

Engaging & Dynamic - Role-playing, visual aids, activities, discussions. Computer
networking, systems security, cyber operations, defense, AI, virtual reality

Jackson Laboratory's Summer Student Program - 12th Grade & College Students

Farmington, CT - Develop & execute research, analyze data, present findings;
$6,500 stipend along with room, board, and travel to and from the lab

Science and Engineering Apprenticeship Program (SEAP) – US Navy – Groton

8-weeks, 300 openings, 30 research labs nationwide, $4,000-$4,500 salary. HS
students must be 16+ years old. Apply starting in August for following summer.

Summer Studio: Discovering Graphic Design (AIGA) – Bridgeport, CT

Free 4-week hands-on program for Bridgeport rising juniors and seniors
Week 1 – Music Festival Poster, Week 2 – Digital Media Poster
Week 3 – Animating Your Ideas, Week 4 – Portfolio Art for College Applications

Yale Summer Program in Astrophysics (YSPA) - Rising HS Seniors

Research/enrichment at the Leitner Family Observatory & Planetarium; 2-
week online prelim & 4-week on-campus program w/ research project

Yale Young Global Scholars - 2-Week HS Program; 150 countries; 50 states

Residential sessions June, July, & August - Apps due in January - Environmental
Studies/Issues, Innovations in Science & Technology, Literature, Philosophy, &
Culture, Politics Law & Economics, and Solving Global Challenges

Yale Young Global Scholars - HS Students - Biological & Biomedical Science

This 2-week program reviews topics in psychology, neuroscience, and
biomedical sciences in lectures and seminars with renowned faculty.

Delaware

Bank of America Student Leaders Program - 3+ DE Cities - HS Students - 8 Wks

Paid internships with nonprofits. Work experience & leadership development.
Week long all-expense-paid Student Leaders Summit in Washington, DC in July.
Submit application essays, recommendations, and resume in January.

District of Columbia

American Chemical Society - Project SEED Program - Washington, D.C.

Hands-on summer research/mentor chemistry prog. for low income students; 8-week program - Virtual summer opp. for 11,000 students in 40 U.S. states

Bank of America Student Leaders Program - DC - HS Students - 8 Wks

Paid internships with nonprofits; work experience & leadership development. With week long all-expense-paid Student Leaders Summit in Washington, DC in July. Submit application, essays, recommendations, and resume in January.

Catholic University School of Architecture and Planning

Summer High School Program - 2-week Residential (Two Session Options)

Defense Intelligence Agency Summer College Internship-Engineering/Technology

10-14 Week Summer Internship Program Intelligence/Tech Apply in Feb Washington, D.C. - College Jr/Sr or Grad Student

Federal Summer Internship Program - Paid - High School & College Students

National Institutes of Health (NIH) - Biomedical, behavioral, & social science research for 11th grade to grad school. Interns work w/a Principal Investigator.
Pathways Internship Program - HS to grad school - Hands-on w/govt agencies.
U.S. Fish & Wildlife Service Internships - Work in wildlife conservation and visitor services. Practical experience may lead to permanent federal positions.

GenCyber – 5-day Nat Security Agency-Sponsored Cybersecurity Camp for HS Students - Gallaudet University – Taught by Cyber Industry Professionals

Engaging & Dynamic - Role-playing, visual aids, activities, discussions: Computer networking, systems security, cyber operations, defense, AI, virtual reality

George Washington University Digital Storytelling Pre-College Program – July

Produce stories w/smartphones, learn storyboarding, & social media broadcast craft ideas, capture images, & create compelling content, w/character devt.

Georgetown University – 1-week – Creative Writing – Publishing

Fiction, Short Story, Poetry, and Professional Writing; visit literary hubs

National Air and Space Museum in Washington, D.C. – HS and College Students

The Explainers Program offers ~$15/hr year-round paid position for students to help visitors better understand the Museum and its artifacts and exhibitions.

U.S. Department of Education - Internships for HS & College - Fall, Winter, Spring, & Summer; Must be 16+; 8-Week Program

Human Resources/Project Mgmt, Educational Policies, Data Analytics, Training/Development; Grants Management; Communications; Information Technology

Florida

Bank of America Student Leaders Program - 20+ FL Cities - HS Students - 8 Wks

Paid internships with nonprofits. Work experience & leadership development. Week long all-expense-paid Student Leaders Summit in Washington, DC in July. Submit application essays, recommendations, and resume in January.

Cyberpatriot - Air Force Assn National Youth Cyber Education Program - 1 Week

HS Students - Multiple camp locations, incl FL SW Col, DoD StarBase, & USF

Defense Intelligence Agency Summer College Internship-Engineering/Technology

10-14 Week Summer Internship Program Intelligence/Tech Apply in February Miami & Tampa - College Jr/Sr or Grad Student

Disney Dreamers Academy - 4-Day HS Program - Walt Disney World

Mentorship program with workshops and seminars to connect students with Disney executives, celebrities, and educators. Apply online in October w/essays and video introduction.

Earthwatch Teen Expeditions - 8 days - 15-18 year olds - Sarasota, FL

Tracking Sharks and Rays - Conduct research alongside scientists in one of the oldest and largest shark/ray programs. Students consider overexploitation & environmental threats. Mote Marine Laboratory & Aquarium.

Eglin Air Force Base - Valparaiso, FL - Air Force Research Labs - 8-12 Weeks

Students participate in mentored in ongoing research. Paid internships: comp sci, physics, materials science, & aerospace. Workshops, seminars, presentations.

Florida Atlantic University School of Architecture– Boca Raton & Ft. Lauderdale

July 3-week program for HS students & first 2 years of college - Portfolio development, fabrication, architectural education, portfolio display, & critiques

Certificate of Completion Awarded – Enrollment is first-come, first-served basis.

Florida International University - Journalism Jumpstart - FREE - Miami, FL

Partnership & grant from the Dow Jones News Fund. Student work is showcased on the Jumpstart Journal Webpage. This program promotes a diverse national media. Participants work closely with media professionals.

GenCyber – 5-day Nat Security Agency-Sponsored Cybersecurity Camp for HS Students - Florida Inst of Technology, FL International University, Innovation Tech Academy, Univ. of West Florida – Taught by Cyber Industry Professionals

Engaging & Dynamic - Role-playing, visual aids, activities, discussions: Computer networking, systems security, cyber operations, defense, AI, virtual reality

Ringling College of Art and Design –Sarasota, FL - Intensive 4-week Program

Art/Design - computer animation, virtual reality, creative writing, digital sculpting, entertainment design, fabrication, film directing/production, game art, game design, illustration, painting, photography, and storyboarding

Science and Engineering Apprenticeship Program (SEAP) – US Navy Patrick SFB, Jacksonville, Orlando, Panama City

8-weeks, 300 openings, 30 research labs nationwide, $4,000-$4,500 salary. HS students must be 16+ years old. Apply starting in August for following summer.

SpaceX – Summer Engineering/Co-op Program – Cape Canaveral, FL

Paid Internship - Must be an undergraduate in a STEM subject.

University of Florida Design Exploration Program (DEP) - 3 Weeks

On-campus immersion into architecture. Construction of studio design projects, teamwork, seminars, field trips, architectural theory.

University of Florida - Student Science Training Program (SSTP) 6-Weeks

Rising seniors; 16+ years old; UF-SSTP is a rigorous, fast paced program for academically talented, and self-motivated students.

University of Miami Summer Scholars, Explorations in Architecture & Design

3-week Residential program; 6 college credits; Design, Graphics, and Theory. Architecture, Landscape Architecture, Historic Preservation; Urban Planning. Studio experience with drawing, model making, drafting, CAD, visual analysis.

Georgia

Bank of America Student Leaders Program - 10+ GA Cities - HS Students - 8 Wks

Paid internships with nonprofits. Work experience & leadership development. Week long all-expense-paid Student Leaders Summit in Washington, DC in July. Submit application essays, recommendations, and resume in January.

Centers for Disease Control - Atlanta, GA - CDC Disease Detective Day Camp

11th & 12th Grade - Lectures on global health, interventions, infectious diseases, chronic disease, & injury prevention. Students participate in mock press conferences, re-created outbreaks, lab sessions, & disease surveillance.

Cyberpatriot - Air Force Assn National Youth Cyber Education Program - 1 Week

HS Students - Multiple camp locations, including GA Cyber Innovation/Training Center, Middle GA State U., Ft Valley State U., & Wesley Community College

Emory University – Atlanta, GA – 2-, 4-, 6-Week Writing Programs

Journalism, Dramatic Writing, Media & Politics, Psychology & Fiction

GenCyber – 5-day Nat Security Agency-Sponsored Cybersecurity Camp for HS Students - Columbus State Univ., Savannah State Univ. , Univ. of North Georgia, Westminster Schools of Augusta - Taught by Cyber Industry Professionals

Engaging & Dynamic - Role-playing, visual aids, activities, discussions: Computer networking, systems security, cyber operations, defense, AI, virtual reality

Georgia Institute of Technology Pre-College Design Program – Atlanta, GA

2-week Residential program – College of Design – Grades 11 & 12 (Two Sessions); Architecture, Building Construction, Industrial Design, and Music Technology

Georgia Tech Summer Engineering Institute - Atlanta, GA - 3-Week

Residential engineering/tech prog. Grades 11-12, underrepresented students

Mentorship for Environmental Scholars (MES) Program - 10 Wk Paid - HS/College

Savannah State Univ. - Dept of Energy - Research in Environmental Science/STEM

National Security Agency (NSA) – Paid Computer Internship – Augusta

Students must be at least a junior in high school with interest in business, engineering, or computer science. Apply between September 1 & October 31.

Savannah College of Art & Design – 5-Week Rising Star & SCAD Courses

2-week College of Design Residential program –– Grades 11 & 12 - Courses include Advertising, Animation, Virtual Reality, Illustration, Storyboarding, Photography, Painting, Fashion, Digital Film, Graphic Design, and Industrial Design.

University of Georgia - Women Experience Creativity, Excitement, & Learning (ExCEL)

1-Week - Engineering Discovery Laboratory & Fabrication Studio

Hawaii

COPE Scholars Program – Healthcare Internship – 280 Hrs Training in Kailua

Health Scholars must be 18+. Students assist w/basic healthcare for medical or nursing school, etc. Certificate of Completion - Keck Graduate Institute.

Defense Intelligence Agency Summer College Internship-Engineering/Technology

10-14 Week Summer Internship Program Intelligence/Tech Apply in February Honolulu - College Jr/Sr or Grad Student

GenCyber – 5-day Cybersecurity Camp for HS Students - UH, Hilo, UH Kahului, UH Kaunakakai, UH Lihue-UH Wahiawa: Taught by Cyber Industry Professional

Engaging & Dynamic - Role-playing, visual aids, activities, discussions: Computer networking, systems security, cyber operations, defense, AI, virtual reality

Maui Optical & Super Computing Site - Maui, HI - Air Force Research Labs: 8-12 Wks

Students participate in mentored ongoing research teams. Paid internship: comp sci, physics, materials science, & aerospace. Workshops, seminars, presentations.

National Security Agency (NSA) – Paid Computer Internship – Oahu

Students must be at least a junior in high school with interest in business, engineering, or computer science. Apply between September 1 and October 31.

Science and Engineering Apprenticeship Program (SEAP) – US Navy – Honolulu

8-weeks, 300 openings, 30 research labs nationwide, $4,000-$4,500 salary. HS students must be 16+ years old. Apply starting in August for following summer.

Science Camps of America - Land & Sea Camp - 9-day HS Residential Camp

Practical exploration of volcanos, turtles, fish, & geological/marine conservation

STEMworks Innovation Internship Program - HS Students - $2,000 stipend

Focus areas include: 3D design, architecture, biomedical tech & engineering

University of Hawaii, Manoa College of Engineering Summer HS Student Program

Hands-on engineering & STEM program in robotics and interactive learning.

Idaho

Bank of America Student Leaders Program - 3+ ID Cities - HS Students - 8 Wks

Paid internships with nonprofits; work experience & leadership development. With week long all-expense-paid Student Leaders Summit in Washington, DC in July. Submit application, essays, recommendations, and resume in January.

GenCyber – 5-day Nat Security Agency-Sponsored Cybersecurity Camp for HS Students - Boise State University – Taught by Cyber Industry Professionals

Engaging & Dynamic - Role-playing, visual aids, activities, discussions: Computer networking, systems security, cyber operations, defense, AI, virtual reality

Idaho National Laboratory Internships - Idaho Falls, ID - 6-Week Paid Program

Nuclear Energy, Renewable Energy, and/or National Security. Interns apply STEM to solve real-world problems with experts in the nuclear field.

Illinois

After School Matters - 6-8 WeekSummer Program - Chicago

Internships and apprenticeships in areas like science, sports, technology, and communications.

Argonne National Laboratory - 8-Week - College Bound Research Program

STEM Lab/lecture w/interactive programs. Students take part in real-world problem-solving. This program is FREE, plus $500 per week stipend.

Bank of America Student Leaders Program - 5+ IL Cities - HS Students - 8 Wks

Paid internships with nonprofits. Work experience & leadership development. Week long all-expense-paid Student Leaders Summit in Washington, DC in July. Submit application essays, recommendations, and resume in January.

Cass County CEO Program - HS Summer & Academic Year - Cass County

HS students gain work experience with local business owners to develop and implement their business ideas.

Cyberpatriot - Air Force Assn National Youth Cyber Education Program - 1 Week

HS Students - Camp locations include Elmhurst University

Defense Intelligence Agency Summer College Internship - Engineering/Technology

10-14 Week Summer Internship Program Intelligence/Tech Apply in February Scott Air Force Base, IL - College Jr/Sr or Grad Student

GenCyber – 5-day Nat Security Agency-Sponsored Cybersecurity Camp for HS Students - College of Dupage – Taught by Cyber Industry Professionals

Engaging & Dynamic - Role-playing, visual aids, activities, discussions: Computer networking, systems security, cyber operations, defense, AI, virtual reality

Great Books Summer Program - Northwestern University - Grades 6-8 and 9-12

Great Books & Big Ideas, Writer's Workshops, and Literary Travel Programs Read, Write, & Discuss Big Ideas in Literature and Philosophy with scholars

Illinois Institute of Technology - HS Summer Introduction to Architecture

2-week - Comprehensive overview; 1-week Exploration in Architecture for middle school students – studio-based, firm visits, field trips, projects.

Northwestern University Center for Talent Development Rigorous/Accel - Grades 9-12

Medical Pharmacology, Neuroplasticity, Cybersecurity, Data Science, Astrophysics, Quantum Mechanics, IoT, Build Your Own Computer, & Machine Learning

Northwestern University – National High School Institute

5-week Film & Video, Music, Speech & Debate, Theatre, and Dramaturgy

Pathway Summer Program Dept of Energy RENEW Initiative-HS/College Students

Mentorship, hands-on engineering/technology - Argonne National Lab

School of the Art Institute of Chicago – Early College Program for HS Students

1-, 2-, 4-week Residential programs in Painting, Drawing, Animation, Comics/ Graphic Novels, and Fashion Design. Portfolio development programs; earn college credit. Full-tuition scholarships are available.

Southern Illinois University Carbondale – Kid Architecture

1-week Elementary Grades, Middle School & High School Architecture Camp

University of Chicago Creative Writing Immersion - HS Writing Program

"Collegiate Writing: Awakening Into Consciousness"

University of Chicago Psychology Summer Program - Understanding the Mind

This 3-4 week program explores cognitive psychology and neuroscience to understand how the mind works.

University of Chicago Research in the Biological Sciences (RIBS) 4 week Intensive

Highly competitive project-based training in molecular, microbiological, & cell biology; weekly writing assignments & lunch seminars; intependent project

University of Illinois at Chicago Architecture - HiArch Summer HS Program

1 & 2-week (July) - Culture of architecture, design, thinking, and artmaking.

University of Illinois at Urbana-Champaign - Women in Engineering - 6th-12th

The Grainger College of Engineering introduces engineering to teenage girls.

Univ of Illinois, Urbana-Champaign - HS Students Discover Engineering Camp

STEM-focused camps - 7th-12th grade - Specialized Aerospace, Chemical Electrical, Computer, Mechanical, Nuclear, Radiological, Materials Science, AI, Programming, Molecule Making camps. 20+ camps from June to August

Young Scholars Summer STEMM Research Programs at Univ of Illinois (UIUC)

6-weeks, Rising 10th-12th graders collaborate on cutting-edge research in cancer, immunology, neuroscience, artificial intelligence, physics, quantum mechanics, bioengineering, electrical engineering - Final Symposium held in early August.

Indiana

Bank of America Student Leaders Program - 5+ IN Cities - HS Students - 8 Wks

Paid internships with nonprofits. Work experience & leadership development. Week long all-expense-paid Student Leaders Summit in Washington, DC in July. Submit application essays, recommendations, and resume in January.

Cyberpatriot - Air Force Assn National Youth Cyber Education Program - 1 Week

HS Students - Camp locations include Ivy Tech Community College

GenCyber – 5-day Nat Security Agency-Sponsored Cybersecurity Camp for HS Students - Purdue Univ. Northwest – Taught by Cyber Industry Professionals

Engaging & Dynamic - Role-playing, visual aids, activities, discussions: Computer networking, systems security, cyber operations, defense, AI, virtual reality

Indiana University Bloomington Summer Science Program - HS Students 5-6 Wks

Biochemistry and molecular biology research - highly competitive, hands-on, collaborative; mentors; student teams; analysis, scientific writing, presentations

Purdue University Summer Programs for HS Students

Seminar for Top Engineering Prospects (STEP) - 1 Week
Program for rising seniors to explore engineering opportunities.
Minority Engineering Program - 7th - 9th Grade Students
This summer camp introduces to engineering careers and the design process.
Summer Science Program - HS Students 5-6 Wks
Biochemistry and molecular biology research - highly competitive, hands-on, collaborative; mentors; student teams; analysis, scientific writing, presentations

Rose-Hulman Institute of Technology - Operation Catapult - 2 Weeks

Engineering projects, robotics, research, and STEM design projects - Rising HS juniors or seniors participate in hands-on engineering activities.

Science and Engineering Apprenticeship Program (SEAP) – US Navy – Crane

8-weeks, 300 openings, 30 research labs nationwide, $4,000-$4,500 salary. HS students must be 16+ years old. Apply starting in August for following summer.

University of Notre Dame Summer Scholars Program - 2-weeks HS Students

Film, Photography, Performing Arts - studios, seminars, and field trips STEM: Climate Change, Artificial Intelligence, Engineering, Chemistry, Medicine

Iowa

Bank of America Student Leaders Program - Polk County - HS Students - 8 Wks

Paid internships with nonprofits. Work experience & leadership development. Week long all-expense-paid Student Leaders Summit in Washington, DC in July. Submit application essays, recommendations, and resume in January.

Iowa State University – College of Design - Design Camps - HS Students

1-week – Architecture, Studio/Fine Arts, Graphic, Interior, & Industrial Design

Kansas

Bank of America Student Leaders Program - 2 KS Cities - HS Students - 8 Wks

Paid internships with nonprofits. Work experience & leadership development. Week long all-expense-paid Student Leaders Summit in Washington, DC in July. Submit application essays, recommendations, and resume in January.

Kentucky

Bank of America Student Leaders Program - 10+ KY Cities - HS Students - 8 Wks

Paid internships with nonprofits. Work experience & leadership development. Week long all-expense-paid Student Leaders Summit in Washington, DC in July. Submit application essays, recommendations, and resume in January.

GenCyber – 5-day Nat Security Agency-Sponsored Cybersecurity Camp for HS Students - Big Sandy Community & Technical College – Taught by Cyber Industry

Engaging & Dynamic - Role-playing, visual aids, activities, discussions: Computer networking, systems security, cyber operations, defense, AI, virtual reality

Louisiana

Bank of America Student Leaders Program - 20+ LA Cities - HS Students - 8 Wks

Paid internships with nonprofits. Work experience & leadership development. Week long all-expense-paid Student Leaders Summit in Washington, DC in July. Submit application essays, recommendations, and resume in January.

Barksdale Air Force Base - Bossier Parish, LA - Air Force Research Labs - 8-12 Weeks

Students participate in mentored ongoing research. Paid internship: comp sci, physics, materials science, & aerospace. Workshops, seminars, presentations.

GenCyber – 5-day Nat Security Agency-Sponsored Cybersecurity Camp for HS Students - Louisiana Tech University – Taught by Cyber Industry Professionals

Engaging & Dynamic - Role-playing, visual aids, activities, discussions: Computer networking, systems security, cyber operations, defense, AI, virtual reality

Science and Engineering Apprenticeship Program (SEAP) – US Navy – New Orleans

8-weeks, 300 openings, 30 research labs nationwide, $4,000-$4,500 salary. HS students must be 16+ years old. Apply starting in August for following summer.

Maine

Bank of America Student Leaders Program - Cumberland - HS Students - 8 Wks

Paid internships with nonprofits. Work experience & leadership development. Week long all-expense-paid Student Leaders Summit in Washington, DC in July. Submit application essays, recommendations, and resume in January.

Earthwatch Teen Expeditions - Acadia National Park, Maine - 1 week
students must be 16+ years old. Apply starting in August for following summer.

Climate Change: Sea to the Trees science exploration program; understand patterns and make observations regarding how humans are changing the ecosystem; wildlife diversity, bird migration, ocean acidification, sea warming

GenCyber – 5-day Nat Security Agency-Sponsored Cybersecurity Camp for HS
Students - Northeastern Univ Portland, Maine – Taught by Cyber Industry Prof

Engaging & Dynamic - Role-playing, visual aids, activities, discussions: Computer networking, systems security, cyber operations, defense, AI, virtual reality

Jackson Laboratory's Summer Student Program - 12th Grade & College Students

Bar Harbor, ME - Develop & execute research, analyze data, present findings; $6,500 stipend along with room, board, and travel to and from the lab

Maryland

Bank of America Student Leaders Program - 10+ MD Cities - HS Students - 8 Wks

Paid internships with nonprofits. Work experience & leadership development. Week long all-expense-paid Student Leaders Summit in Washington, DC in July. Submit application essays, recommendations, and resume in January.

Defense Intelligence Agency Summer College Internship - Engineering/Technology

10-14 Week Summer Internship Program Intelligence & Tech Apply in February Ft. Meade, MD - College Jr/Sr or Grad Student

GenCyber – 5-day Nat Security Agency-Sponsored Cybersecurity Camp for HS
Students - Anne Arundel CC, Harford CC, PGCC – Taught by Cyber Industry

Engaging & Dynamic - Role-playing, visual aids, activities, discussions: Computer networking, systems security, cyber operations, defense, AI, virtual reality

Goddard Space Flight Center (NASA) - High School & College

Summer Aerospace and Climate Change Internship at GISS - Greenbelt, MD Research, Mentorship, Experiential Learning Opportunities

Johns Hopkins Engineering Summer Programs in Innovation Sustainable
Energy, and Biomedical Engineering - Online and In-Person

Biomedical, chemical, civil, electrical, environmental, and mechanical

Maryland Institute College of Art (MICA) – 2-, 3-, 5-week - HS Students

Live studio workshops, artist talks, collaboration, feedback, critique, evaluation

National Institute of Health – 8-week Paid Internship– Bethesda, Baltimore, and
Frederick. MD Research Group Locations - Apply by mid February

Biomedical research internship for students 17 years or older by June 15th. HS-SIP for high school juniors & seniors - June to August - hands-on research.

90

National Security Agency (NSA) – Paid Computer Internship – Ft. Meade
Students must be at least a junior in high school with interest in business, engineering, or computer science. Apply between September 1 and October 31.

Naval Academy Summer STEM Program - Annapolis, MD - HS Students
Three week-long sessions for students interested in coding, game design computer projects, robotics, & engineering. Collaborate in world-class labs.

Science and Engineering Apprenticeship Program (SEAP) – US Navy – Bethesda, Patuxent River, Silver Spring, Indian Head, and Annapolis
8-weeks, 300 openings, 30 research labs nationwide, $4,000-$4,500 salary. HS students must be 16+ years old. Apply starting in August for following summer.

Terp Young Scholars - University of Maryland - 3-Week High School Program
Immersion into computer science with projects, exams, and collaboration.

University of Maryland – 4-week ESTEEM/SER-Quest Summer Program
Rising seniors undertake engineering-focused projects while conducting research

University of Maryland - Discovering Engineering - 1 week (additional programs also)
Exploration of engineering with faculty to learn about the various disciplines.

United States Naval Academy - Summer STEM Program for Students in 9th - 11th
Design and build STEM projects with USNA Faculty and Midshipmen
1 week residential program, $700, includes lodging, meals, transport from airport

Massachusetts

Bank of America Student Leaders Program - 5+ MA Cities - HS Students - 8 Wks
Paid internships with nonprofits. Work experience & leadership development. Week long all-expense-paid Student Leaders Summit in Washington, DC in July. Submit application essays, recommendations, and resume in January.

Bentley University - Wolfram Math/Computer -2 Week - HS Summer Program
Intensive training in programming, computation, & technology. Students produce a project from ideation to completion (Wolfram Emerging Scholars).

Boston College - Cognitive & Affective Neuroscience Lab (CANLab)
One HS Student is chosen each year to intern in the lab learning aging, memory, brain health, sleep, and both cognitive and affective neuroscience.

Boston College - Boston, MA – Creative Writing Seminar Program
3-week (July) Residential Program – HS Students – nonfiction, fiction, poetry Create & edit the class literary journal and present writings at a public reading.

Boston University Math, Engineering, Technology, Media, and Journalism

AMP - Academy of Media Production – Cinematic/journalistic in visual storytelling (Grades 10 – 12)

Code Breakers – 10th & 11th Grade Females - Cybersecurity, Cryptography, Computer Programming, and Ethical Hacking (Free)

Girls Get Math@BU – 5-day Non-residential summer program for enthusiastic 10th – 11th graders

Neuroscience - 6-Weeks - 11th & 12th Grade - Lectures and discussions cover psychology, neuropharmacology, neurology, and neuropsychology.

Journalism Academy – 2-week Writing, Photography, Reporting ages 14-18

PROMYS – Program in Mathematics for Young Scientists – 6 weeks 80 high school students 14+ years old (scholarships available); seminars in number theory, cryptography, linear algebra, matroids, graphs, and data visualization.

RISE – Research in Science & Engineering - 6-week   Research in Science & Engineering program in astronomy, chemistry, neuroscience, and medicine. Engineering Research Options: Biomedical, Computer, Electrical, Mechanical

U-Design – 2-week Engineering Design Prog – hands-on workshop - 6th - 10th

Forsyth Student Scholars Summer Internship Program - 8-Weeks - 11th & 12th grades

Science research mentor program for underserved Massachusetts HS students.

GenCyber – 5-day Nat Security Agency-Sponsored Cybersecurity Camp for HS Students - Assumption University & Cape Cod CC – Taught by Cyber Industry

Engaging & Dynamic - Role-playing, visual aids, activities, discussions: Computer networking, systems security, cyber operations, defense, AI, virtual reality

Great Books Summer Program - Amherst College - Grades 6-8 and 9-12

Great Books & Big Ideas, Writer's Workshops, and Literary Travel Programs Read, Write, & Discuss Big Ideas in Literature and Philosophy with scholars

Harvard Medical School - MEDscience Simulation Lab - Grades 9-12

Students learn biotech/medicine in an immersive, hands-on clinical research lab. This 1-week program offers medical simulations and research with DNA extraction, PCR, Gel Electrophoresis, ELISA, and disease diagnosis and treatment

Harvard University GSD Design Discovery– Cambridge, MA (Ages 18+)

3-week Residential Program – Architecture, Landscape, Urban Planning & Design Students participate in physical modeling, fabrication, and assembly.

Harvard Summer Program for High School Students Credit/Non Credit Classes

7-week college credit (campus dorms) include: Creating Comics & Graphic Novels; Advertising, Visual Imagery, Creative Writing, Physics, Chemistry, Biology, Medicinal Topics, Calculus, Economics, and Computer Science

Massachusetts College of Art & Design – 4-Week Art Immersion Program
Students take 3 foundation courses and participate in a closing exhibition.

Massachusetts Institute of Technology – HS Students – Cambridge

Beaver Works Summer Institute – 4-week intensive program for first-generation high school juniors. Programs include Autonomous Underwater Vehicles to Quantum Software and to Serious Game Design with AI.

Lincoln Laboratory Radar Introduction for Student Engineers (LLRISE) - FFREE - 2-week project-based workshop to teach students how to build small Doppler and range radar systems. HS Juniors. Applications open in January.

MITES – Minority Introduction to Engineering and Science – Intensive 6-week residential program for 80 high school juniors who intend to enter STEM programs, especially from underrepresented groups. The program is free.

MOTSTEC - Hands-on, in-depth STEM mentorship for HS seniors; courses/projects; present research at 5-day event (FREE) Work w/MIT faculty/researchers. Six-month hybrid learning program with 2-week STEM Immersion June-August.

RSI – Research Science Institute – Free. Competitive/Intensive 6-week program for 70 HS juniors who research/study advanced theory in math, science, & engineering. Distinguished Lectures/Alumni Network. Apply by early December.

THINK Scholars Program - 4 months HS students apply between Nov 1-Jan 1, accepted in Feb, join program in June. Pair with MIT researcher. Summer 4-days at MIT, All Expenses Paid + $1,000. Submit detailed proposals for novel ideas.

WTP – Women's Technology Program – 4-wk engineering focus - EE, ME, EECS

Urbanframe Summer Design - Build Project - CAD, drafting, sketching, mapping and context study, historical research, carpentry & construction.

Additional MIT Hosted Programs: LaunchX, OSC, iD Tech Camps, National Geographic Student Expeditions

National Institute of Health – Paid Internship - Apply in Feb– Framingham, MA
8-week - Biomedical research internship for students 17 years or older by June. HS-SIP for high school juniors & seniors June to August hands-on research.

Northeastern University - Drug Discovery to Clinical Care - HS Students
This 2-week hands-on interactive program describes the life cycle of medications from drug discovery to use in humans. Students visit facilities, engage in compounding, and learn the therapeutic and toxicological background.

Northeastern Univ Young Scholars Program w/field trips - Rising HS Seniors
Intro to Engineering - Chemical, Civil, EE, Computer, Mechanical & Industrial Radar, batteries, energy, robotics, lasers, microwave, biotech, medicine, bldgs

Tufts University – 6-Week Writing Intensive - HS Students - Develop Papers
Writing exercises, evaluation from professors, revise, and build on a theme.

Tufts University Summer Accelerator - 2-Weeks for HS Students in 10th-12th
Students take 2 college-level seminars in neuroscience, coding, physiology, criminal justice, international affairs, chaos theory, engineering, artificial intelligence, astrochemistry, and mythology.

University of Massachusetts Amherst Pre-College – Amherst, MA
1-, 2-, 3-week Residential Intensives Grades 10-12; 3-D Design, 3-D Animation, Building & Construction Technology; Combatting the Climate Crisis Summer Engineering Institute, Design Academy, Programming for Aspiring Scientists

Wellesley College – 2-week Residential Program - Wellesley, MA
EXPLO Pre-College + Career for Grades 10-12 Three session options; Topics include – AI, Entrepreneurship, Engineering, Medicine, Law, CSI

Wentworth Institute of Technology - 2-4 Week Impact Lab - HS 11th & 12th
On-Campus Comp Sci, Engineering, Info Technology, Architecture, & Construction

WPI Frontiers Program - Worcester Polytechnic Institute - Two 2-Week Sessions
This residential program allows HS students to explore comp sci & data science.

Youth Design Boston (AIGA) – Boston, MA
Summer Graphic Design Internship & Mentoring Program

Michigan

Andrews University School of Architecture & Interior Design - Renaissance Kids
Virtual Studio Projects; lecture; community build projects

Bank of America Student Leaders Program - 5+ MI Cities - HS Students - 8 Wks
Paid internships with nonprofits. Work experience & leadership development. Week long all-expense-paid Student Leaders Summit in Washington, DC in July. Submit application essays, recommendations, and resume in January.

GenCyber – 5-day Nat Security Agency-Sponsored Cybersecurity Camp for HS Students - Northern MI U. & Oakland U. – Taught by Cyber Industry Professionals
Engaging & Dynamic - Role-playing, visual aids, activities, discussions: Computer networking, systems security, cyber operations, defense, AI, virtual reality

Interlochen Center for the Arts – Summer Arts Camp – 1-6 Weeks
Creative Writing, Dance, Art, Motion Picture, Music, Theatre, Visual Arts

Michigan State University - HS Honors Science, Math, Engineering Program
7-week intensive, hands-on summer research program & engineering projects.

National Institute of Health – 8-week Paid Internship - Apply in Feb– Detroit
Research biomedical internship for students 17 years or older by June.
HS-SIP for high school juniors & seniors June to August hands-on research.

University of Michigan – Stamps School of Art & Design – 3-Week BFA Preview
HS Students – Creative retreat w/state-of-the-art facilities & museum excursions

University of Michigan – Summer Engineering Exploration (SEE) - 1 Week
On-campus - engineering design challenges - Apply Jan-Feb – Grades 10-12

Minnesota

Bank of America Student Leaders Program - 10+ MN Cities - HS Students - 8 Wks
Paid internships with nonprofits. Work experience & leadership development.
Week long all-expense-paid Student Leaders Summit in Washington, DC in July.
Submit application essays, recommendations, and resume in January.

GenCyber – 5-day Nat Security Agency-Sponsored Cybersecurity Camp for HS Students - Alexandria Tech & CC & Lake Superior College – Cyber Industry Prof
Engaging & Dynamic - Role-playing, visual aids, activities, discussions: Computer networking, systems security, cyber operations, defense, AI, virtual reality

Summer Liberal Arts Institute (SLAI) Computer Science Program - HS Jr & Sr
Hands-on, project-based residential program in computational solutions to problems, research, and a final symposium to present findings.

Mississippi

GenCyber – 5-day Nat Security Agency-Sponsored Cybersecurity Camp for HS Students - Univ. of Southern MS – Taught by Cyber Industry Professionals
Engaging & Dynamic - Role-playing, visual aids, activities, discussions: Computer networking, systems security, cyber operations, defense, AI, virtual reality

Science and Engineering Apprenticeship Program (SEAP) – US Navy – Stennis
8-weeks, 300 openings, 30 research labs nationwide, $4,000-$4,500 salary. HS students must be 16+ years old. Apply starting in August for following summer.

Missouri

Bank of America Student Leaders Program - 10+ MO Cities - HS Students - 8 Wks
Paid internships with nonprofits. Work experience & leadership development.
Week long all-expense-paid Student Leaders Summit in Washington, DC in July.
Submit application essays, recommendations, and resume in January.

GenCyber – 5-day Nat Security Agency-Sponsored Cybersecurity Camp for HS Students - Univ. of MO, Kansas City – Taught by Cyber Industry Professionals

Engaging & Dynamic - Role-playing, visual aids, activities, discussions: Computer networking, systems security, cyber operations, defense, AI, virtual reality

Univ of Missouri Kansas City – Dept of Architecture, Urban Planning & Design

Design Discovery Program – Architecture, Interior Design, Landscape Architecture 3-day (July) Non-Residential Program – HS Students/Current College Students

Washington University in St. Louis - HS Programs

Biology of the Brain - 4-5 week summer - Grades 11, 12 - Students learn brain anatomy, composition, changes, development, memories, and injury

Creative Writing Program – 2-weeks - fiction, nonfiction, and poetry. Morning writer's workshops. Students edit, share ideas, and discuss work

Arts & Journalism Program - 5-8 week – Dance, Journalism, Photography, Music, Drama, Photojournalism

Young Scientist Program - Rising Seniors - Summer Focus is an 8-week paid summer research internship.

Shaw Institute for Field Training (SIFT) and Tyson Environmental Research **Apprenticeship** (TERA) programs.

BOLD@Olin - 1-week Business Leadership/Entrepreneurship Program

Whiteman Air Force Base - Knob Noster, MO - Air Force Research Labs - 8-12 Weeks

Students participate in mentored ongoing research teams. Paid internship: comp sci, physics, materials science, & aerospace. Workshops, seminars, presentations.

Montana

Cyberpatriot - Air Force Assn National Youth Cyber Education Program - 1 Week

HS Students - Camp locations include Montana State University

GenCyber – 5-day Nat Security Agency-Sponsored Cybersecurity Camp for HS Students - Univ. of Montana, Missoula – Taught by Cyber Industry Professionals

Engaging & Dynamic - Role-playing, visual aids, activities, discussions: Computer networking, systems security, cyber operations, defense, AI, virtual reality

National Institute of Health – 8-week Paid Internship – Hamilton, MT

Biomedical research internship for students 17 years or older by June.
HS-SIP for high school juniors & seniors June to August hands-on research.

Nebraska

Bank of America Student Leaders Program - 3+ NE Cities - HS Students - 8 Wks

Paid internships with nonprofits. Work experience & leadership development. Week long all-expense-paid Student Leaders Summit in Washington, DC in July. Submit application essays, recommendations, and resume in January.

Cyberpatriot - Air Force Assn National Youth Cyber Education Program - 1 Week

HS Students - Multiple camp locations include Bellevue University.

GenCyber – 5-day Nat Security Agency-Sponsored Cybersecurity Camp for HS Students - Univ. of Nebraska, Omaha – Taught by Cyber Industry Professionals

Engaging & Dynamic - Role-playing, visual aids, activities, discussions: Computer networking, systems security, cyber operations, defense, AI, virtual reality

University of Nebraska College of Architecture – 6-day (June) - Grades 11-12

6-day (June) Residential Program – Grades 11 & 12 – Studio training; architectural design; scholarships

Nevada

AFWERX - Las Vegas, NV - Air Force Research Labs - 8-12 Weeks

Students participate in mentored ongoing research teams. Paid internship: comp sci, physics, materials science, & aerospace. Workshops, seminars, presentations

Bank of America Student Leaders Program - 3+ NV Cities - HS Students - 8 Wks

Paid internships with nonprofits. Work experience & leadership development. Week long all-expense-paid Student Leaders Summit in Washington, DC in July. Submit application essays, recommendations, and resume in January.

GenCyber – 5-day Nat Security Agency-Sponsored Cybersecurity Camp for HS Students - University of Nevada, LV – Taught by Cyber Industry Professionals

Engaging & Dynamic - Role-playing, visual aids, activities, discussions: Computer networking, systems security, cyber operations, defense, AI, virtual reality

University of Nevada - Hands-On Engineering & Cybersecurity Camps - HS Students

UNR Engineering Exploration - Projects/activities - design, engineer, build, & test
UNLV Cybersecurity Camp - Interactive labs/projects on cyber threats & defense.

New Jersey

Bank of America Student Leaders Program - 10+ NJ Cities - HS Students - 8 Wks
Paid internships with nonprofits. Work experience & leadership development.
Week long all-expense-paid Student Leaders Summit in Washington, DC in July.
Submit application essays, recommendations, and resume in January.

New Jersey Institute of Technology – Hillier College of Architecture & Design
1-week (July) Residential Program – HS Students – Architecture, Interior Design,
Industrial Design, Digital Design - Architecture + Design Programs (2 Start Dates)

Pathway Summer Program Dept of Energy RENEW Initiative-HS & College Students
Mentorship, hands-on engineering/technology - Princeton Plasma Physics Lab

Princeton Summer Journalism Program (PSJP) - FREE Residential Prog for HS Juniors
Year-long college prep program for HS juniors from low-income backgrounds.
Summer intensive at Princeton University (10 days); tours, seminars, writing project.

Princeton University Laboratory Learning Program 5-6 Weeks, 16+ years old
Summer science/engineering research for HS students; lab experience; write paper

Science and Engineering Apprenticeship Program (SEAP) – US Navy – Lakehurst
8-weeks, 300 openings, 30 research labs nationwide, $4,000-$4,500 salary. HS
students must be 16+ years old. Apply starting in August for following summer.

New Hampshire

Bank of America Student Leaders Program - 2 NH Cities - HS Students - 8 Wks
Paid internships with nonprofits. Work experience & leadership development.
Week long all-expense-paid Student Leaders Summit in Washington, DC in July.
Submit application essays, recommendations, and resume in January.

Sustainable Summer @ Dartmouth - Environmental Leadership Academy
Students ages 15-18 attend 2-week program; bootcamp, research/development
environmental problem, and then convert abstract ideas into real initiatives.

University of New Hampshire InterOperability Lab - HighTech Bound - 4-6 Weeks
Paid summer program for rising HS seniors pursuing careers in technology.
Real-world mentored projects, visit tech companies, Apply between Jan & Feb

New Mexico

Bank of America Student Leaders Program - 2 NM Cities - HS Students - 8 Wks
Paid internships with nonprofits. Work experience & leadership development.
Week long all-expense-paid Student Leaders Summit in Washington, DC in July.
Submit application essays, recommendations, and resume in January.

Cyberpatriot - Air Force Assn National Youth Cyber Education Program - 1 Week
HS Students - Multiple camp locations include San Juan College

GenCyber – 5-day Nat Security Agency-Sponsored Cybersecurity Camp for HS Students - San Juan College – Taught by Cyber Industry Professionals

Engaging & Dynamic - Role-playing, visual aids, activities, discussions: Computer networking, systems security, cyber operations, defense, AI, virtual reality

Kirtland Air Force Base - Albuquerque, NM - Air Force Research Labs - 8-12 Weeks

Students participate in mentored ongoing research. Paid internship: comp sci, physics, materials science, & aerospace. Workshops, seminars, presentations.

Mentorship for Environmental Scholars (MES) Program - 10 Wk Paid - HS/College

Sandia Nat Lab Dept of Energy Albuquerque - Environmental Science & STEM

New Mexico State Summer Science Program - 5-6 Weeks - HS Students

Astrophysics calculations, astronomy, original research program; mentors, workshops; collaborative community - highly selective - transformative

Pathway Summer Program Dept of Energy RENEW Initiative-HS & College Students

Mentorship, hands-on engineering/technology - Sandia National Laboratories

Sandia National Labs - Albuquerque - Engineering/Tech Internship - HS/College

* Ages 16+ - FT HS Student - Work on STEM Projects with mentors
* 10-12 Week College Summer Internship, Year-Round Internship, & Co-Ops

New York

AIA New York – Center for Architecture 1-week (July) – HS Students

Grades 3-12 include Architectural Design Studio, Drawing, Rooftop Dwelling, Dream House, Treehouses, Skyscrapers, Green Island Home, Neighborhood Design, Subway Architecture, Waterfront City, Parks & Playground Design

Bank of America Student Leaders Program - 10+ NY Cities - HS Students - 8 Wks

Paid internships with nonprofits. Work experience & leadership development. Week long all-expense-paid Student Leaders Summit in Washington, DC in July. Submit application essays, recommendations, and resume in January.

Brookhaven National Laboratory - Upton, NY - US Dept of Energy - Rising HS Seniors
Ensure America's energy security, environment, nuclear challenges by researching solutions. 6-week High School Research Program (HSRP) STEM research

Brooklyn College STEM Research Academy - Urban Ecology & Design for HS Students
This 6-week environmental science research program includes lab, fieldwork, and methodology. Students dive into data collection and analysis.

Canon Insights Summer Internship – Canon USA – PR/Marketing - Huntington, NY
Public Relations & Marketing Majors – 10 Week Paid Position

City College of New York - STEM Institute Research/Project for HS Students
Build 3D Printers, Robot, Rockets, & Drones - Free Supercharged Program

Cold Spring Harbor Laboratory - Partners for the Future Program - HS Students
Long Island HS seniors engage in biomedical research - min 10 hrs/wk from Sept - March of their senior year. State-of-the-art molecular biology - present findings.

Columbia University Summer Programs for HS Students
BRAINYAC - Zuckerman Institute's Brain Research Apprenticeships for HS students in NYC. Weekends and 7 weeks in the summer.
Neuroscience of Psychiatric Disorders - Grades 9-12 - Students learn brain anatomy and explore case studies of neuropsychiatric disorders.
School of Engineering - HS Maker Lab - 6-Weeks - Free - Students address a health problem - design, prototype, & test a biomedical device. Final presentation given to leading biomedical executives.
SHAPE (3-Wk - Summer HS Program in Technology & Engineering) - Build 3D Printers, Robots, Rockets, & Drones - Free Supercharged Program - This engineering program is for HS students pursuing technology-focused subjects.
Science of Psychology - Introduction to the theory & science of psychology.
Summer Art Immersion - 3-week July-August Residential Program – Drawing Architecture, Creative Writing, Filmmaking, Photography, Theater, Visual Arts

Cooper Union - New York, NY – Summer Art Intensive - 4-Week July-August
Residential Prog – Portfolio Devt, Exhibition, Anthology Publication; Drawing Animation, Creative Writing, Photography, Graphic Design, & Stop Animation

Cornell University – 3-Week Transmedia: Image, Sound, Motion Program
3-, 6-, 9-week June-August Residential Program; Drawing and New Media (collage, drawing, digital photography, screen printing, & video)
Architecture: Design Studio, Culture, and Society, Architectural Science & Technology

Cornell University – CURIE Academy High School females entering 11th and 12th
Students who excel in math & science break the rules to make new discoveries.

Cornell University - CATALYST Scholars - 1-Week STEM Academy (diverse students)
Cornell Engineering faculty/students participate in ten field sessions.

Corning Summer Internships for College Students – Corning, NY

Advanced optics, Gorilla Glass, emerging innovations, life sciences, pharmaceuticals. Internships offered in engineering, science, & business

Environmental Studies Summer Youth Inst-Hobart & William Smith Colleges

2-week, college experience for HS Students - Immerse in discussions, fieldwork in the Adirondacks, and projects on the environment and sustainability.

Federal Bureau of Investigation - Future Agents in Training - Teen Academy

FBI classes on terrorism, cyber crime, public corruption, polygraph exams, evidence response, and SWAT. Meet w/special agents and intelligence analysts.

GenCyber – 5-day Nat Security Agency-Sponsored Cybersecurity Camp for HS Students - Mohawk Valley CC, RIT, & SUNY Buffalo – Taught by Cyber Industry

Engaging & Dynamic - Role-playing, visual aids, activities, discussions: Computer networking, systems security, cyber operations, defense, AI, virtual reality

Goddard Institute for Space Studies (GISS) New York City - Climate Change Research Initiative (CCRI) Summer Internship - High School & College

Research, Mentorship, and Experiential Learning Opportunities

Hofstra University Summer Science Research Program (HUSSRP) - 5-Week HS Prog

Students conduct research with matched faculty mentors, culminating in a poster session; students attend weekly seminars.

Jacobs Institute 8-week Paid Biomedical Internship (Apply Nov.-Jan.)

HS Jr/Sr or College Student – Gates Vascular Institute, Buffalo, NY Niagara Medical Campus; Lunch and Learn, weekly grand rounds, research, presentations

John Jay College of Criminal Justice - 4 week - Introduction to Psychology

New York high school students - Learn research methods in thought, memory, learning, personality, socialization, development, disorders, and the biological basis of behavior.

Lamont-Doherty Earth Observatory Secondary School Field Research Program

6-week - research, lab, and fieldwork - HS students - $1,400 stipend. Students follow through a research process to resolve environmental problems.

Manhattan College Engineering Summer Camp - 1-Week - HS Students

Campers explore five engineering specialties: mechanical, electrical, civil, chemical, and environmental engineering.

Mount Sinai - Icahn School of Medicine - Internship Program - FREE - Rising Senior

African-American/Black or Hispanic/Latino w/demonstrated interest in medicine 6-Week summer program. Dept of Neurosurgery. Applications open in January

New York University Engineering Innovation and Computer Science Programs

Applied Research in Science and Engineering (ARISE) - ARISE is a Free 7-week STEM program focused on Biomedical, Chemical Civil, Computer, Electrical, Mechanical, & Aerospace Engineering
Cyber Security Awareness Week (CSAW) - Cybersecurity Games & Conference NYU Center for Cyber Security - World's largest student-run event for students of

all ages, evolving to keep pace w/the changing threat landscape & innovations.

Computer Science for Cyber Security (CS4CS) - 3-week Immersive CS Intro for HS students w/no cybersecurity/programming exp - Learn data usage, hacking, digital forensics, privacy, cryptography, steganography & relevant cyber issues

Innovation, Entrepreneurship and the Science of Smart Cities (ieSoSC) - Advancing Technology & Engineering - FREE 5-week program focused on 'smart city' design, prototypes, & research Lessons: circuits, electronics, coding, complex tasks, team projects/presentation

SPARC - Summer Prog in Automation, Robotics, & Coding - Three 2-week, programs for HS Students in robotics, mechatronics, AR, AI, IoT, computer science, electrical engineering, mechanical engineering, machine learning

Pace University - 2-Week STEM Summer Institute for HS Students - In-Person

Coding w/Python, Data Analytics, Design Thinking

Parsons School of Design – New York and Paris - 4-Week Online & On-Campus

NYC summer programs for students from 3rd grade to 12th grade - Portfolio building in 3-credit immersive design, studio art, photography, illustration, and game design
Paris Program – Design & Mgmt, Explorations in Drawing & Painting, Fashion Design

Pathway Summer Program Dept of Energy RENEW Initiative- HS/College Students

Mentorship, hands-on engineering/technology - Brookhaven National Lab

Purchase College - SUNY SummerTech - HS Students w/day camp & overnight options

This tech camp offers Python, Java, animation, 3D modeling & individual instruction.

Rensselaer Polytechnic University – Summer Architecture Program - Troy, NY

2-week Program in July or August, building 3D models, drawings, image editing

Rochester Institute of Technology - FREE - Stipend - Army Laboratory Research Program

Dissect brains, conduct research, meet scientists, interactive lectures - age 16+

Rockefeller University Summer Neuroscience Program - 2-Week, NYC Students

Dissect a brain, research, meet scientists, interactive lectures - 16+ years old

Rome Laboratory - Rome, NY - Air Force Research Labs - 8-12 Weeks

Students participate in mentored ongoing research. Paid internship: comp sci, physics, materials science, & aerospace. Workshops, seminars, presentations.

Roswell Park Cancer Research Institute for HS Juniors - Poster Presentation

Independent research, classroom instruction on cancer, seminars w/invited speakers
Cancer biophysics, genetics, pharmacology, cancer therapeutics, tumor immunology

School of Creative & Performing Arts (SOCAPA) – New York (13-18-year-olds)

2-, 3-week - Learn Filmmaking, Screenwriting, Dance, Music, Photography

Sotheby's Summer Institute – Pre-College, Undergrad, Graduate, and Professional

New York, London, and virtual programs; Intensives in painting & drawing, curating, luxury marketing, art crime/art law, fashion, and art business

Spotify – Summer Internship with The Journal – New York (Remote Eligible)

Research, writing, news stories, podcasts: Partnership w/Gimlet and WSJ

Stony Brook University - Simons Summer Research Prog - FREE/Stipend HS Outreach

Simons Fellows conclude the internship by writing a research abstract & poster. Weekly faculty talks; research workshops, tours, events, poster symposium.

Stony Brook University - Garcia Center for Polymers at Engineered Interfaces

7-Week Program for HS/college students (June-Aug); Apply (Jan-March) projects, possible recognition in national competitions & publication in refereed journals

Syracuse University - Neuroscience: Introduction to the Brain - HS Students

This 2-week program provides a foundation to study the nervous system's structure, function, and disorders, including lectures, reading, and lab exercises.

Syracuse University – 2-, 3-, 6-week On-Campus & Online Programs for HS Students

3-D studio art; sculpture; architecture; design studies; writing immersion

University at Buffalo School of Pharmacy and Pharmaceutical Sciences (SPPS)
Pharmacy Summer Institute (PSI) - 3-days - Buffalo, NY - HS/College Students

Hands-on experiences, exposure to research, career pathways

University of Rochester - Laboratory for Laser Energetics - 16 Rising Seniors Selected

Attend weekly seminars on LLE research, write reports, present research results

Wave Hill Forest Project - 7-week Environmental Proj - HS NYC Resident (16+ yrs old)

Paid Summer Internship/Fieldwork in ecological restoration & urban ecology. Build/maintain wooded trails, remove invasive plant species, fix eroded slopes.

North Carolina

Bank of America Student Leaders Program - 10+ NC Cities - HS Students - 8 Wks

Paid internships with nonprofits. Work experience & leadership development.
Week long all-expense-paid Student Leaders Summit in Washington, DC in July.
Submit application essays, recommendations, and resume in January.

Corning Summer Internships for College Students – NW Charlotte, NC

Advanced optics, Gorilla Glass, emerging innovations, life sciences,
pharmaceuticals. Internships offered in engineering, science, & business

Cyberpatriot - Air Force Assn National Youth Cyber Education Program - 1 Week

HS Students - Multiple camp locations include Central Piedmont CC & Wayne CC

Duke University Summer Program in Psychology & Neuroscience for HS Students

4-Week Hands-on research program in psychology & neuroscience labs.

Duke University Summer Workshop in Math (SWiM) - Free - 1-Week Program

Focused on advancing female participation in math, SWiM participants
attend 2 math courses, afternoon lectures by professors and social activities.

GenCyber – 5-day Nat Security Agency-Sponsored Cybersecurity Camp for HS Students - NC Central University – Taught by Cyber Industry Professionals

Engaging & Dynamic - Role-playing, visual aids, activities, discussions: Computer
networking, systems security, cyber operations, defense, AI, virtual reality

National Institute of Health – 8-week Paid Internship – Research Triangle Park

Biomedical research internship for students 17 years or older by June.
HS-SIP for high school juniors & seniors June to August hands-on research.

North Carolina State University - Residential Engineering Camp for HS Students

11th & 12th graders explore engineering - Three 1-week Sessions Available
Topics include: robotics, AI, bioenergy, agriculture, sustainability, paper science,
industrial & systems eng, textile eng, aerospace, biomedical eng, comp sci, civil
eng, ecological, computer networking, chemical eng, & materials science

Science & Engineering Apprenticeship Program (SEAP) – US Navy – Cherry Point

8-weeks, 300 openings, 30 research labs nationwide, $4,000-$4,500 salary. HS
students must be 16+ years old. Apply starting in August for following summer.

University of North Carolina Summer Science Program - HS Students 5-6 Wks

Biochemistry and molecular biology research - highly competitive, hands-on,
collaborative; mentors; student teams; analysis, scientific writing, presentations

Wake Forest University - Highly Selective Cancer, Bioscience, and Sports Medicine

These in-person and virtual programs offer HS students hands-on experience
with medicine. Passionate students will find this first-hand experience inspiring.

North Dakota

GenCyber – 5-day Nat Security Agency-Sponsored Cybersecurity Camp for HS Students - Bismark State College – Taught by Cyber Industry Professionals
Engaging & Dynamic - Role-playing, visual aids, activities, discussions: Computer networking, systems security, cyber operations, defense, AI, virtual reality

Ohio

Bank of America Student Leaders Program - 4+ OH Cities - HS Students - 8 Wks
Paid internships with nonprofits. Work experience & leadership development. Week long all-expense-paid Student Leaders Summit in Washington, DC in July. Submit application essays, recommendations, and resume in January.

Cyberpatriot - Air Force Assn National Youth Cyber Education Program - 1 Week
HS Students - Camp locations include the National Museum of the U.S. Air Force

Science and Engineering Apprenticeship Program (SEAP) – US Navy – Dayton
8-weeks, 300 openings, 30 research labs nationwide, $4,000-$4,500 salary. HS students must be 16+ years old. Apply starting in August for following summer.

Wright-Patterson AF Base - Dayton, OH - Air Force Research Labs - 8-12 Weeks
Students participate in mentored ongoing research. Paid internship: comp sci, physics, materials science, & aerospace. Workshops, seminars, presentations.

Oklahoma

Bank of America Student Leaders Program - 5+ OK Cities - HS Students - 8 Wks
Paid internships with nonprofits. Work experience & leadership development. Week long all-expense-paid Student Leaders Summit in Washington, DC in July. Submit application essays, recommendations, and resume in January.

GenCyber – 5-day Nat Security Agency-Sponsored Cybersecurity Camp for HS Students - Rose State College – Taught by Cyber Industry Professionals
Engaging & Dynamic - Role-playing, visual aids, activities, discussions: Computer networking, systems security, cyber operations, defense, AI, virtual reality

University of Oklahoma Architecture Summer Academy - HS Students - 1 week
Residential Program: Architecture, interior design, construction science design in action: creativity, innovation, & sustainability shaping the built environment

Oregon

Bank of America Student Leaders Program - 4+ OR Cities - HS Students - 8 Wks
Paid internships with nonprofits. Work experience & leadership development. Week long all-expense-paid Student Leaders Summit in Washington, DC in July. Submit application essays, recommendations, and resume in January.

GenCyber – 5-day Nat Security Agency-Sponsored Cybersecurity Camp for HS Students - Chemeketa CC, Oregon State, Portland CC – Taught by Cyber Industry
> Engaging & Dynamic - Role-playing, visual aids, activities, discussions: Computer networking, systems security, cyber operations, defense, AI, virtual reality

Pennsylvania

Bank of America Student Leaders Program - 10+ PA Cities - HS Students - 8 Wks
> Paid internships with nonprofits. Work experience & leadership development. Week long all-expense-paid Student Leaders Summit in Washington, DC in July. Submit application essays, recommendations, and resume in January.

Carnegie Mellon University - Art, Math, Science, and Game Design Programs
> **National HS Game Academy - 6-Week Game Design Program** - Design video games from ideation, development, & pitch, to final product.
> **AI Scholars Program** - FREE - 4-Week Program for HS Students - AI, seminars, discussions, research, projects, and engagement with tech companies
> **Pre-College Residential Art Program:** 3-, 4-, 6-week (July-August) Intensive Studio Studies Portfolio development in Drawing, Sculpture, Animation and Concept Studio Art Chestnut Hill College Global Solutions Lab
> **Summer Academy for Math & Science (SAMS)**-Free Hands-on STEM program for underrepresented students, explore science w/projects & class instruction.

Cyberpatriot - Air Force Assn National Youth Cyber Education Program - 1 Week
> HS Students - Multiple locations include Univ. of Pittsburgh, Gannon University, Community College of Beaver County, & Pittsburgh Technical College

Drexel University Westphal College of Media Arts & Design – Discovering Architecture
> 2-week Residential Program – HS Students – Intensive Studio Architecture Program Visit prominent architectural, multi-disciplinary design offices; meet architects

GenCyber – 5-day Nat Security Agency-Sponsored Cybersecurity Camp for HS Students - Indiana U. of Pennsylvania – Taught by Cyber Industry Professionals
> Engaging & Dynamic - Role-playing, visual aids, activities, discussions: Computer networking, systems security, cyber operations, defense, AI, virtual reality

Gettysburg College - Camp Psych - 1-Week HS Student Program
> In-person summer camp in psychology gives an insider's view of the field.

Great Books Summer Program - Haverford College - Grades 6-8 and 9-12
> Great Books & Big Ideas, Writer's Workshops, and Literary Travel Programs Read, Write, & Discuss Big Ideas in Literature and Philosophy with scholars

Interactive Global Simulation, Electrifying Africa, & UN Sustainable Growth
> 1-week – HS Students – Intensive collaborative team solutions to big problems

Lehigh University - IGEI (4 Weeks) and SEI (2 Weeks) - HS Programs for 11th & 12th

Iacocca Global Entrepreneurship Intensive(IGEI) - HS Entrepreneurship Program Sustainable design, global citizenship, design challenges, business hackathons, teams

Summer Engineering Institute (SEI) - Intensive classroom study, discussions, team projects, problem-solving, integrated technology

Maywood University Pre-College Summer Workshop School of Architecture

2-week (July) Residential Program – HS Students – Design/Build Your Future

Penn Summer Coding Academy - Univ of Pennsylvania 3-Week HS Program

Students learn HTML, Cascading Style Sheets, JavaScript, and webpage creation

Pennsylvania State University Architecture & Landscape Architecture Summer Camp

1-week (July) – HS Students – Architecture, graphics, design, built environment

Pennsylvania State University Summer Discovery Program in Engineering & STEM, Also Engineering Ahead (Free 4-Week Program for Minorities)

Students are introduced to engineering disciplines, design, and research.

Science and Engineering Apprenticeship Program (SEAP) – US Navy – Philadelphia

8-weeks, 300 openings, 30 research labs nationwide, $4,000-$4,500 salary. HS students must be 16+ years old. Apply starting in August for following summer.

Temple University Tyler School of Art and Architecture Pre-College Program

2-week (July-August) Residential Program – HS Students – Studio Architecture

University of Pennsylvania TREES Program - Environmental Science Research

Tuition-free at the UPenn Center of Excellence in Environmental Toxicology Two Weeks training, followed by independent research for high school students

University of Pennsylvania 3 Week Engineering Summer Academy at Penn (ESAP)

Rigorous on-campus program for highly motivated high school students; Focus biotech, computer graphics, computer science, aanotechnology, & robotics.

University of Pittsburgh Medical Center - FREE - Hillman Cancer Center Academy

Immersive 7-week mentored medical research program for high school students (15+ yrs). Research in biology, medicine, and computer science.

Wistar Institute High School Fellowship in Biomedical Research - Philadelphia

4-week - cancer biology, genetics, vaccine development, infectious diseases, and bioinformatics. Work in state-of-the-art training lab; literature review.

Rhode Island

Bank of America Student Leaders Program - 5+ RI Cities - HS Students - 8 Wks

Paid internships with nonprofits. Work experience & leadership development. Week long all-expense-paid Student Leaders Summit in Washington, DC in July. Submit application essays, recommendations, and resume in January.

Brown University – 1-4 Weeks – Art Themed Courses & the Environmental
Leadership Lab (Climate Change 2-week hand's on program for HS Students
  Creative writing, music, studio art, art history, & environment/sustainability

Cyberpatriot - Air Force Assn National Youth Cyber Education Program - 1 Week
  HS Students - Multiple camp locations include the Comm College of Rhode Island

GenCyber – 5-day Nat Security Agency-Sponsored Cybersecurity Camp for HS
Students - Rhode Island College – Taught by Cyber Industry Professionals
  Engaging & Dynamic - Role-playing, visual aids, activities, discussions: Computer
  networking, systems security, cyber operations, defense, AI, virtual reality

Rhode Island School of Design Pre-College School of Design – Providence, RI
  6-week (June-July) Residential Program – High school students – Foundational
  Art & Design Studies. Figure drawing, projects, trips, & exhibitions.

Roger Williams University High School Summer Academy in Architecture
  4-week (July-August) Residential Program – Grades 11 & 12 – Explore Studio
  Architecture - Seminars, fieldwork, studio, portfolio development

South Carolina

Bank of America Student Leaders Program - 7+ SC Cities - HS Students - 8 Wks
  Paid internships with nonprofits. Work experience & leadership development.
  Weeklong all-expense-paid Student Leaders Summit in Washington, DC in July.
  Submit application essays, recommendations, and resume in January.

Clemson University Pre-College School of Architecture Program
  1-week (July-August) Residential Program – Grades 7-12 - Engineering design,
  mechanical/civil engineering, intelligent vehicles, materials engineering

Cyberpatriot - Air Force Assn National Youth Cyber Education Program - 1 Week
  HS Students - Multiple camp locations, including USC Upstate & USC Aiken

GenCyber – 5-day Nat Security Agency-Sponsored Cybersecurity Camp for HS
Students - The Citadel – Taught by Cyber Industry Professionals
  Engaging & Dynamic - Role-playing, visual aids, activities, discussions: Computer
  networking, systems security, cyber operations, defense, AI, virtual reality

Mentorship for Environmental Scholars (MES) Program - 10 Wk Paid - HS/College
  Savannah River Site Dept of Energy - Aiken, SC - Environmental Science & STEM

Students - The Citadel – Taught by Cyber Industry Professionals
  Engaging & Dynamic - Role-playing, visual aids, activities, discussions: Computer
  networking, systems security, cyber operations, defense, AI, virtual reality

Science and Engineering Apprenticeship Program – US Navy – Charleston
  8-weeks, 300 openings, 30 research labs nationwide, $4,000-$4,500 salary. HS
  students must be 16+ years old. Apply starting in August for following summer.

University of South Carolina HS Summer Computer Tech & Engineering Programs

Carolina Master Scholars Adventure Series - 1 Week Hands-on design thinking in VEX Robotics, digital content creation, and green engineering
Partners for Minorities in Eng & Comp Sci (PMECS) 9th-12th AI, Cyber, Coding

South Dakota

GenCyber – 5-day Nat Security Agency-Sponsored Cybersecurity Camp for HS Students - Dakota State Univ. – Taught by Cyber Industry Professionals

Engaging & Dynamic - Role-playing, visual aids, activities, discussions: Computer networking, systems security, cyber operations, defense, AI, virtual reality

Tennessee

Arnold Air Force Base - Tullahoma, TN - Air Force Research Labs - 8-12 Weeks

Students participate in mentored ongoing research. Paid internship: comp sci, physics, materials science, & aerospace. Workshops, seminars, presentations.

Bank of America Student Leaders Program - 8+ TN Cities - HS Students - 8 Wks

Paid internships with nonprofits. Work experience & leadership development. Week long all-expense-paid Student Leaders Summit in Washington, DC in July. Submit application essays, recommendations, and resume in January.

Mentorship for Environmental Scholars (MES) Program - 10 Wk Paid - HS/College

Oak Ridge Nat Lab Dept of Energy Site - Research in Environmental Science/STEM

University of Memphis Discovering Architecture + Design - 1-day – HS Students

Design programs on architecture, interior design, and the built environment.

University of Tennessee, Knoxville College of Architecture + Design

1-week UT Summer Design Camp (July) Residential – HS Students
Immersive architecture, graphic design, and professional practice program

Vanderbilt Summer Academy – Nashville, TN – 3-Week Program

" Digital Storytelling", "Writing Fantasy Fiction", "Math & Music", "Writing Short Stories"

Vanderbilt Research Experience for High School Students (REHSS) - 6-Week Intensive

Only for specific Nashville STEM HS - 40 hrs/wk, weekly workshops, final symposium

Texas

AFWERX Air Force Innovation - Austin, TX - Air Force Research Labs - 8-12 Weeks

Students participate in mentored ongoing research teams. Paid intern: comp sci, physics, materials science, & aerospace. Workshops, seminars, presentations.

Aggie STEM Summer Camps - Texas A&M - Grades 6-8 & 9-12 - 1 & 2 Week

STEM topics include robotics, rockets, coding, and engineering design principles. Students also meet professors & tour STEM labs on the TAMU campus.

Bank of America Student Leaders Program - 10+ TX Cities - HS Students - 8 Wks

Paid internships with nonprofits. Work experience & leadership development. Week long all-expense-paid Student Leaders Summit in Washington, DC in July. Submit application essays, recommendations, and resume in January

Baylor Engineering & Computing Summer Academy (BECSA) - 10th - 12th

Focus on rolling, electrical, calculating energy, energy in flight & harvesting energy

Baylor University - CASPER HS Scholars Program - EE/Aerospace - 11th & 12th

Astrophysics, gravitation, condensed matter, plasmas & beam physics

Boeing Summer Internship – HS & College– Lewisville and San Antonio

Hands-on industry experience - Aviation and engineering Internships

Corning Summer Internships for College Students – Keller, TX

Advanced optics, Gorilla Glass, emerging innovations, life sciences, and pharmaceuticals Internships offered in engineering, science, and business.

Cyberpatriot - Air Force Assn National Youth Cyber Education Program - 1 Week

HS Students - Locations include Angelo State U. South Texas College, UTEP, Baylor Collaborative, Texas Women's University, St. Philip's College Texas State

GenCyber – 5-day Nat Security Agency-Sponsored Cybersecurity Camp for HS Students - San Antonio College, Texas A&M – Taught by Cyber Industry Prof.

Engaging & Dynamic - Role-playing, visual aids, activities, discussions: Computer networking, systems security, cyber operations, defense, AI, virtual reality

Jacobs Engineering Internship – Summer Internship (College) - Dallas

Civil, electrical, environmental, geotechnical, & transportation engineering; sustainability, cybersecurity, mobility, and R&D with worldwide projects.

National Security Agency (NSA) – Paid Computer Internship – San Antonio

Students must be at least a junior in high school with interest in business, engineering, or computer science. Apply between September 1 and October 31.

Rice University Summer Scholars Programs - Middle & High School Students

Aerospace Academy - 12 days - Hands-on in industry facilities w/NASA reps Immersion attend flight school w/flight prep simulation, launch a satellite.
Creative Writing Camp - Develop writing skills while living on campus.
National Youth Leadership Forum: Medicine & Health Care - 8 days hands-on HS students gain clinical training in medical diagnostics, surgery & first aid
Pre-College Programs - Economics, Entrepreneurship, Genome Engineering, Global Affairs, Law, Physiology, & Psychology
Rice Center for Engineering Leadership (RCEL) Rice ELITE Tech - Real world advanced engineering & technology - AI, IoT, machine learning, data science
Rice U School Mathematics Project (RUSMP) - Summer Math Camps
Tapia Camps - 1 Week on campus - STEM projects, presentations, field trips

SpaceX – Summer Engineering/Co-op Program – Brownsville & McGregor
Paid Internship - Must be in an undergraduate in a STEM subject.

Southern Methodist University - STEM Works, Kids Ahead, TEDXKids@SMU
Introduction to Engineering - 7th & 8th - Basic hands-on project approach
Advanced Engineering - 9th & 10th - Project-based engineering design
Engineering Design Experience - 11th & 12th - Civil, EE, Comp Sci, Mechanical

Tesla Internships – Ave. $33/hour – Full-Time Automotive Design/Engineering
Austin – Manufacturing Engineering; Waco - People Analytics - Vehicle Service
Research/Training

Texas Tech Anson L Clark Scholars Program – Research Areas: Advertising, Architecture, Art, Dance, Engineering, or Theatre - 7-week – Grades 11 & 12
Residential Program (must be 17 years old by start date) – No program fee.
Intensive research-based program; $500 meal card; $750 tax-free stipend.

University of Houston & Wonderworks Pre-College Summer Discovery Program
Hines College of Architecture & Design – Intro to Architecture 6-week – HS
Students – Design in hands-on studio, field trips, & portfolio workshop.
UH Coding and AI Camp - Hands-on programming with AI applications.

University of Texas at Austin Summer Programs for HS Students
Computer Science Summer Academy - 1 Week - HS Students learn C++,
project management, machine learning, artificial intelligence, & Python.
My Introduction to Engineering (MITE) - 5-day camp for 11th grade students to
work on team-based engineering projects
Digital Design - 2-D Game Design, 3-D Game Design, 3-D Animation/ Motion - School
of Design & Creative Technologies - 1-week – HS Students – portfolio development &
3D Game design

STEM Enhancement in Earth Science (SEES) - NASA, Texas Space Grant Consortium, Center for Space Research Summer Program - Interpret NASA satellite remote sensing data while working w/NASA scientists & engineers. Field investigation - HS Juniors/Seniors 16+ years old by July 1 - FREE

Welch Summer Scholar Program (WSSP) - 5-Week - HS Jr/Sr from Texas
@UT Austin, UT Arlington, UT Dallas, University of Houston, & Texas Tech
Hands-on chemical research, mentorship, research paper, presentation, poster

Utah

Bank of America Student Leaders Program - 4+ UT Cities - HS Students - 8 Wks
Paid internships with nonprofits. Work experience & leadership development. Week long all-expense-paid Student Leaders Summit in Washington, DC in July. Submit application essays, recommendations, and resume in January.

Cyberpatriot - Air Force Assn National Youth Cyber Education Program - 1 Week
HS Students - Multiple camp locations, including Utah Valley University.

Edwards Lifesciences Summer College Internship Program - Draper, Utah
Currently enrolled in college - Interested in healthcare related programs
Proficient in engineering drafting software, writing, or business/leadership

GenCyber – 5-day Nat Security Agency-Sponsored Cybersecurity Camp for HS Students - Brigham Young University – Taught by Cyber Industry Professionals
Engaging & Dynamic - Role-playing, visual aids, activities, discussions: Computer networking, systems security, cyber operations, defense, AI, virtual reality

Vermont

Columbia Climate School in the Green Mountains - Green Mountains - HS Students
2-week program on Climate and Sustainability - discussions, seminars, fieldwork, hands-on projects, critical thinking, & problem solving

School of Creative & Performing Arts (SOCAPA) – Burlington, VT (13-18-year-olds)
2-week, 3-week - learn filmmaking, screenwriting, dance, music, photography

Virginia

Bank of America Student Leaders Program - 25+ VA Cities - HS Students - 8 Wks
Paid internships with nonprofits. Work experience & leadership development. Week long all-expense-paid Student Leaders Summit in Washington, DC in July. Submit application essays, recommendations, and resume in January.

Cyberpatriot - Air Force Assn National Youth Cyber Education Program - 1 Week
HS Students - Locations, incl Mtn Gateway CC & Lynchburg Nat Guard Academy

Defense Intelligence Agency Summer College Internship - Engineering/Technology

10-14 Week Summer Internship Program Intelligence/Tech Apply in February Arlington, Charlottesville, Quantico, Reston - College Jr/Sr or Grad Student

Federal Bureau of Investigation - Future Agents in Training - Teen Academy

FBI classes on terrorism, cyber crime, public corruption, polygraph exams, evidence response, and SWAT. Meet w/special agents and intelligence analysts.

GenCyber – 5-day Nat Security Agency-Sponsored Cybersecurity Camp for HS Students - Marymount Univ. & Virginia Tech - Taught by Cyber Industry Prof.

Engaging & Dynamic - Role-playing, visual aids, activities, discussions: Computer networking, systems security, cyber operations, defense, AI, virtual reality

NASA Langley Research Center Paid Internship Program (16+ years old) 8-10 weeks

Aerospace program in public affairs, multimedia, statistics, aerial robotics, apace hardware design, testing, Mars surface habitat, & high temperature materials

NASA's Wallops Flight Facility Summer Internship - High School & College

Research, mentorship, and experiential learning opportunities

Northrop Grumman – Engineering Intern– Space Systems R & D Team

Graduating HS Seniors – Join an engineering team to design, develop and test space systems and satellites; R & D - land, sea, air, space, and cyberspace.

Pentagon - Arlington, VA - Air Force Research Labs - 8-12 Weeks

Students participate in mentored ongoing research. Paid internship: comp sci, physics, materials science, & aerospace. Workshops, seminars, presentations.

Science and Engineering Apprenticeship Program (SEAP) – US Navy Hampton Roads and Dahlgren

8-weeks, 300 openings, 30 research labs nationwide, $4,000-$4,500 salary. HS students must be 16+ years old. Apply starting in August for following summer.

Virginia Commonwealth University (VCUArts) Pre-College - 3-Week

On-Campus Program – 2D Portfolio devt, photography; Clay: More Than Just Mud, Sketchbook to Controller, animation workshop, sculpture, jewelry & fashion design, stage combat, musical theatre, & Acting From Page to Stage

Virginia Tech Inside Architecture + Design & Imagination Camp

1-week – HS Students – Hands-on design studio architecture program 1-week Electrical & computer engineering; drone, build, & fly program.

Washington

Bank of America Student Leaders Prog - Various WA Cities - HS Students - 8 Wks

Paid internships with nonprofits. Work experience & leadership development. Week long all-expense-paid Student Leaders Summit in Washington, DC in July. Submit application essays, recommendations, and resume in January.

COPE Scholars Program – Healthcare Internship – 280 Hours Training Locations in Puyallup, Seattle, Spokane, and Tacoma

> Health Scholars must be 18+. Students assist w/basic healthcare for medical or nursing school, etc. Certificate of Completion - Keck Graduate Institute

Cyberpatriot - Air Force Assn National Youth Cyber Education Program - 1 Week

> HS Students - Multiple camp locations, including Marysville NUROTC.

DigiPen Academy – K-12 Animation, Film, Music, Game Design Summer Programs – Redmond, WA

> 1-week and 2-week programs, including Teen Art & Animation; Film Scoring Music & Sound Design; Video Game Development; Animation Masterclass

Fred Hutchinson Cancer Research Center's Summer HS/College Internship Program

> Seattle - 8-Week, FT, Paid Internship - Mentored research, seminars, workshops

GenCyber – 5-day Nat Security Agency-Sponsored Cybersecurity Camp for HS Students - Eastern Washington Univ., Spokane Falls CC, & Whatcom CC – Taught by Cyber Industry Professionals

> Engaging & Dynamic - Role-playing, visual aids, activities, discussions: Computer networking, systems security, cyber operations, defense, AI, virtual reality

Microsoft Discovery Program - 4 Weeks - HS Students - Redmond, Washington

> Work on real-world projects during the summer at Microsoft to gain business skills and mentorship. Students must live & attend high school within 50 miles of Redmond or Atlanta. Resume, application, & questions; apply in February.

Mentorship for Environmental Scholars (MES) Program - 10 Wk Paid - HS/College

> Hanford Dept of Energy Site Richland, WA Environmental Science/STEM Research

NatureBridge Summer Programs - Olympic National Park - 1-2 weeks

> Environmental science education, & hands-on fieldwork while backpacking for students in 7th - 12th grades. Connect to nature with trail building, habitat restoration, and wilderness exploration.

Pacific Northwest National Laboratory - Summer STEM Programs for HS/College

> HS - 10-Week Student Research Apprenticeship Prog & Young Women in Science College - 10 Week Science Undergrad Lab Internship, National Security Internship Program, Energy & Environment Internship Program

Pathway Summer Program Dept of Energy RENEW Initiative- HS/College Students

> Mentorship, hands-on engineering/technology - Pacific NW National Laboratory

Seattle Children's Research Institute STEM Internships - Biomedical Research

> *   4 Week Paid 10th Grade HS Research Training Program - Bio lab - July/Aug
> *   Yearlong HS Program - biomedical research in healthcare - Lab exp, guest lectures
> *   College - 9 & 12 Week Paid Summer Scholars & STAR Biomedical Research Prog

University of Washington – Seattle, WA – Middle and HS Students

> 1-Week - Neurotechnology Young Scholars Program, DawgBytes Computer

Science Camp, Material Science Camp, and summer session art classes STEM - Summer program in Engineering and Technology

Wilderness Awareness School's Summer Camps - 5-days for 6-12 year olds

Nature and environmental activities, including survival skills training in St. Edward State Park, Cougar Mountain Park, Seward Park, Tolt MacDonald Park, and Carnation Farms. These are day camps for kids.

Youth Engaged in Sustainable Systems (YESS) - HS Student Summer Program

This hands-on paid internship includes natural resources, conservation, ecological restoration, & sustainable environmental practices. Replace invasive plant species to restore ecological environments. Highline & Riverview School Districts

West Virginia

NASA Independent Verification and Validation Facility, Fairmont, WV

Research, Mentorship, and Experiential Learning Opportunities
HS Students - Focus on robotics, programming, engineering, & STEM projects.

National Youth Science Academy - FREE - Camp Pocahontas, WV - STEAM

Two delegates (high school juniors or seniors) are selected to attend from each state and D.C. attend for 3 weeks. Housing, meals, transportation, and supplies are provided at no cost. Washington, D.C. trip included.

West Virginia Governor's STEM Institute (GSI) - high-achieving 8th & 9th Graders

Hands-on computer science, cybersecurity, & AI program to advance science exp

Wisconsin

Bank of America Student Leaders Prog - Various WI Cities - HS Students - 8 Wks

Paid internships with nonprofits. Work experience & leadership development. Week long all-expense-paid Student Leaders Summit in Washington, DC in July. Submit application essays, recommendations, and resume in January.

Cyberpatriot - Air Force Assn National Youth Cyber Education Program - 1 Week

HS Students - Camp locations include Marquette University

Experimental Aircraft Association - 1 Week Aviation Camps for students 12 - 18

Young Eagles Camp - 12-13-year-olds - Aeromodeling, Wing Construction, basic flight, interactive computer simulator ground school, fly designed missions
Basic Camp - 14-15-year-olds Ground School, Tech Workshop, Models, Demos
Advanced Camp - Action-packed aviation ground instruction & flight experience

GenCyber – 5-day Nat Security Agency-Sponsored Cybersecurity Camp for HS Students - U. of Wisconsin-Whitewater – Taught by Cyber Industry Professionals

Engaging & Dynamic - Role-playing, visual aids, activities, discussions: Computer networking, systems security, cyber operations, defense, AI, virtual reality

University of Wisconsin - Madison - Engineering Summer Program - 11th & 12th

Free, 3-week residential program for students interested in engineering. Mechanical engineering & electrical/computer engineering

University of Wisconsin Milwaukee School of Architecture & Urban Planning

1-week – HS Students – Online architectural design & interior design activities, lectures, workshops, and interactive architectural concepts and design thinking.

Wyoming

Sierra Club's Summer Outings - Gros Ventre Wilderness - Yellowstone Ecosystem

Trail restoration trip - 7 days - Forest Service personnel drive gear to the trailhead. Hike the rugged landscape to scenic rivers while working on the trail.

TAKE ADVANTAGE OF THIS TIME TO EXPLORE

During high school and college, explore your interests through summer programs, skill-building camps, and internships. Try out different fields you might not have considered before. You never really have the same chance to consider alternatives in quite the same way. Learn something new. There are hundreds of career areas you may never have considered. Have some fun while you are at it!

Everything has its beauty, but not everyone sees it.

– Andy Warhol

Make next summer a summer to remember!
Apply early. Some deadlines are in the fall and others fill fast.

CHAPTER 7

COLLEGE DEGREES, TIMING, LOCATION, & COSTS

"Between stimulus and response there is a space. In that space is our power to choose our response. In our response lies our growth and our freedom."

– Viktor E. Frankl

Some people insist the best universities are those with large lecture halls. However, some students work better in small, project-based environments with hands-on activities and field trips to labs, research centers, and events.

Every student is different. You need to find a school that fits you. Large, fiercely competitive schools can be motivational or they can leave you with a pit in your stomach and a sense of failure. If graduate school is your goal, you may want to attend a university where you can get research opportunities, master your classes, and get involved. Thus, the best university is the one where you will thrive. Fortunately, there are many colleges and variables to consider.

Here is the big picture data for U.S. college student enrollment:

- 19.25 million college students
- 2,691 4-year colleges
- 1,496 2-year colleges
- 5.2 million attend private colleges
- 13.7 million attend public colleges

In another interesting statistic, undergraduate enrollment dropped more than 8% from fall 2019 to fall 2022, representing nearly 2,000,000 loss of students during the pandemic. However, in 2024, enrollment grew 1.2% with greatest increase in community colleges. Test-optional admissions opened the door to students without test scores or those who test poorly. Thus, more students applied to the top schools. Beware, though, some colleges are moving back to requiring tests.

The secret of getting ahead is getting started.
The secret of getting started is breaking your complex, overwhelming tasks into small manageable tasks, and then starting on the first one.

– Mark Twain

CONSIDER MORE THAN JUST RANKINGS

Rankings can help you start your search. However, they miss important factors that determine whether the school is a good fit for your circumstances. Here are a few variables to consider:

Ability to Enroll in Required	Internships
Classes Acceptance Rates	Intramural Sports
Access to Professors	Majors
Book Costs	Research Opportunities
Competitiveness	Safety
Diversity	Scholarship Money
Dorm Life	School Spirit
Financial Aid	Security
Graduate School Acceptance	Size of Lower Division Classes
Housing Availability	Social Life
Inclusiveness	Study Abroad

Note: Colleges with 400 students in first and second year classes often say their "average class size" is somewhere around 25. Do not be deceived by statistics that deviate from reality. Also, almost every school offers study abroad, though in many cases the study abroad programs are under another school's or program's umbrella and rarely include students or professors from your university.

Ask students at a school you are interested in attending if they are able to register for the classes they need, get support for internships or summer programs, and have access to professors and not just graduate school assistants who, frankly, have a full load of their own classes.

ADMISSIONS DATA TO CONSIDER

The Ivy League Schools
Comparison of Early vs Regular Decision Admit Rates and Waitlist Data

Ivy League University	ED Admit Rate – Class of 2027	RD Admit Rate – Class of 2027	ED Admit Rate – Class of 2026	RD Admit Rate – Class of 2026	Number Waitlist Admits
Brown	13%	4%	14.6%	3.71%	15
Columbia	11.3%	3%	10.3%	3%	N/A
Cornell	18%	6%	21.4%	6.7%	260
Dartmouth	19.2%	5%	20%	4.8%	N/A
Harvard	7.6%	3%	7.9%	2.34%	65
UPenn	15%	4%	15.6%	4.2%	N/A
Princeton	Princeton did not publish its data				
Yale	10%	3%	11%	3.4%	N/A

ADMISSIONS DATA FOR TOP SCHOOLS - EARLY VS. REGULAR DECISION

University	ED1/EDII/EA Admit Rate – Class of 2027	RD/Total % Admit Rate – Class of 2027	ED/EDII/EA Admit Rate – Class of 2026	RD/Total % Admit Rate – Class of 2026	Number Waitlist Admits
Amherst College	26%	9%	32%	6.1%/7%	36
Boston College	30%	19%/15.1%	28%	16.7%	13
Boston Univ	29%	18.9%/10.7%	26%/25.3%	13.4%/14.15%	3
Cal Poly SLO	N/A	28.1%	N/A	30%	345
Claremont McK	32%	11%	28.2%/29.5%	7.5%/10.3%	11
Colgate Univ	22.4%	12%	25.2%	11.1%/17%	0
Colorado College	40%/22%	19.9%	49.3%/26%/15%	11%/13.6%	2
Duke University	16.5%	4.8%	21.3%	4.3%/4.9%	N/A
Emory University	37.4%/11.7%	10%	36.5%/14%	9.5%/10.7%	107
Georgetown	11.8%	13%	10%	12.11%	40
GWU	66%	50%	66.1%/65%	48.2%/49%	N/A
Georgia Tech	40%(in-state) 10.5% (out)	16%	39% (in-state) 12% (out)	17.14%	41
Harvey Mudd	21%	10%	19.1%	12.6%/13%	17
Johns Hopkins	19.7%	8%/6.3%	21%/14.8%	5.9%/7.2%	0
MIT	5.7%	4%/4.7%	4.7%	4%	0
Northeastern	39% ED	6%	32.6%/6%	6%/6.8%	N/A
Northwestern	21%	6%	22.1%/12.8%	5.6%/7.2%	83
Notre Dame	15.2%	10%/12%	17.3%	13%	N/A
NYU	38%	8%	38%	12.2%/12.4%	N/A
Rice University	18%	7%	24%/18.8%	7.7%/8.6%	0
SMU	N/A	53%	70.9%	50%/51.6%	2
Stanford	N/A	5%	N/A	3.7%	8
Texas Christian	N/A	41%	70.4%	55.3%/56%	2
Tufts University	N/A	9.5%	N/A	9.7%	183
Tulane University	60%/15%	13%	67.9%/17%	7.9%/8.4%	3
UChicago	N/A	5%	N/A	5.4%	N/A
Univ of Miami	61%/37%	19%/28%	56.7%	17.6%/18.9%	115
Univ of So Cal	6%	9.9%	N/A	11.9%/12%	N/A
Univ of Virginia	31% (in-state) 12.4% (out)	15%/16.3%	37.8% (in-state) 18.1% (out)	18.7%	N/A
Vanderbilt	15.7%	4%/5.6%	24%/17.6%	5.3%/6%	~200
Wash U St Louis	35%	11%	26.2%/17.6%	9.3%/11.3%	168
Wesleyan	41%	12.4%/15.7%	44%/31%	13.9%	81
William & Mary	45%	42% (in-state) 28% (out)	N/A	42% (in-state) 28% (out)	4
Williams College	27%	8%	31%	8.5%	0

UNIVERSITY OF CALIFORNIA

The University of California Fact Sheet data below from UC Admissions, says, "Data are Subject to Change". Nonetheless, here is a comparison between admissions to the class of 2024 and admission to the classes of 2026 and 2028.

The increase in applications to the University of California is in large part due to changes in testing requirements. Policies, prices, and class sizes also allowed for more students to be admitted. For the class of 2028, the University of California received 250,436 applications, an increase of 1.5% from the previous year.

UNIVERSITY OF CALIFORNIA ADMISSIONS DATA				
University of California Campus	Residency of Applicants	Number of Undergraduate Applications		
		Class of 2024	Class of 2026	Class of 2028
Berkeley	California	50,223	72,417	72,129
	Out-of-State	20,659	32,580	29,755
	International	17,114	23,195	22,320
	Total	88,026	128,192	124,204
Davis	California	54,570	65,367	67,912
	Out-of-State	6,505	10,748	12,267
	International	15,798	18,610	18,655
	Total	76,873	94,725	98,834
Irvine	California	72,391	84,743	87,517
	Out-of-State	8,000	14,309	15,732
	International	17,525	20,113	19,412
	Total	97,916	119,165	122,661
Los Angeles	California	67,877	91,544	92,290
	Out-of-State	23,016	34,627	31,841
	International	17,944	23,608	22,119
	Total	108,837	149,779	146,250
Merced	California	22,244	22,516	23,691
	Out-of-State	598	1,319	1,539
	International	1,534	2,208	4,121
	Total	24,376	26,043	29,351
Riverside	California	43,151	46,456	48,633
	Out-of-State	1,473	2,492	2,753
	International	4,628	5,417	6,034
	Total	49,252	54,365	57,420
San Diego	California	66,350	84,326	88,392
	Out-of-State	14,364	23,778	24,169
	International	19,320	23,112	21,878
	Total	100,034	131,226	134,439
Santa Barbara	California	63,269	73,575	75,523
	Out-of-State	10,988	18,432	17,466
	International	16,690	18,984	17,247
	Total	90,947	110,991	110,236
Santa Cruz	California	43,893	53,051	57,503
	Out-of-State	3,897	6,878	7,691
	International	7,213	5,937	6,503
	Total	55,003	65,886	71,697

LEARNING OBJECTIVES

Communication – Social, behavioral, and cognitive scientists must present clear, engaging writing and speaking that transmits information appropriately and effectively to those with no technical or scientific background. However, effectively translating complex scientific topics into written text is not as easy as it sounds. Listening is equally important since team members often provide valuable suggestions. By encouraging students to work together and give class presentations, colleges train students to be able to communicate with a wide range of audiences in seminars, poster sessions, and journal articles.

Teamwork - Group projects provide opportunities to communicate, cooperate, and integrate, helping to develop the necessary skills for team membership, leadership, and inclusivity. As such, students discover member's strengths and weaknesses while establishing group goals, dividing tasks, and creating a plan for the delivery of performance outcomes.

Creativity – Psychologists and neuroscientists must think differently. In compiling statistical data in charts, articles, and presentations. Creativity is essential. Psychologists and neuroscientists envision, test, and evaluate. Collaboration stimulates ideas, percolating new avenues to accomplish the same task.

Problem Solving – Students identify opportunities along with challenges that need to be resolved. With a solutions-oriented approach, psychologists formulate best-fit alternatives by applying lessons learned in their math and science classes. Furthermore, since multiple perspectives may achieve optimal solutions given critical variables and project specifications, consensus is necessary.

Analysis – Students are taught statistics, laboratory, and technology skills that rely on statistics, visual analysis, and scientific analysis. To improve judgment, process, and analysis, students apply comprehensive analysis and data-informed decision-making.

Ethics – Psychologists have an ethical responsibility to society and a professional responsibility to universities, research centers, and employers. Thus, as specialized researchers, Psychologists must use ethical practices, good judgment, and transparent communication, while also considering consequences. They must balance the needs of everyone on the collaborative team.

Lifelong Learning – Students soon discover that their knowledge and skills are quickly outdated. From the moment a student begins college until the moment they graduate, technological transformations take place that require information renewal, like learning new software and using state-of-the-art materials. Yet, like a time warp, some projects may use decades-old equipment. Thus, you may need to use 'old school' techniques and work with antiquated materials, tools, and processes. Even so, you should keep up with the latest technologies without complaining even when your bosses or supervisors do not.

UNDERGRADUATE AND GRADUATE DEGREES

AA – Associate of Arts: 2-year degree

AS – Associate of Science: 2-year degree

BA – Bachelor of Arts: 4-year degree

BArch – Bachelor of Architecture: 5-year professional credential program

BDes – Bachelor of Design: 4-year degree with classes focused on design

BEd – Bachelor of Education: 4-year program focused on teaching & learning

BEng – Bachelor of Engineering: 4-5-year engineering-focused program

BESc – Bachelor of Engineering Science: 4-year science & engineering program

BFA – Bachelor of Fine Arts: 4-year degree with classes focused on art/design

BID – Bachelor of Industrial Design: 4-year Industrial Design-focused degree

BS – Bachelor of Science: 4-year STEM-focused degree

BSCE – Bachelor of Science in Civil Engineering

BS Chem E – Bachelor of Science in Chemical Engineering

BS Comp Sci – Bachelor of Science in Computer Science

BSEE – Bachelor of Science in Electrical Engineering

BSIE – Bachelor of Science in Industrial Engineering

BSME – Bachelor of Science in Mechanical Engineering

EdD – Doctor of Education: 3-5-year program focused on teaching & learning

MA – Master of Arts: 1-2-year specialized degree

MArch – Master of Architecture: 1-3-year professional credential program

MDes – Master of Design: 1-2-year design-focused specialized degree

MEd – Master of Education: 1-2-year education-focused program

MEng – Master of Engineering: 1-2-year engineering program

MFA – Master of Fine Arts: 1-2-year degree earned after the BA, BS, or BFA

MID – Master of Industrial Design

Minor – Students take 6 to 10 additional classes in an interest area

MS – Master of Science: 1-2-year STEM-focused degree

MSID – Master of Science in Industrial Design

Ph.D. – Doctor of Philosophy: doctorate in any field (typically 3 – 8 years)

AA (ASSOCIATE OF ARTS) & AS (ASSOCIATE OF SCIENCE)

The AA or AS degree is typically a 2-year general studies degree offered online or in-person through a community college. However, some universities offer AA or AS degrees as well. Often, the Associate of Arts degree, while focused on the liberal arts, has no barrier to entry, meaning that students can enter most AA programs with a high school diploma or the equivalent.

The AS degree frequently includes additional science and math requirements. Some students take more or less time to complete the AA or AS based upon their skills upon entering the program, certainty of their direction, and the transfer requirements. For example, students majoring in engineering or business have additional science and math requirements and need to create an academic plan early in their program to finish in two years.

BA (BACHELOR OF ARTS) & BS (BACHELOR OF SCIENCE)

The BA and BS degrees are 4- or 5-year undergraduate degrees that typically offer a liberal arts foundation along with a major or concentration in a specific subject. The BA and BS degrees frequently require students to take lower-division (first and second-year) liberal arts courses before taking specialized courses focused around a major or concentration in their third and fourth years.

For engineering and architecture, there is typically a fifth year due to the additional experiential requirements. Classes may be taught online or in person. Some students complete their BS in fewer years depending upon AP/IB credit, dual enrollment, and summer/intersession classes.

A BFA is considered a professional arts-focused degree with fewer courses in English, science, math, social science, and the humanities. Thus, the BFA, BDes, BID, and BArch are specialist qualifications. The BEng focuses on engineering, while the BEd focuses on education. The BA and BS degrees include significantly more liberal arts classes and thus are more general degrees.

The intention of the BFA, BDes, BID, and BArch degrees is for students to pursue a focused curriculum with uniquely tailored courses. Finally, BA and BS degrees are often interchangeable depending upon the college and additional STEM requirements. Thus, a BFA may be seen as different since there is typically more coursework focused on art with fewer liberal arts classes; students concentrate on their specialty area.

MASTER'S DEGREES & DOCTORAL DEGREES

The master's and doctorate are graduate degrees for students who have completed their bachelor's degree. These degrees can take between one and eight years depending upon coursework, research, practicum, capstone, thesis, qualifying exams, and experiential requirements. Students immerse themselves to gain in-depth practical, coursework, and research training.

A graduate degree in psychology can be helpful in advancing your career goals since most research, clinical, and academic positions require additional education. The extra training combined with internship and networking opportunities will strengthen your resume and career opportunities.

I have nine graduate degrees so far. Each set of requirements was distinct. Their programs and processes were designed differently as well. Do not expect standardization in coursework, thesis requirements, or comprehensive exams. However, one consistency is that you graduate with a much deeper knowledge of the specialty. Gaining admission into these programs is competitive. Thus, planning, preparation, and a solid resume of experiences are required. Search for a program that fits your needs. There are numerous options to pursue your interests.

THE SEVEN MAJOR DIFFERENCES BETWEEN THE ASSOCIATE, BACHELOR'S, AND MASTER'S DEGREES

1. Starting Point
2. Academic Discipline
3. Time to Completion
4. Location of the Education
5. Educational Costs
6. Earning Power
7. Professional Opportunities

STARTING POINT

Most students who begin in an Associate of Arts (AA) or Associate of Science (AS) program typically have no college credits. Starting a college education from scratch, students accumulate 60+ units beginning at a community college and take lower division courses. While most students earn AA or AS degrees at the community college, a few earn this degree at a 4-year college or university.

The AA or AS is either a terminal degree, meaning the student will not seek a higher degree, or a steppingstone to their BA, BS, or BFA. An associate's and bachelor's degree is just the starting point. Meanwhile, a student must earn a bachelor's degree to begin a master's degree (MA, MS, or MFA) program.

ACADEMIC DISCIPLINE

Every degree encompasses different requirements. Requirements for the AA differ from an AS. Similarly, the requirements for the BA, BS, and BFA also differ. With two additional years of coursework, the BA, BS, and BFA are more thorough. The MA, MS, and MFA build upon the bachelor's degree and pursue topics even deeper.

Furthermore, students in different majors rarely take the same courses or class sequence. For example students studying neuroscience will not take the same classes as those pursuing psychology, though some may overlap. While both disciplines are related to the brain, cognition, and behavior, the necessary skills for each career area are distinct. Thus, the course requirements are also unique. Even the same major at different universities can vary significantly. Degrees may include a different number of credits in psychology, statistics, calculus, science, and computer programming depending upon the major's course specifications.

TIME TO COMPLETION

Associate of Arts (AA) and Associate of Science (AS) degrees typically take two years, while most BA, BS, and BFA degrees are 4- or 5-year programs, depending upon full-time or part-time status. Students who transfer credits, earn credits through CLEP, or test out can reduce their time to completion.

The time required to earn a bachelor's degree depends upon each student's skills and advanced credit. Still, some students change their chosen major which frequently extends the time to completion based on the additional requirements.

According to the National Center for Educational Statistics, college advisors aid students in finishing "on time", though less than half of all students in the United States who start a bachelor's program finish their degree in four years.

Time in college can be reduced. Some students enter bachelor's degree programs with college credits because they were either dual-enrolled or they took college classes outside of their high school or college during the summer or school year as allowed. Some students who earn qualifying scores on AP/IB tests from advanced classes taken in high school can be granted credits by the college or university. Policies regarding AP/IB credit vary. Look on each college's website to determine what scores and subjects qualify.

Other ways students can enter at a different starting point include credit-by-exam, CLEP tests, experiential credits, and units granted in the military. Colleges and universities are keenly aware of the challenges students face today with work, illness, and family responsibilities. Thus, many schools of higher education offer flexible enrollment with opportunities for part-time, evening, weekend, and online classes.

LOCATION OF THE EDUCATION

The AA and AS are earned at colleges that grant 2-year degrees. The location may be at a local community college or a university. BA, BS, and BFA programs are offered at a 4-year college or university. However, with online classes, students have the flexibility to take classes from colleges farther away as well. With the added variable of students taking classes on multiple campuses, the location in which students study is not as set as it once was. Nevertheless, in-person internships are often situated in corporate hubs and, thus, require grounding in a specific location.

Online internships have become more prevalent with companies downsizing location-based jobs and seeking assistance from remote workers. With virtual offices and people becoming more comfortable with online work, students may find alternative job options that offer more flexibility with less in-person activities.

EDUCATIONAL COSTS

Since the AA or AS takes less time than the BA or BA and is typically completed at a lower-cost community college, the cost of an associate's degree is typically less than a bachelor's degree. Master's programs often cost more per credit but take less time than a bachelor's degree. Don't be surprised. Graduate students in research-based majors often do not pay tuition since they frequently receive grants, tuition waivers, fellowships, teaching opportunities, or research assistantships to cover their tuition.

On the other hand, many students obtain financial aid in the form of grants, loans, and both merit and need-based scholarships. This aid can help pay for school and reduce debt after college.

We must be willing to let go of the life we planned
to have the life that is waiting for us.

- Joseph Campbell

EARNING POWER

Education pays off. According to national data, suggest the median income for degree attainment in 2025 is as follows.

- Master's Degree or Higher - $82,000
- Bachelor's Degree - $70,000
- Associate's Degree - $51,000
- High School - $43,000
- Engineering MS - $115,000
- Engineering BS - $95,000
- STEM Associates - $58,000

Median incomes do not tell the whole story. There is significant variation in annual salaries ranging from those with low salaries to those who are paid high six-digit incomes. Thus, the median salary may seem low though the range is huge.

PROFESSIONAL OPPORTUNITIES

Earning a BA, BS, or BEng opens more doors than an AA or AS. Similarly, an MA, MS, or MFA opens more doors than a BA, BS, or BEng. You can also obtain skills from workshops, symposia, and conferences. With a scholarship to pay for college, you might take advantage of professional training, conferences, and study abroad programs to broaden your knowledge. Besides, you will also gain skills that will enhance your value throughout your career.

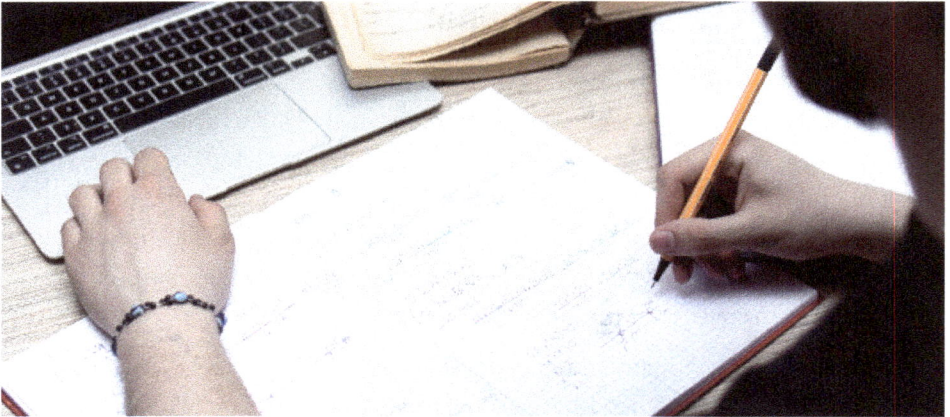

The beautiful thing about learning is that no one can take it from you.

- B.B. King

Professional opportunities depend on your career direction, degree of independence, and country of potential employment. Many graduate schools, educational organizations and companies are incorporating AR, VR, and machine learning. However, some focus on counseling, lab testing, and the pharmaceutical industry. Scroll through the firms that hire scientists in your field of interest or work environment preference to get a sense of the hundreds of professional options available to you.

Universities, organizations, or industries may also be a factor in your decision-making. While large firms may have more diversity of function and upward mobility, you might also be tasked with a specialized or limited role. On the other hand, a smaller treatment center or counseling firm may give you the chance to multitask on a wide range of projects and have a greater stake in the big picture of the operation. Whatever you decide, by taking internships, you will discover your preferences and, at a minimum, know the questions to ask during interviews.

Some areas of interest may include Internet of Things (IoT) design. You might spend time reviewing brain scans or use technology in an integrated system that allows computers to monitor, collect/relay information, and revise processes. This specialization will transform ideas into comprehensive strategies that embed, sense, track, and provide more ubiquitous flow of cloud-based data. In addition, neurotechnology companies will increasingly rely on 3D-printed parts.

Law school might be another direction you could take your education. One of the biggest challenges facing scientists is the control of intellectual property.

While filing for a patent is not terribly difficult, maintaining control of that property is much more challenging. In our copycat world, globalization delivers products worldwide to places that do not conform to international law. Materials, processes, and technologies are taken apart, reconfigured or modified, and put into the marketplace. Some organizations focus on protecting intellectual property by seeking out and prosecuting violators.

Jump at chances to gain real-world experiences. You may be in the workforce for fifty years. That is a really long time if you do not feel fulfilled. Sure, internships may mean sacrificing a summer holiday for a month somewhere, but it could make a significant difference in your future lifestyle and happiness.

CHICAGO
HANOVER COLLEGE
Bucknell
PENNSTATE
your feet,
Coe College
Bucknell

CHAPTER 8

THE COLLEGE ADMISSIONS PROCESS

"The best years of your life are the ones in which you decide your problems are your own. You do not blame them on your mother, the ecology, or the president. You realize that you control your own destiny."

– Albert Ellis

Apply to the colleges with the curriculum, clubs, activities, and opportunities that best fit your goals. Stanford, Harvard, Princeton, Yale, UChicago, UPenn, UC Berkeley, and UCLA are eight colleges with amazing faculty, excellent facilities, exciting research, entrepreneurial students, and relatively easy access to job opportunities.

While most students consider Atlanta, Boston, Chicago, New York, Los Angeles, and Silicon Valley, as locations for internships, do not discount other metropolitan areas like Austin, Cleveland, Houston, Seattle, and Research Triangle. You cannot go wrong attending schools like UT Austin, Case Western, Duke, UNC, Rice, Vanderbilt, and the University of Washington for their deep dive into the worlds of psychology and human-centered science. These colleges offer rigorous courses of study and socially responsible projects on the cutting edge of experimentation, technology, and forward-thinking optimism.

However, planning is required before you apply. Let's look at a few terms you should know, then move on to community service, connecting with the colleges, and whether or not you should take standardized tests. Then, I offer some data, a checklist, and some tips for applying to and succeeding in college.

Best wishes on your journey!!!

ADMISSIONS TERMS TO KNOW

Admissions Tests – Universities use standardized tests like the SAT, ACT, GMAT, GRE, and MCAT to compare student's aptitude in basic academic skill areas.

Admit Rate – The percentage of applicants admitted to a school.

Articulation Agreement – This is the agreement between 2-year and 4-year colleges determining whether credits transfer from one institution to another.

Candidate Reply Date – For freshman admissions, students must reply back to colleges by May 1 with their choice of college or university they will attend from those in which they were accepted.

Class Rank – Most high schools no longer rank students. However, a few still do. This ranking puts students in order of GPA, though the criteria vary from school to school. Some schools rank in percentiles or deciles.

Coalition Application – This application can be sent to multiple schools within their network of approximately 150 colleges. Many of the affiliated colleges also require supplemental applications with additional essays and requirements.

College Credit – Most colleges require 120 – 130 semester credits to graduate with a bachelor's degree. Students earn credits upon successful completion of classes.

Colleges may award college credit for qualifying AP/IB scores, CLEP exams, and military training courses.

Common Application – This standardized digital application may be submitted to multiple schools within their network of approximately 1,100 colleges. Most colleges also require supplements with additional essays and requirements.

Deferred Admission – After the EA/ED admissions cycle, students are accepted, denied, or deferred to regular decision. Typically, the chance of acceptance during the regular admissions cycle after being deferred is 5–10%.

Deferred Enrollment – Colleges allow a student to postpone their attendance for up to one year. Note: Not all colleges allow students to defer. If they do, there may be restrictions and other requirements. Check the college's website to be sure.

Domestic Student – U.S. citizens or permanent residents at the time of admission are considered domestic students, irrespective of the country in which they live.

Early Action (EA) – EA is an early application submission in which a student also finds out their admission status before regular decision students. Early action is typically not binding, meaning that students do not need to enroll if accepted. Most EA application due dates are between October 15th and November 15th. Almost all EA decisions come back between December 1st and February 1st, with most responses between December 10th and 20th.

Early Decision (ED) – A few colleges have ED, whereby a student commits to one school should they be accepted. Students agree to attend when they apply, and they can only apply to one ED school. If admitted, students pay the deposit and withdraw their applications from other schools. ED applications are typically due November 1 and decisions typically come back in mid-December.

Financial Aid – This monetary award is given to students to help pay for college. The amount may be composed of scholarships, grants, loans, and work-study. Financial aid may be granted from the government, college, or private organizations. Complete the FAFSA for the possibility of receiving federal aid.

First-Generation – Students are 'first-gen' if neither parent earned a four-year college degree. Some colleges specify that that the parents also never attended college. A few students consider themselves first-generation U.S. college students since neither of their parents attended college in the United States. The underlying notion in each case is that these parents lack the knowledge to fully advise their child.

High School GPA – This number is considered or recalculated differently by each college depending upon whether they include 9th – 11th, summers, middle school, AP/IB/Honors credit, college classes, and courses like health, leadership, computer applications, sports, MUN, journalism, religion, etc. Some colleges like the University of California cap their weighted GPA for admissions purposes with only 8 semesters of 'honors' points. No more than 4 of these can be from 10th grade.

In-State – Students are 'in-state' if they have residency in the state with evidence like driver's license, taxes, bills, school attendance, etc., no matter where they physically live. Rules regarding DACA students differ.

International – International applicants are not citizens or permanent residents of the U.S. This designation can vary based upon college/state rules.

Legacy Candidate – A child of a close relative (usually a parent) who graduated from a given college. A few colleges give preference to legacy applicants.

Lower Division – These are courses typically taken during your first two years of college. Most community college classes are lower division. At a university, lower division courses for a BA or BS degree are primarily liberal arts classes.

Need-Aware Admissions – The policy where admissions teams consider financial circumstances in the admissions process.

Need-Blind Admissions – The policy where admissions teams do not consider financial circumstances in the admissions process.

Open Admissions – A college opens enrollment to all students until all seats are filled without consideration of past academic performance or minimum requirements.

Placement Tests – Most colleges require certain levels of mastery before entering a class. Upon enrolling in a college, students take placement tests to determine the level in which they are placed. Since information recall may not be strong from a class taken years before, you should review the material before you take the test or else you may need to take additional remedial classes which may prolong graduation one or more years.

Portal – This online admissions site, connected to a specific college, is a centralized information area. Students log in to determine next steps, including missing items (transcripts, test scores, portfolio, letters of recommendation, FAFSA, CSS Profile, etc.), financial aid, scholarship opportunities, and admissions status

Registrar's Office – This is the office of college officials who are responsible for your student records, including recording final grades, checking remaining payments, certifying completion of requirements, and sending transcripts.

Residency – This is the determination of the state where you legally reside and determines residency, non-resident U.S., DACA, or international status.

Rolling Admission – This is the college policy to accept students as applications are received rather than waiting for a specific date to review each applicant's records. Many colleges with rolling admissions will determine your admission result within a month of receipt of your application materials.

Summer Melt – This is the phenomenon whereby students submit an intent to enroll at a college after being admitted, pay the deposit, and decide not to attend during the summer. While this situation may have increased during the pandemic, the phenomenon has recurred for decades. The primary reasons for summer melt include the inability to pay, illness, family matter, change of heart, acceptance of a job, or getting off the waitlist at another college.

Transfer Student – A student who has taken college classes after completing high school and applies to a 4-year university is considered a transfer student. Typically, if a student takes college classes during high school and then applies to college they are still considered as freshman for admissions purposes.

Upper Division – These are courses typically taken in a student's second two years of college. At a university, upper division courses for a BA or BS degree are primarily major-specific classes.

Waitlist – Admissions offices accept, deny, or waitlist students. Those students on a waitlist must wait until a spot opens. If there is a vacancy, the student may be taken off the waitlist on a priority basis, ranking system, or admissions review.

Yield – This is the percent of admitted students who pay the deposit with the intent to enroll (enrolled/admitted x 100).

PRESIDENT'S VOLUNTEER SERVICE AWARD

Students can support their communities through volunteer service. Some students are recognized for their volunteer efforts as they support others via scouting, charity organizations, service-oriented events, or self-designed passion projects. There are numerous ways to serve society and make a difference by earning a certificate of acknowledgment at the same time. A few of these are listed below.

5K Walks	Drug Awareness	Medical Missions	Salvation Army
Africa Cries Out	Elder/Hospice Care	Medical Research	Schools
Animal Shelters	Feed America	Musical Events	Soup Kitchens
Beach Cleanup	Fire Prevention	Nursing Homes	Special Olympic
Boating Safety	Food Banks	Operation Smile	Sports Camps
Carnivals	Forest Renewal	Park Cleanups	Suicide Prevention
Charity Events	Habitat for Humanity	Political Campaigns	Theater Docent
Church Events	Homeless Shelters	Red Cross	Veterans Events
Club Dust	Human Trafficking	Refugee Centers	Wetlands Conservation
Doctors w/o Borders	International Service	Rescue Missions	Working Wardrobes
Domestic Violence Ctrs	Marine Life Asst	Ronald Mcdonald	Youth Action Teams

... along with organizations supporting medical conditions like Alzheimer's, cancer, cleft palate, cystic fibrosis, dementia, diabetes, heart disease, leukemia, and muscular dystrophy. By starting now and accumulating hours, you can earn one of the following Presidential awards.

Hours Required to Earn Awards in Each Age Group

Age Group	Bronze	Silver	Gold	Lifetime Achievement Award
Kids (5–10 years old)	26–49 hours	50–74 hours	75+ hours	4,000+ hours
Teens (11–15)	50–74 hours	75–99 hours	100+ hours	4,000+ hours
Young Adults (16–25)	100–174 hours	175–249 hours	250+ hours	4,000+ hours
Adults (26+)	100–249 hours	250–499 hours	500+ hours	4,000+ hours

COLLEGE ADMISSIONS:

Success in the Face of Uncertainty

There are no guarantees in college admissions. However, planning is essential for success. The most beneficial advice is to pursue your passions with gusto, train to be the best you can be, take advantage of internships and experiences, and meet lots of people along the way.

Remember, "life is a journey, not a destination." Often the journey is more exciting, leading to lessons, friendships, and unforgettable moments. However, the fact is, in the end, if college is your goal, then you need to recall a few action items for success.

Should you worry about grades? Of course. You should also take classes that will challenge you. Colleges pick the best candidates from those who apply. Students must be academically prepared, socially conscious, and talented in a few different areas in which they are passionate. For example,

App Development	Cultural Activities	Gaming	Public Speaking
Athletics	Dance	Graphics Art	Robotics
Clubs	Debate	Hiking	Sports Camps
Coding	Elder/Hospice Care	Human Trafficking	Sustainability
Community Service	Entrepreneurship	Leadership	Theatre
Competitions	Environment	Multiculturalism	Travel
Computer Repair	Fashion	Music	Water Sports
Construction	Fire Prevention	Photography	Winter Activities

The college selection process is not that much different than companies picking employees. While colleges are more or less competitive, companies may have only one job, and a hundred resumes. Discover your unique drive and internal motivations that make you the very best you can be. Be exceptional at what you choose to do academically, personally, and professionally.

Most of all, You Do You!

TALENT FOCUSED

Not all schools require high grades and test scores. Many are simply interested in selecting students who are the most talented, most driven, and the most willing to be team players on the college campus. Thus, you should take a solid set of courses and fulfill the standard requirements. Some students are late bloomers!

Hundreds of thousands of students attend college with high school GPAs between 2.5 and 3.5. Furthermore, most college students today (more than ten million) never take a standardized test. If you are applying to highly competitive schools, you should take the ACT or SAT. However, there are hundreds of colleges that do not require test scores and probably never will in the future.

I pulled some 2024-2025 data you may find informative.

1. As of 2024, the U.S. student loan debt reached $1,77 trillion with over 92%in federal loans. The average graduate has $37,000 in student loans.
2. College tuition costs surged by 148% since 1980 with costs of over $100,000. Some top schools are around $90,000/year.
3. Only 41% of students complete their 4-year degree in four years.
4. Approximately 40% of students drop out of college; 30% of freshmen do not return for a second year.
5. Students spend nearly $1,500 on textbooks and reading materials per year.
6. College enrollment for 18-24-year-olds is trending downward, though the

top colleges continue to have expanding enrollments.

7. U.S. college enrollment is expected to reach a turning point in 2025. Afterward, an "enrollment cliff" is anticipated with large fall off. Low birth rates during this period will plunge down student enrollment. As a result, student population shifts are expected.

2024-2025 DEMOGRAPHIC CHARACTERISTICS

Caucasian – 42.2%

LatinX (Hispanic/Latino) - 17.5%

Black or African American - 10.6%

Asian or Asian American – 5.8%

American Indian/Alaska Native – 0.7%

Pacific Islander – 0.3%

Foreign Born - 5.6%

Women - 57.5%

Men - 41.5%

Other Gender - 1%

Under 18 years old - 5%

18 - 24 years old - 64%

25 - 50 years old – 28%

Over 50 years old – 3%

DEGREES AND MAJORS
2024-2025 Distribution of Students/Graduates

49.2 million students attended K-12 schools

*3.7 million earned a high school diploma

*19.7 million students attended college

*15.5 million undergraduates

*4.2 million graduate students

*Approximately 2 million earned

U.S. Census Bureau Degrees Earned

*22.5% BA or BS

*13.1% MA or MS

*1.3% JD

*0.8% MD

*2.1% Ph.D, or Ed.D

2024 DISTRIBUTION OF MAJORS

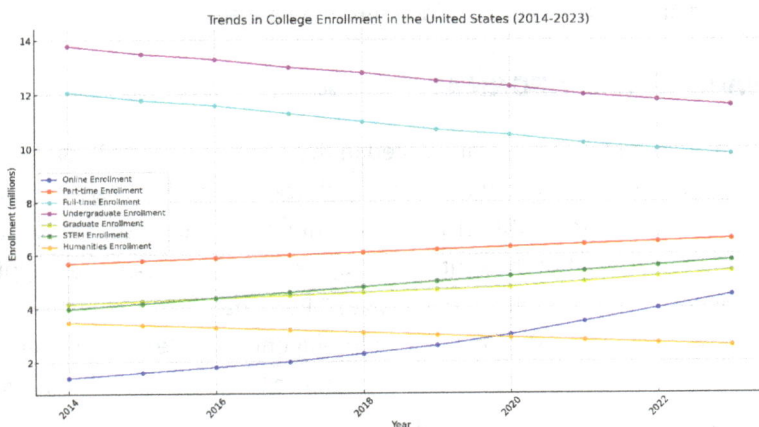

Trends in College Enrollment in the United States (2014-2023)

COMPETITIVE COLLEGE ADMISSIONS

A few highly selective colleges seek extraordinary artistic or athletic talent over academics, but most zero in on a student's academic record of AP, IB, and college prep courses. To gain admission into the most selective academic colleges, you must take the most challenging course load in which you can manage the assignments and succeed with high grades. Don't overwhelm yourself. If you cannot handle the difficulty, give yourself a break. Just know that admissions to top colleges is competitive and you may not attend a high ranking school. Highly selective colleges want disciplined scholars AND remarkably talented students.

Determine what you can handle, knowing that some colleges with extremely competitive admission will only take students who have completed more than ten AP, IB, or honors classes during high school. Still, a top college may pose significant academic challenges when the coursework is tremendously difficult, you are away from home, and you are either underprepared academically or emotionally.

Why would some top colleges require AP Calculus or AP Physics? No matter how daunting these classes may seem, remember, the top colleges have lots of applicants. They need to draw the line somewhere. For the class of 2029, UCLA had 173,297 applicants (145,058 1st year, 28,239 transfer); UC Berkeley had 150,109 total applicants. The numbers are truly staggering. For the 2024-2025 school year, approximately 5,700 freshman attended UCLA and 5,500 attended UC Berkeley.

The college admissions process can feel like a rollercoaster of energy, rigor, and emotion. Creating a portfolio of talent, training, and experience is just the beginning. Meanwhile, some colleges want to see standardized test scores. You may need to practice. Managing your application, essays, and deadlines can be difficult. This moment is a good time to get a calendar and organize your tasks. Caution: Using AI on your essays could result in an automatic rejection.

BEWARE OF MISINFORMATION & ARTIFICIAL INTELLIGENCE

The University of California announced in their November 13, 2024 Counselors & Advisors Bulletin that they would randomly check applications for verification in mid-December and then notify students via their portal and other methods that they will need to verify what they submitted by January 31 or else their application would be canceled. Additionally, the essays (UC Personal Insight Questions) would also be reviewed for plagiarism or artificial intelligence. Students will have two weeks to respond with proof of authenticity. Failure to respond will result in their application being canceled. Check your portals!

REQUEST INFORMATION

Almost every college has a location, a link, or a contact us page where you can request additional information. If you are considering a college or university, use the link and request information. They may send materials, updates, scholarship opportunities, application fee waiver, exclusive invites, and other information that could be valuable even though you may already be receiving information from the school. Still, I recommend filling out their form to show you are reaching out to them. Then, since you are likely to be inundated with e-mails, make a file folder in your e-mail for all colleges you are considering. When you get an e-mail from one of those schools, file it away.

STANDARDIZED TESTING

Though some colleges remain test-optional, many schools are returning to standardized test requirements. Check first. While test optional means you are not required to take the SAT or ACT, if you have a good score, submit! Your test results may make all the difference in gaining admission. College admissions officers are studying this topic and reconsidering their policies. Their concern began with worldwide test cancellations due to the pandemic and the inability to find test locations and supervisors.

144

During the pandemic, school administrators did not want to let possibly-infected students onto their campus to take the test, nor were they able to ensure student safety. In addition, social distancing requirements limited the number of students at any testing site. Yet, for decades, college admissions decisions centered around grades and test scores. This change in the decision-making landscape rattled admissions directors and enrollment managers.

Meanwhile, some colleges proclaim that test-optional truly means the test is not considered. Yet, evidence proves otherwise. Thus, many students still take the test and work around test preparation and test site hurdles amid the confusion.

Data show that students who submitted scores within the college's range were accepted at a higher rate than those without a score. Meanwhile, some schools are test blind, meaning they do not consider test scores. Even so, a few of these same colleges still provide a place to input scores. Thus, they are not truly blind. Nevertheless, the decision regarding whether you should take the test or submit your scores is yours. If the school does not require an admissions test, you can choose to take and submit the test as you like. If your academics are solid and you are willing to prepare for the test, you should take the test.

Competition continues to drive students to present evidence demonstrating they are worthy candidates. In the end, colleges need to make a final decision between very good candidates. If one student has a high standardized test score, that student may have a higher likelihood of admission depending upon the admissions committee's formal or subliminal decision-making process.

APPLYING EARLY
Early Action (EA), Restricted Early Action (REA), and Early Decision (ED)

With low acceptance rates, the chance to obtain additional scholarship money, and the chaos surrounding the cancellations and changes in AP, IB, SAT, and ACT testing, students clamor to apply early to schools. In addition, applications to the top schools increased during the pandemic, resulting in colleges needing to make difficult admissions decisions in their quest to build a diverse, talented, and engaged class of students. Furthermore, students applying early have access to many more scholarship options. Some require test scores. This confluence sent students in droves to apply early. This trend is likely to continue.

In Early Action (EA), Restricted Early Action (REA), and Early Decision (ED), students apply to college in late summer or early fall and generally find out around winter break, though some decisions come out earlier and a few arrive later. This advantage not only gives students a chance for more scholarship money in some cases but the benefit of finding out early reduces the tension of the long waiting period until Regular Decision results arrive.

Early Action (EA) and Restricted Early Action (REA) are different. In Restricted Early Action, a limitation is placed on either how many or what colleges you can apply to simultaneously. Many REA schools do not allow students to apply to other Early Action schools, though some will allow students to apply early to public colleges. Check the colleges to be sure. In addition, some schools like Georgetown will allow students to apply EA elsewhere but not to a binding Early Decision (ED) program where the student commits to attending if they are accepted. However, most EA schools do not have these restrictions. Some students apply to a handful of EA schools during the admissions process.

Early Decision (ED) is a binding agreement between the student and college with signatures from the student, the student's parents, and the high school counselor, ensuring the student is committed to their first-choice ED school and will attend if accepted. Each of these parties acknowledges and agrees that, if granted admission, the student will fulfill their agreement. There are caveats, though you should go into the agreement fully committing to your ED school.

There are incentives to applying ED. Frequently, acceptance rates are higher. Also, at some schools, a large percentage of their class is filled with students who profess their unequivocal love for their dream school. Students who can commit to their top choice school, filled the necessary prerequisites, and are willing to accept the binding agreement to attend, should apply ED.

COMMON APPLICATION, COALITION APPLICATION, OR COLLEGE-SPECIFIC APPLICATION

Every college's process is unique. However, there are a few commonalities. In 2025, approximately 1,100 colleges used the Common App; about 150 colleges used the Coalition Application. A few used both. The University of California system has its own application as do the California State Universities and the Texas schools. UT Austin and Texas A&M joined the Common App in 2023.

The Common App and Coalition App may be started early. In your junior year, consider getting a head start reviewing requirements. College-specific questions may change each year. However, the basic application is generally the same and can be created ahead of time. The application rolls over August 1. Toward the end of July, make a copy of the application you completed just in case.

Some schools admit on a rolling basis. 'Rolling' means that periodically, after all materials are received, the admissions committee determines who they will accept, and then sends the notification of the admissions decision. Some students are accepted as early as August. The thrill of acceptance cannot be overstated.

ESSAYS

The Common Application and Coalition essays are often posted months ahead of time. Since this main essay is required or recommended for nearly all Common Application and Coalition Application schools, the personal statement is an excellent place to start thinking about what you might want to say to colleges.

In addition to the main essay on the Common Application and Coalition Application, half of the colleges have their own specific questions or essays. In August, most admissions applications are open and ready for you to dive into the supplemental college-specific questions, though many of the essay topics are available earlier, and some schools hold out until later for their big essay reveal.

Essays can be prepared ahead of time too. One popular question is, "What activity is most important to you and why?" Another is "Why did you choose your major?" A third common question is, "Why do you want to attend our school?" For others, you should prepare or at least consider the topics of diversity, adversity, and challenges since these topics have become increasingly important in the admissions process. Everyone has a challenge they needed to overcome, especially during the pandemic. What did you learn from your experiences?

Complete the application fully. Think carefully about optional sections. Typically, universities offer you the chance to provide the school with just the right cherry on top of the sundae, allowing you to share something unique about you. If you have absolutely nothing to say, leave it blank. There is an additional information section on the main Common App, Coalition Application, and University of California application. This location is not a place to write another essay, but you can include information that cannot be adequately explained in the rest of the application.

There are also schools that include scholarship essays within the supplement part of the application. Start early.

TIPS FOR THE COLLEGE ESSAY

Let's look at some step-by-step advice on college entrance essays.

Step 1: Read the Prompt Carefully

Answer the question fully and completely.

Check the word or character count.

Re-read the prompt to understand themes.

Teamwork, diversity, challenges, community, or goals are important.

Where do you fit into that college?

What is the intersection of your interests and what they offer?

Step 2: Brainstorm Ideas

List hobbies, passions, and influences.

Reflect on your life stories and events.

What areas fit with the college's culture?

What were pivotal moments, challenges, or achievements?

Step 3: Find a Unique Angle

Be creative and interesting but also authentic.

Do not copy, augment, or adapt someone else's story.

Going outside of the box is fine, but remember, simple is fine too.

They just want to get to know you.

Some students focus on uniqueness at the cost of being relatable.

Step 4: Focus on Key Moments

Focus on key moments rather than generalities.

Remember: Show, don't tell.

Make the story compelling and meaningful.

What experience changed your perspective?

Step 5: Create an Outline

This is an essay after all.

What is your catchy introduction?

What body paragraphs provide examples for your thesis?

Conclude with a reflection that ties the story together.

Step 6: Start with a Hook

A quote, shock, epiphany, or idea can help introduce your story.

Connect your story to the prompt.

Step 7: Write a Draft and Wrap it with a Bow

Tie the hook with a story.

Tie the story to your life experiences.

Tie the body paragraphs to the prompt.

Tie the loose ends in a bow and memorable idea.

Avoid cliches and generalities.

Step 8: Edit for Clarity

Check spelling, grammar, and ideas.

Make sure your essay aligns with the college.

Remember, readers have thousands of essays.

Create smooth paragraph transitions.

Maintain focus.

Sept 9: Seek Feedback

The reader is not a teenager.

What you think is funny or amusing may not appeal to an adult.

However, parents may not be in-tune with colleges.

Think through the feedback. Trust your instincts.

Step 10: Revise, Proofread, and Submit

Remember to use your unique voice.

Format as directed – font, spacing, word count.

Read it over one more time and submit.

Final Notes:

- Optional rarely means optional. In most cases, do it.
- If there is a COVID and Natural Disasters essay, tell your story.
- Write in complete sentences.
- Research the school. Every school is different.
- Do not just write the same essay for each school.
- Don't complain about a teacher, even if it is true.
- Don't lie or tell untruths in your essay or application.

Additional Information Section

Do not put essays in the additional information section, but you can use this section to clarify elements in your application that need explanation, like low grades, a bad semester, family emergencies, or why you did not take a class that you really should have completed.

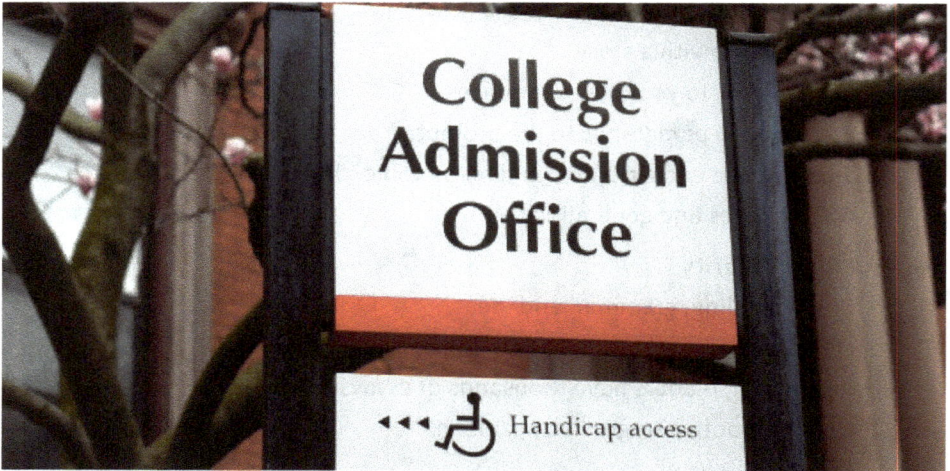

STUDENT RESUMES FOR COLLEGE ADMISSION

1. **Decide on a clean, easy-to-read format**
   - One page is best.
   - Most people will only read the first page.
   - Being long-winded and wordy is not helpful.
   - Arial, Calibri, or Times New Roman are the best.
   - Font sizes should not be too small.

2. **Pictures are okay for a freshman admissions resume**

3. **Name, E-Mail, and Phone Number**
   - Do not include your home address

4. **Educational Experiences or Academic Background**
   - High School(s), dates, location(s)
   - Colleges Attended, dates, location(s)
   - Academic Programs/Training
   - Languages

5. **Honors, Awards, Certifications**
   - Academic Honors
   - Awards
   - Certificates
   - Acknowledgments
   - Extraordinary Accomplishments

6. **Extracurricular Activities**
   - Clubs/Activities
     - Bulletpoint each accomplishment with past tense verbs.
     - Focus on achievements, consistency, and leadership.
   - Sports/Athletics – Separate if extensive

7. **Community Service**

8. **Work Experience**

9. **Hobbies**

Final Notes
- You might add a goal/vision statement at the top or a quote that defines your destiny or vision.
- Avoid writing paragraphs since people will not read these.
- Proofread by double-checking for spelling and errors.
- Ask for feedback.
- If you have time, tailor the resumes to each school.
- Add a LinkedIn URL, Portfolio Link, or Personal Website

LETTERS OF RECOMMENDATION

Most colleges on the Common App and Coalition App, though not all, request letters of recommendation from a counselor and one or more teachers. For science programs, university admissions offices may want academic teachers in mathematics, science, or humanities. Plan for this.

Occasionally, there is a section for optional recommendations too. In this location, you might request a recommendation from a summer program leader or someone with whom you held a job or completed an internship. If you were in a sport, you might choose a coach, art teacher, or religious leader.

SUPPLEMENTAL APPLICATIONS

Some schools require a supplemental application with additional essays. You may also be able to add a research abstract. For students with creative talents art, music, and theatre, a SlideRoom application may be required with separate recommendations and materials reviewed by the college's talent experts.

COLLEGE APPLICATION CHECKLIST

☐ **Calendar** - Keep a calendar of due dates for summer program applications, contests, AP tests, SAT/ACT, applications, scholarships, and financial aid.

☐ **Career Interest Survey** - Take a career interest/aptitude test. Learn more about the majors and career options that best fit your interests and abilities

☐ **Consider College Majors** – What classes are required in your chosen major? Many students who dislike math are surprised to learn that top colleges require both calculus and statistics while incorporating math in nearly every class. STEM degrees typically require physics. Research course requirements.

☐ **Investigate Colleges** – Consider colleges based on their programs. Research opportunities, internships, clubs, activities, sports, and personal interests. Visit if possible. Ask questions to students who are currently in the program.

☐ **National College Fair** – In the spring, colleges send representatives to events, typically held in large convention centers, where you can meet admissions staff. Walk from booth to booth to learn more about the colleges and ask questions. Get the representative's business card and write them a thank you note.

☐ **Request Information** – Fill out "request information" forms for each college you are considering. They will keep you informed of opportunities you may not have considered. They may send you a fee waiver or streamlined application.

☐ **Summer Programs** – Consider skill-building events, coding/robotics camps, tours, research, internships, and college courses. Investigate these opportunities, applications, and deadlines. Apply and consider your options.

☐ **Narrow Your List** – Narrow down your choices during the summer before your senior year so you have target, reach, and safety schools.

☐ **Communicate With Your Counselor** – Your counselor can be a helpful guide who not only helps you select courses but also advocates for you in the admissions process. Counselors write recommendation letters and sometimes communicate with admissions officers on your behalf. Get to know them.

☐ **SAT/ACT** – Look up each college you are considering to determine their test requirements. While low scores are not helpful, high scores can improve your chances. Don't forget to send your scores from the testing agency if required.

☐ **Extended Time** – Determine if you qualify for extended time on tests.

☐ **Fee Waivers** – Ask your counselor if you qualify for fee waivers for the SAT/ACT, CSS Profile, or college applications.

☐ **Resume** – Create a resume whether or not the college requests one – some do. First, you may need one for a job. However, a resume allows you to gather your activities and accomplishments in one place so you can determine what you want to present to a school.

☐ **Essays and Short Answer Questions** – Consider aspects of your life that stand out. Give colleges the best impression of your goals, passions, pursuits, interests, inspirations, commitment, and life journey.

☐ **Counselor Recommendation Form** – Determine if your high school requires a special form to obtain a counselor recommendation.

☐ **Recommendations** – Ask your teachers in the spring of your junior year or when school starts in your senior year.

☐ **Early Action/Early Decision** – ED and EA applications are due early in your senior year, typically between October 15th and November 15th.

☐ **Regional Representative** – Some colleges have a regional representative. If you have specific questions not apparent from the college website, contact them.

☐ **Transcripts** – Order transcripts to be sent to colleges from your high school(s) and any colleges you have attended. Note: Some colleges like the University of California do not want transcripts sent until you are admitted.

☐ **Deadlines** – Keep your eye on the deadlines.

☐ **Portals** – You must log into your portal after you submit your application and then every couple of weeks afterward to see if the college is missing something from your file. Some colleges will dismiss your application if you do not log in or will move your early application to regular decision.

☐ **Scholarships** – Scholarship due dates vary and continue throughout your senior year. Some consider students in the spring of your junior year. The Coca-Cola Scholarship is due September 30th. Look for scholarships on www.fastweb.com and www.bigfuture.collegeboard.org/scholarship-search.

☐ **Regular Decision** – Most RD due dates are between Thanksgiving and the first two weeks of January with responses in from March 15th to April 7th.

☐ **FAFSA** – Free Application for Federal Student Aid - This application is required for federal financial aid (grants, work study, and loans).

- ☐ **CSS Profile** – About 300 colleges require this form in addition to the FAFSA to obtain financial aid.

- ☐ **Student Aid Report (SAR)** – Approximately 4 weeks after completing your FAFSA you should receive your SAR. Follow the instructions to complete any updates or add schools.

- ☐ **Update Colleges** – Make sure you update colleges with your continued interest.

- ☐ **Keep Copies** – Keep copies of your application materials in a folder.

- ☐ **Visit Colleges** – If possible, visit colleges to which you were accepted. Since you are going to live there for four years, you should get a feel for the campus and not just judge a school by its rankings or images in the school's website.

- ☐ **Communicate With Students** – Find students currently attending the university who are willing to answer a few questions. How hard is it to change your major? Are students friendly? What do students do on the weekends? Ask your counselor, teachers, or admissions officers if they can refer you to a current student or one who just graduated.

- ☐ **Waitlisted Schools** – Good news. You still have a chance. This list is created by colleges to fill in the gaps. Most schools allow you to write a letter updating them on your accomplishments during your senior year and your continued interest. Read the instructions since every school has a different format and set of requirements. Demonstrate your commitment.

- ☐ **Candidate Reply Date** – By May 1st you must choose one school and place a deposit.

- ☐ **Senior Year Grades** – Colleges rescind admissions offers for students who do poorly in their senior year. Do not slack off. You will regret it.

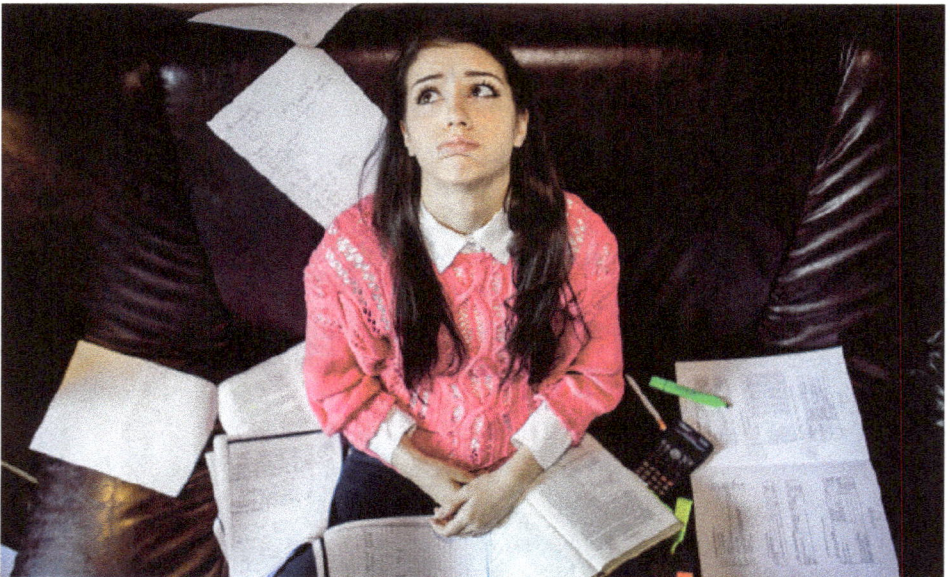

DECISIONS, DECISIONS: WAITING FOR A RESPONSE

The period between submitting your application and getting your admissions results requires patience and diligence. Most schools will send you a link to a portal where you will see what the college is missing, follow through with honors programs or scholarships, and check the results. Go into the site every couple of weeks in case the college requires a recommendation or has offered you the chance to apply for an extra scholarship.

Check your portal regularly. Additionally, read the college's correspondence sent through your e-mail. Waiting from November to April is agonizing. Your life is on the line and you just want to know where you are headed. However, colleges typically list the date they will send admissions results on the portal. Other popular sites post their decision notification dates too. You will find out soon.

THICK OR THIN ENVELOPE

Students eagerly check each day as winter turns to spring, waiting to hear via e-mail, the college portal, or the mail for a welcome packet or denial letter. You know spring has come as regular decision admissions results steadily roll in, one at a time. In March, every day seems to last 26 hours. Two extra for the period that lingers until that day's announcement. With each school announcing, one-by-one, the slow drip torture as you wait is exacerbated by the uncanny way each college picks a different day in March or April to announce their decision.

At some point you will know. That statement seems like little solace in the middle of the fray. You have until May 1 to make a decision, though with limited housing available and a first-come, first-served basis of selection, the pressure is on to choose. Even so, visiting the college is vital, despite the fact that AP tests and finals are just around the corner and there seems to be no time. However, this decision influences where you will live, eat, study, make friends, take classes, and get involved for four years. Do you want to base your next four years on a few college-selected pictures and the tweets or news feeds of other people?

There are many variables to consider. This is why forward thinking at the beginning of the application process is valuable and even necessary to seek scholarships, merit money, or opportunities for financial aid. This proactive planning is especially needed with the spike in college applications at selective schools and the ever-changing landscape of test-optional admissions. MIT, Stanford, and Ivy League schools, for example, resumed their test requirement.

Plan ahead. The college application period is not a good time to procrastinate. The fall of your senior year is tough, especially with a demanding course load. It is even tougher for athletes who compete in a fall sport. However, throughout your life you will work on time management, organization, and goal setting. This is a good time to start so you do not miss thousands of dollars in financial aid and scholarships. Time management proved challenging for students who adjusted their lifestyles with self-paced classes, Zoom meetings, and online assignments.

CELEBRATING ACCEPTANCES AND DEALING WITH REJECTION

Acceptance is not guaranteed. Colleges seek students who are wholly committed to their education, talents, and learning experiences. Unfortunately, even for dedicated students, the probability of acceptance is low at the most highly selective schools. Your commitment, work ethic, and planning make the outcome sweeter when you are accepted. Celebrate the next step along the way. You can do this. Get help. Think critically and logically. Be willing to work for it.

Congratulations! When you are accepted, you have colleges on your list of options. Check your financial aid and scholarship packages. Money is often an important factor in making your decision. Even if you cannot visit the campus, ask the college for contact names for students in your major. Many students apply to college merely by someone's recommendation, *U.S. News and World Report* ranking, Google photos, or posts on a website.

Nothing replaces the actual campus visit. After all, you will spend a few years there. Be selective as to where you apply, You may decide after visiting you do not want to apply. Understandably, the pandemic's uncertainty added more question marks to an already complicated set of admissions processes.

The buzzword for 2025-2035 is resilience. It is never easy to be rejected. However, rejection happens. You will survive this. Note: Many colleges still accept applications in April, May, and June long after most school's applications are closed. If you did not get accepted, look up colleges that still have openings. Some schools on the list may surprise you and may be good options. In April and May, Google "College Openings Update" to see schools that still have open spots.

WAITLISTS: THE ART OF WAITING

Immediately confirm if you are given a waitlist spot and still want to attend. There is often a deadline. You do not want to miss this. If you are no longer interested or have selected another school, go into the portal and turn down the offer. Someone else is bound to be thrilled by your anonymous gift.

If you are still interested, find the designated location on the portal and update them on what you have done since applying – accomplishments, awards, extra classes, honors, art shows, or films. Only add what they have not yet seen, but if you have taken the initiative to do something more than what you originally stated on the application, by all means, tell them. Some let you write a "love letter."

You could just wait for their decision, but you are better off being proactive and showing that you really want to be at their school. Students do get off the waitlists at most schools. How much do you want to attend? Meanwhile, you will have to deposit somewhere else before the May 1st deadline. Stay hopeful. This next year is a significant step along your journey. Relax!

ACCEPTANCE IS JUST THE BEGINNING

Once you are accepted to college, you begin your journey toward your future. They call graduation "commencement" because you start your trek on your own path. The decisions you make now are primarily yours with significantly less input from your parents. For better or worse, your parents taught you lessons that you will keep or discard. Now, your behaviors, attitudes, internships, study abroad, and career choices will determine what you become.

Warning ahead of time…the path is rarely straight and there are pitfalls along the way. Much like Monopoly, you will roll the dice and move ahead a few squares. You may go back a few spaces as well. You might buy a house or save some money. You might lose a property or investment too. Life is full of lessons. Successful adults sometimes look back and forget their wrong turns. Although setbacks sting at the time, they are dismissed over the years as lessons.

I have literally been in college for over fifty years and have degrees that span a multitude of disciplines. I have also taught chemistry, mathematics, engineering, counseling, public relations, and politics. Here are 21 tips as you go forward.

1. Attend class even when other students don't. Surprisingly, many lecture halls are half empty on non test days. Go anyway. Most college professors know if you attend or they can find out from their course assistant.

2. Buy your books and start reading before the semester starts. When classes begin, you live in a blizzard of activities, opportunities, and assignments. Surprisingly, most students do not complete their assigned readings. Some get by without reading at all, but few get As or Bs that way.

3. Work ahead. Finish your paper or project first, then go out and celebrate your friend's birthday, sports team win, or friend-group's successes. Not only can you be more relaxed, but you might even improve on your work later when you come up with a better paper or idea.

4. Most colleges offer free tutoring. Tutors often read over your papers or assignments and almost always give you valuable assistance you would have never considered. Return to #3. To get help, you must complete your assignments ahead of time.

5. Have a backup plan or two. Murphy's Law says: (1) anything that can go wrong will, (2) nothing is as easy as it looks, (3) everything takes longer than you think it will.

6. Save your digital documents – often. The worst thing is when you lose an entire assignment, your computer turns off, or malware attacks your files. Google Drive and iCloud are okay most of the time, but there are pitfalls. Make a backup file if possible, even if your docs are saved in the cloud.

7. Develop solid notetaking and reminder systems that work for you. You will need these for the rest of your life. Small, seemingly insignificant tasks slip through the cracks. Checklists are extremely helpful.

8. There is never enough time. Bring enough clothes so you do not need to wash them often. When you do wash them, take them out when they are done or else someone else will and you may never find them again.

9. Register for classes the minute registration opens for you. Trust me on this one. Otherwise, you get a bad professor at a horrible time that conflicts with your commitments. You might not even get into prerequisites which may extend your time in college an extra semester or year.

10. Petition to get into a class. Begging is fine. The professor can say no, but at least you tried. Good professors will save your sanity. Seriously!

11. If you have any academic problem, particularly with an illness, family matter, or emergency, let your professors know immediately. Most will not help you after the fact if you wait for a month thinking that you can handle it on your own or if you miss an assignment.

12. Make a calendar and keep track of what you need to accomplish. The syllabus is your roadmap. Calendarize due dates on your wall or phone.

13. Teamwork is a mantra in college. You will work on teams. A few team members may be unmotivated slackers or talented, but extreme procrastinators. Determine this ahead of time and set intermediate goals. Remember, your grade is on the line. It's not fair, but go back to #5. In the end, finish the project anyway. The unmotivated slacker will get an A, which may thoroughly frustrate you, but you will earn an A too.

14. Book prices vary widely. The university bookstore prices are high. You pay for convenience. I have friends who swear by certain online sites where they always buy textbooks, get coupons, and then buy more books. An advantage of buying books in digital format is using 'Control F' to find on-demand information which is impossible with a physical copy. I prefer physical books. You choose. Also, renting books is okay unless you forget to return the book.

15. Get involved on campus. Meet students who have similar interests. Join clubs, learn about the school's traditions, try activities you always wanted to learn, ask professors about volunteering on research projects, and get involved with intramural sports.

16. Don't bring a car. A car sounds wonderful, offering you freedom, until your vehicle is broken into, the gas runs out, the car breaks down before a test, or you get a half dozen parking tickets. You will never realized how much trouble a car could be on campus, particularly when there is limited and expensive parking. The college can and will hold your transcripts if you do not pay your parking tickets or clear a violation.

17. Communicate with your professors and TAs. Most have office hours. Well, they probably all have office hours, but sometimes they do not show

up. Either drop by during scheduled times or make an appointment. Especially if you have a question or a problem, speak to them. A professor rarely helps a student after they turn in grades but may have excellent advice during the term if you are struggling. Also, surprisingly, the answer key is occasionally wrong. Professors can be intimidating, standoffish, or mean-spirited. Fortunately, there are only a few bad ones, and even these professors teach you important lessons.

18. Don't get so excited about credit cards. Credit card companies will hound you to sign up with tempting offers. College students are prime targets since they do not yet understand the challenge of paying monthly bills when there is little time and numerous priorities. You will probably have to learn the hard way, but credit cards are not the savior or lifeline they purport to be. Moreover, you will likely spend more than you imagined, and the interest payments alone will dig you into a deep hole.

19. Drinking and drugs are around you 24/7. It does not matter what college you attend. Rarely is a campus void of alcohol or drugs. However, some colleges have more – much more. Some students will even sell illegal drugs in the dorm. Use good judgment. Be careful. Students consume more than they realize, make errors, get seriously injured, spread STDs, and die of overdoses. This section was not written to scare you but to make you aware of the life-changing realities.

20. During Christmas break in your first year, apply for internships, training opportunities, co-ops, or jobs for the summer. Create a resume. Getting real-world experience cannot be understated if you want to jump on the job market. Career fairs are extremely helpful so you can explore jobs. Every college has a career center. Get to know the people who work there. It may mean the difference in getting a coveted interview.

21. Go boldly into this world and try new things. Thomas Edison once said, "I have not failed. I've just found 10,000 ways that won't work."

Scholarship
Application

CHAPTER 9

FINANCIAL AID & SCHOLARSHIPS

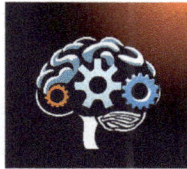

" *The good life is a process, not a state of being. It is a direction, not a destination.* "

– Carl Rogers

Nearly every university in the United States offers financial aid for college. These funds come in the form of grants or scholarships that do not need to be paid back, loans that need to be repaid, and 'work study' for paid work. Students often perform jobs like research, working at the library or assisting with events. The grants or scholarships are either based on need, talent, or grades.

Need-based means the college or government determines what your family can contribute as a function of your family's income. Otherwise, you will be unable to attend without additional resources. Merit-based aid means the college or university will offer students money based on grades, test scores, skills, background, experiences, talent, and/or academic achievement.

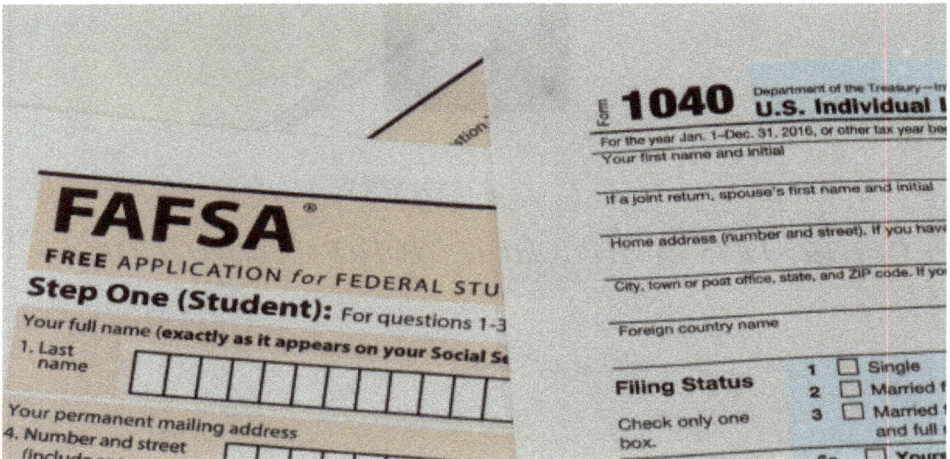

NEED-BASED FINANCIAL AID

To obtain need-based financial aid, almost all colleges require the submission of a Free Application for Federal Student Aid (FAFSA) found at www.studentaid.gov. Some colleges also require students to complete the College Scholarship Service (CSS) Profile, available on the College Board website at www.collegeboard.org.

In both the FAFSA and CSS Profile, students input family income from the tax returns filed with the U.S. federal government.

If your answer is yes to any of the following questions you do not need to declare your parent's income when completing your FAFSA form. There are nuances to this for students who are verifiably independent, ex-pats with a unique situation, and parents who are unavailable for a variety of reasons. The federal government provides free advice to families if they have a unique case.

1. Will you be 24 or older by Jan. 1 of the school year for which you are applying for financial aid?

2. Are you married or separated but not divorced?

3. Will you be working toward a master's or doctorate degree (such as MA, MBA, MD, JD, Ph.D., Ed.D., etc.)?

4. Do you have children who receive more than half of their support from you?

5. Do you have dependents (other than children or a spouse) who live with you and receive more than half of their support from you?

6. Are you currently serving on active duty in the U.S. armed forces for purposes other than training?

7. Are you a veteran of the U.S. armed forces?

8. At any time since you turned age 13, were both of your parents deceased, were you in foster care, or were you a ward or dependent of the court?

9. Are you an emancipated minor or are you in a legal guardianship as determined by a court?

10. Are you an unaccompanied youth who is homeless or self-supporting and at risk of being homeless?

SCHOLARSHIPS

Merit scholarships are frequently available through colleges, private donors, or corporations. These are based upon academic success, background, talent, or life experiences. Scholarships may require additional forms, recommendations, essays, and proof of academic success. Note: A few universities, particularly the highest-ranked schools, do not offer merit scholarships, though most colleges do.

Merit scholarships based on talent typically require a research abstract, video, audition, website, or some other skill demonstration. Check the requirements for art, dance, music, writing, debate, theatre, research, robotics, or engineering. Each college or university has a different set of rules to demonstrate your mastery.

Please review the profile section at the back of this book for scholarships and requirements. Additionally, look up the college website for their financial aid process. For example, some colleges may require you to submit the CSS Profile to be awarded any merit scholarship. To help you get a sense of available scholarships, I selected three schools from the options listed in the profile section.

ENGINEERING SCHOLARSHIPS

Air & Space Forces Association

AFA contributes $230,000 per year to Airmen, Guardians, their spouses, and their children through 12 unique scholarships that help fund college tuition, flight school, dental school, Arnold Air Society, Silver Wings, and full rides to universities. Apply between December 1 and April 30 each year.

Air Traffic Control Association

The 2024 Scholarship will open for application submissions in March 2024 and will close on May 1, 2024. ATCA awards $75,000 in scholarships annually; each scholarship recipient receives between $5,000 and $15,000.

Aircraft Electronics Association

Approximately 20 scholarships are given to members of the AEA. See https://aea.net/educationalfoundation/scholarships.asp for list of scholarships.

American Council of Engineering Companies (ACEC)
Research Institute Scholarships

Apply through the ACEC Research Institute scholarship portal. There are more than 100 scholarships totaling $1 million, including a $5,000 award given to one student in every state and D.C. These scholarships are for both undergraduate and graduate study.

American Electric Power Scholarship ($4,000)
& ASME Power Division Scholarship ($3,000)

These scholarships are granted to college student members of ASME whose goal is to pursue a career in power engineering. Applications are due in February.

American Institute of Aeronautics and Astronautics

AIAA has given out 1,300 scholarships to students at more than 150 colleges worldwide. Students must be an AIAA student member who has completed 1 year of engineering coursework with a 3.30+ GPA. See website for a list of scholarships.

American Institute of Chemical Engineers (AIChE) Minority Affairs

Minority Scholarship Awards are available for underrepresented Chemical Engineering Students (Multiple Awards). Applicants who are African-American, Hispanic, Native American, Alaskan Native, or Pacific Islander are invited to apply. The $1,000 award is renewable each year.

American Water Works Association

The AWWA supports students who seek a future in preserving, protecting, and providing water to communities. Scholarships of $5,000 are offered to approximately ten students each year. Applications open in September.

Astronaut Scholarship Foundation

In 2023, ASF awarded 68 scholarships to students from 45 different U.S. universities. Astronaut Scholarships are awarded to college students in their junior and senior years who are completing STEM majors with the intent to pursue research or advance science.

Biomedical Engineering Society Student Design Competition

In addition to student chapter awards and the Rita Schaffer Young Investigator Award, BMES offers Student Design & Research Awards.

Boeing Scholarships

Boeing offers engineering scholarships along with $500,000 for 25 students to attend pilot training with organizations such as Boeing Fly-Compton, Aircraft Owners & Pilots Association, Latino Pilots Association, Organization of Black Aerospace Professionals, Sisters of the Skies, and Women in Aviation International. Boeing also donates $450,000 to Fly Compton, a Los Angeles-based nonprofit that introduces minority youth to career opportunities in aerospace.

Chevron Scholarships - AISES, UNCF, REACH, REC Foundation

Chevron offers scholarships to students (Native American, African American, children of employees, robotics competitors, etc.) with awards of varying amounts.

Environmental Engineering & Science Foundation

Graduate/Master's level scholarships are awarded to students pursuing environmental engineering/science (eight are awarded per year).

Experimental Aircraft Association

EAA scholarships encourage aviation enthusiasts to pursue post-secondary education. EAA offers scholarships for college, flight training, and the camp academy. Apply between Nov 1 and March 1.

Eugene C. Figg, Jr. Civil Engineering Scholarship

This $3,000 scholarship is awarded to engineering students who pursue bridge design and construction. Students submit an application, resume, transcripts, recommendations, and an essay regarding bridge design/construction.

Federal Water Quality Association

FWQA provides at least three scholarships for high school students pursuing careers in wastewater and environmental science.

Ford Fund Scholarships for Automotive/Mechanical Engineering

These scholarships are offered to students to assist with laptops, software, tools, books, uniforms, and other supplies.

General Aviation Manufacturers Association

GAMA Edward W. Stimpson Aviation Excellence Award - A $2,000 scholarship is awarded to a graduating high school senior to be enrolled in an aviation degree.

ICAS Foundation/GAMA Scholarship – A $2,000 award is given to students seeking an aviation-related degree, such as professional pilot, maintenance/engineering, or aviation business.

Whirly-Girls Scholarship Fund - Whirly-Girls offers 16 scholarships ranging from $950 to $14,000. Applicants must be members.

The Aviation Youth Empowerment Fund (AYEF) STEM Scholarship Award – Students are encouraged to apply for $4,000 scholarships for aviation, sciences, technology, engineering, and math fields. Students must live in Washington, Oregon, or Northern California.

Google Scholarships
Google Scholarships for Disabled Students
Scholarships for Students in India
Student Veterans
Women Techmakers
Google Travel & Conference Grants
Generation Google Scholarship

Students majoring in Computer Science, Computer Engineering, or related field and are members of an underrepresented group will receive special consideration. Need-based awards of $10,000 are given to students. Apply in April.

Barry Goldwater Scholarship

Hundreds of scholarships are awarded to college sophomores and juniors pursuing research careers in STEM subjects. A $9 million grant seeks to double the number of awards.

Dan & Vicky Hancock Scholarship - Mechanical Engineering Excellence

One $5,500 scholarship is awarded yearly to applicants pursuing mechanical engineering. Students must submit an application, FAFSA form, two letters of recommendation, and a resume with demonstrated leadership. Applications are due in March.

Ralph K. Hillquist Honorary SAE Scholarship

This $1,000 award, offered every other year at the SAE Noise & Vibration Conference, is for junior mechanical engineering majors who are interested in noise, vibration, statics, dynamics, and physics. Applications are due in March.

Institute of Electrical & Electronics Engineers

The IEEE Power & Energy Society (PES) provides $7,000 scholarships toward college expenses while also offering connections, mentoring, and internship opportunities.

Intel Scholarship Program

These scholarships are for students pursuing engineering and computer science. Nearly $2 million is distributed annually.

Stephen T. Kugle Scholarship

This $3,000 scholarship is for an active ASME student member who attends college in AZ, AK, CO, LA, NM, OK, TX, UT, or WY. Applications are due in February.

John Lenard Civil Engineering Scholarship

Student members of the American Society of Civil Engineers (ASCE) whose primary civil engineering interest is in water supply or environmental engineering can apply in February. Scholarship amounts vary.

Lockheed Martin Scholarships
STEM Scholarship Program

In 2024, Lockheed Martin awarded 100 students a grant for $10,000 to study at a 4-year college or university. This scholarship is renewable each year. Apply by April 1.

Guglielmo Marconi Engineering Scholarship

This $1,250 engineering scholarship is available to full-time undergraduates who have at least one parent of Italian ancestry. The application is due in April.

John J. McKetta Undergraduate Scholarship

College juniors or seniors who are members of the American Institute of Chemical Engineers and plan to pursue chemical engineering can submit an application for this scholarship along with a career essay, transcript, resume, and two letters of recommendation. The application for this $5,000 award is due in June.

Frank & Dorothy Miller Scholarship (2 - $2,000); F.W. "Beich" Beichley Scholarship (1 - $3,000); Garland Duncan Scholarship (2 - $5,000), Irma and Robert Bennett Scholarship (2 - $3,000); John & Else Gracik Scholarships (5 - $5,000); Allen J. Baldwin Scholarship (2 - $3,000); Berna Lou Cartwright Scholarship (2 - $3,000); Sylvia W. Farny Scholarship (2 - $3,000); Agnes Malakate Kezios Scholarship (2 - $3,000); Charles B. Scharp Scholarship (1 - $3,000), Kenneth Andrew Roe Scholarship (1 - $13,000); Melvin R. Green Scholarship (1 - $8,000)

Up to 23 awards are given yearly to college student members of ASME. Considerations include integrity, leadership, academics, and the potential to contribute to the mechanical engineering profession. Applications are due in February.

Microsoft Scholarships, Internships, & Competitions for Students in Computer Science & STEM Disciplines

See website for details.

Lawrence W. and Francis W. Cox Scholarship & Robert B.B. and Josephine N. Moorman Scholarship

Applicants for these awards must be student members of ASCE. Students complete an application and essay on why they want to be a civil engineer and how they contributed to ASCE. These applications are due in February.

National Air Transportation Association

Sophomores and juniors interested in aviation and air transportation can apply for the many $1,000 scholarships awarded each year. Applications due in December.

National Oceanic and Atmospheric Administration
Ernest F. Hollings Undergraduate Scholarship Program

Scholars receive up to $9,500 per year during two-years of full-time study. During the summer, they participate in oceanic, atmospheric, and science internships paying $700 per week plus travel expenses.

Northrop Grumman Engineering Scholars Program

These renewable scholarships are for graduating seniors majoring in engineering, computer science, math, or physics. Students must live in CA, IL, MD, NY, OH, or VA.

Donald F. and Mildred Topp Othmer Scholarship Awards (15 Awards)

Undergraduate chemical engineering students may apply for this $1,000 scholarship. Applications are due in June.

Recycling Education & Research Foundation Scholarship (Multiple Awards)

These $2,500 scholarships are open to applicants who are college juniors. The application is due in June.

Allen Rhodes Memorial Scholarships

This scholarship is for college student members of the ASME who are interested in pursuing careers in the oil and gas industry. Applications are due in February.

John Rice Memorial Scholarship

This $3,000 scholarship is for students who attend one of nine NYC area colleges. Students are judged based on transcripts, leadership, integrity, & potential to contribute to the mechanical eng profession. Applications are due in February.

Udall Undergraduate Scholarship

Future leaders in environmental, Tribal public policy, & healthcare, are encouraged to apply. Competitive prog w/school competitions & multi-day Scholar Orientation. In 2024, the Udall Foundation anticipates awarding 55 scholarships of $7,000 each.

Society of Women Engineers All Together Scholarships

SWE awards 280+ scholarships totaling more than $1,200,000 to students in engineering. College students in all areas of engineering are encouraged to apply.

United States Dept of Defense

Science, Mathematics, & Research for Transformation (SMART) Scholarship: STEM undergrad, master's, & doctoral students. Recipients receive full tuition, annual stipends, internships, & guaranteed jobs with Dept of Defense after graduation.

PRIVATE SCHOLARSHIPS

Private individuals, corporations, and endowments off er outside scholarships . Some off er full tuition. Here are a few of the thousands to consider.

AQHA and AQHF – $25,000 - $35,000 (Dec 1) Quarter Horse Members

A few scholarships for journalism, communications, agricultural studies, and equine research.

Alzheimer's Foundation of America

HS seniors impacted by Alzheimer's disease submit a 1,500-word essay or 4-min video describing the impact of Alzheimer's/dementia. Amount: $5,000 Due: April 1.

American Legion National Oratorical Contest

HS juniors/seniors prepare an oration on the U.S. Constitution and citizenship. State Winners: $2,000, National Winner: $20,000 - $25,000.

Ayn Rand Essay Contest - 455,000 student winners; $2,200,000 given out

Read and analyze one of three books (Anthem, Fountainhead, Atlas Shrugged) by Ayn Rand to win this contest. Multiple awards given out. Amount: $2,000 Due: April

Blaze Your Own Trail Scholarship

HS seniors and college students submit a 600-800-word essay describing a challenge you faced, how you overcame it, and your experience. Amount: $1,000 Deadline May

Boren Scholarships ($8,000 - $25,000) and Boren Fellowships ($12,000 -30,000) – Foreign Language Study

The National Security Education Program (NSEP) awards funding for students to study one of about 65 languages the U.S. deems necessary for national security through a study abroad program. Applications open from mid-August to early February. Approximately 300 students are selected.

Brower Youth Awards

Environmental activism awards are granted to 6 winners; each receives $3,000.

Coca Cola Scholarship

1,400 students are selected to receive scholarships. The total amount awarded annually is approximately $3,550,000. 150 students receive $20,000 scholarship.

Comcast NBC Universal Leaders and Achievers Scholarship

More than 800 high school student winners each year win a $2,500 scholarship.

Dell Scholars Program – 500 students selected – $20,000 - First-Generation

This scholarship is awarded to students who exhibit grit, potential, and ambition.

Doodle for Google Contest

This art/imagination contest is for K-12 students. Use any medium to describe your wish for the next 25 years. Amount: $5,000 Due: March 14.

Gates Millennium Scholarship

These scholarships cover the full cost of attendance and are granted to 300 African American, American Indian/Alaska Native, Asian Pacific Islander, or Hispanic American student leaders.

GE-Reagan Foundation Scholarship Program $40,000 (10 students)

Each year, 25 students ages 8 – 18 receive $10,000 for community service projects.

Gloria Barron Prize for Young Heroes

25 students each year ages 8 – 18 receive $10,000 for community service projects

Grit Award Scholarship

HS seniors with a GPA of 3.0+ must show GPA improvement and describe why they now have academic promise. Amount: $500 Due: May.

Hispanic Scholarship Fund

Approximately 10,000 winners - $30,000,000 awarded annually.

K-12 Educator Scholarship

This scholarship is for children with parents who teach in the K-12 system.

Karcher Founders Scholarship

College-bound HS seniors that live near a Carl's Jr. Award: $10,000 Due: April 4.

LULAC (League of United Latin American Citizens)
Ford Driving Dreams Scholarship, ExxonMobil Scholarship
NBC Universal Scholarship

The LULAC National Scholarship Fund along with corporations (Walmart, CocaCola, Nissan, Danaher, etc.) provide hundreds of scholarships for high school and college students.

Minecraft Scholarship

HS/college students submit an essay of 500+ words, detailing how Minecraft can be a positive influence on education and careers. Amount: $2,000 Due July 31.

NAACP – National Association for the Advancement of Colored People

African Americans - about 170 students receive awards of $3,000 to $15,000.

NASSP – National Association of Secondary School Principals

600 Scholarships awarded per year, 1 national winner ($25,000), 24 national finalists ($5,625 each), 575 national semifnalists ($3,200 each). Apply Oct-Dec 1.

Optimist International Essay Contest

HS students submit a 700-800-word essay on how optimism connects people. Amount: $2,500 Due: February 28.

Parent Employment

Many companies offer scholarships for their employees and their children.

Project Yellow Light Video Contest Scholarship

High school juniors and seniors, plus FT undergrads create a 10 or 25 second video that discourages texting while driving. Award: $8,000 Due: April 1.

Prudential Spirit of Community Award (Prudential Emerging Visionaries)

25 students in grades 5 to 12. Amount: $1,000 - $5,000 award for community service.

Questbridge Scholarship

$200,000 is granted to each of 1,464 students to be used over 4 years.

Race to Inspire Essay Contest

Student runners (5k, 10k, half marathons, or marathons) submit a 1,000-2,000 word essay detailing why they run and challenges/lessons. Amount: $500 Due in August.

Rover College Scholarship

HS seniors/college students submit a 400-500-word essay on how growing up with a pet impacted the person they are today. Award: $2,500 Due May 1.

ROTC

These military scholarships are not given to everyone in ROTC. A select group of outstanding candidates is given tuition, fees, textbooks, plus a monthly stipend.

Scholastic Art and Writing Competition

Herblock Award - $1,000 scholarships for editorial cartoons
New York Life Award - $1,000 writing award about personal grief and loss
One Earth Award - $1,000 scholarship for writing about human-caused climate change
PortfolioScholarships – Up to $10,000 granted for top portfolios
Civic Expression Award - $1,000 scholarships for writing on political and social issues
Best-In-Grade – Juror favorite awards receive $500 scholarships
Art & Writing Scholarships - https://www.artandwriting.org/scholarships/

#ScienceSaves High School Video Scholarship

HS seniors create a 20-30 second video about science and what it does for people. Amount: $10,000 Due May 6.

Service/Leadership/Focused Organization Scholarship

Lions Club, Moose Club, Elks Club, Rotary Club, Soroptimists Club, Mensa

Student Veterans of America

These scholarships are awarded to veterans. The funds granted to not interfere with GI Bill grants or other financial aid. Scholarships total over $100,000 yearly.

Susan Thompson Buffet Foundation Scholarships

This scholarship for high school and undergraduate students in Nebraska provides $3,200 plus a book allowance.

Target Scholarship

HBCU Design Challenge for African Americans – Students submit designs for Black History Month. Target Scholars Program – 1,000 students get $5,000 each.

Thurgood Marshall College Fund

Approximately 500 scholarships are awarded per year to engaged and motivated African American students. The average is $6,200 per year.

Unboxing Your Life Video Scholarship

High school seniors and college students create a 5-minute video describing who they are as they unbox their life. Award: $4,000 Due: March 31.

Vegetarian Resource Group Scholarship

HS students who actively promote vegetarianism and peace while demonstrating compassion, courage, and commitment. Amount: $5,000-$10,000 Due Feb 20.

Walgreens Expressions Challenge

High school students between 13 and 18 are challenged to describe their world through words, visual arts, media arts or creative writing. Award: $1,500 - $2,000 This application is due in March.

Walmart Scholarship Program

Employees and dependents can obtain up to $13,000 in scholarships to be used over four years. Complete the online application. Qualified candidates will be considered depending on their financial needs and academic performance.

We The Future Contest

HS/college students submit an essay, song, project, film, social media, or PSA on a topic related to the Constitution. Amount: $1,000-$5,000 Due May 31.

Note: Like Walmart, many corporations offer scholarships for employees and dependents. For example, with Starbucks College Achievement Plan, students can receive 100% upfront tuition coverage for a first-time bachelor's degree through Arizona State University's online program. Starbucks partners can choose from over 100 diverse undergraduate degree programs.

Other prominent examples include AT&T whose deadline is in March. The AT&T Ability ERG Scholarship provides $1,500 to support students enrolling in accredited undergraduate programs. Pepsi provides 400 new scholarships each year for postsecondary education for children of PepsiCo associates. If your parent works for a corporation, check with their human resources department.

Also, many organizations like the American Legion, Elks Club, Exchange Club, Kiwanis International, Knights of Columbus, Lions Club, Moose International, National Grange, Jaycees, National League of Masonic Clubs, Optimist International, and Rotary Club, offer scholarships. These are typically offered through the branch clubs in your local area.

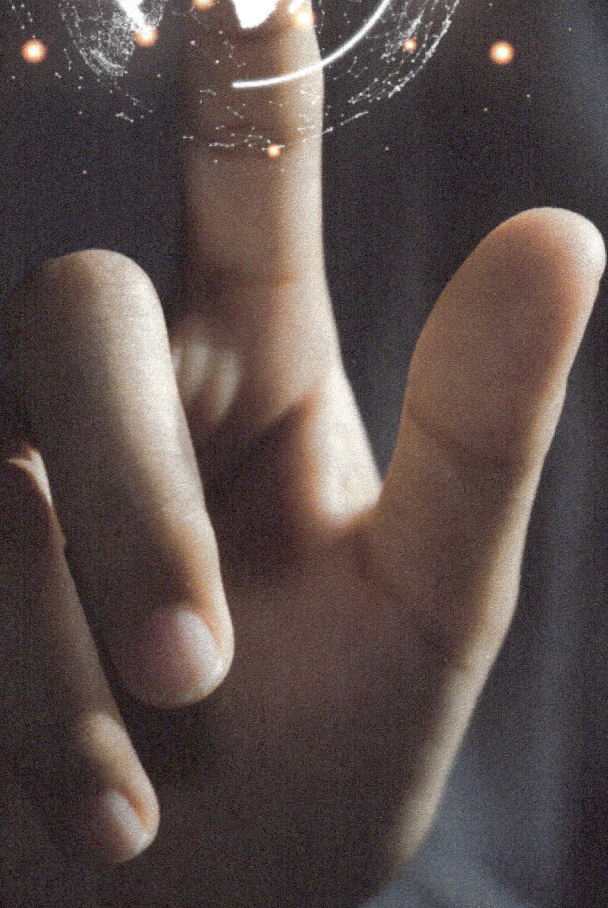

CHAPTER 10
EMPLOYMENT OUTLOOK

"A failure is not always a mistake; it may simply be the best one can do under the circumstances. The real mistake is to stop trying."

– B.F. Skinner

Psychologists play an essential role in mental health, academic research, and social welfare services. They serve in as advisors, counselors, and liaisons. The job requires critical thinking and an analytical mind. Psychologists look for opportunities to improve the community and organizational mental health to help people live longer, healthier, and more productive lives. In research, statistical analysis offers additional avenues for career advancement.

Society seeks solutions to mental health challenges that plague individuals and their families in profound ways. People with addiction, ADD, ADHD, depression, OCD, bipolar disorder, etc. hunger for cures. Thus, psychologists are essential in the interdisciplinary world of cutting-edge discovery. Neuroscience offers additional avenues with stem cell therapies, biotechnologies, computational neuroscience, and brain mapping. Neuroscientists are helping to eradicate brain disorders.

According to the *Occupational Outlook Handbook,* employment of psychologists is projected to grow 7% from 2025 to 2035, which is faster than the average for all occupations. The median annual wage for psychologists in 2025 was about $100,000. The highest 10% earn salaries above $150,000.

The entire set of majors and careers in psychology have expanded. With the challenges society faced during the pandemic and the rollercoaster of employment, eduction, and financial stability, pressure mounted and individuals needed to learn new coping mechanisms to thrive.

Life in 2050 will look nothing like today. With quantum computing's enhanced processing speeds and extraordinary opportunities, the horizon of how we live and work from 2030 - 2050 with dramatically transform. People will need to re-imagine their life with robots, career disruptions, and technologies that do not yet exist today.

Psychology and cognitive science researchers conduct investigations focused on understanding perception, behavior, and disorders to improve overall human health and mental well-being. Psychologist's work encompasses health and human systems using a wide range of methods ranging from brain imaging and statistical models to behavioral experiments and addiction treatment. Alongside fields like medicine and neuroscience, psychologists will explore how humans function, adapt, and journey toward self-discovery.

Positions might include:

Biotechnology

Clinical Support (hospitals or clinics)

Faculty Positions (professor/mentor/researcher)

Health Education

Laboratories

Medicine

Pharmaceutical Industry

Policy, Law, & Compliance

Psychiatry

Public Health

Research & Development

Scientific Writing

Psychologists form hypotheses and both design and carry out rigorous experiments. They may work independently or in clinics, education, corporations, institutions, or governmental agencies. They may collaborate with physicians and scientists to develop interventions that improve mental health, cognition, or sensory-motor function.

Within journal club discussions, departmental colloquia, and conferences, they share findings and review the progress of other research groups. Psychologists publish their results in academic journals. Clear communication is essential, particularly when conveying complex findings in accessible layman's terms.

Psychology researchers often lead teams of lab technicians, research assistants, data scientists, or graduate students. For instance, a cognitive scientist might guide assistants in coding behavioral data, managing MRI sessions, or running simulations.

Many students are drawn to psychology, cognitive science, and neuroscience. These fields offer a profound opportunity to understand thoughts, emotions, behaviors, and biological mechanisms. There is endless fascination with decoding how the brain works, and then using that knowledge to improve mental health, restore lost function, or design life-changing technologies like brain-computer interfaces. This field sits at the intersection of science, technology, and human experience, offering the chance to explore fundamental questions about consciousness and identity while directly impacting lives through innovation, research, and compassionate care.

MANAGEMENT AND EMPLOYEE RETENTION

Skills to Know: New Technologies, Programming, Social Media, Ethics

One of the most significant challenges facing employers from 2025 - 2035 will be locating and retaining talent. Staffing companies within today's changing hiring atmosphere will require rethinking employee dynamics as employees increasingly look elsewhere for better opportunities. This development will require managers to earn employee trust and loyalty.

The digital workforce has also placed demands on human resources. While many academic, corporate, and government institutions want their employees to work in-person, the convenience of working at home and the drudgery of commuting to work created an environment where employees seek greater flexibility. Yet, psychology is more typically done individually. The skills you learn in college will be tremendously valuable in the pursuit of your ultimate goals.

GRADUATE SCHOOL

Nearly all psychology students ultimately attend graduate school. There are numerous options for your graduate school pathway. Each one will take you to a fascinating career.

Choosing a graduate school pathway as a psychology or neuroscience major requires a deep understanding of your long-term goals, personal interests, and the type of impact you want to make in the world. How do you envision your life in the future? What kind of day-to-day work would you prefer? Would you like long hours and high rewards or more flexibility, with weekends off or maybe a 9-5 position or one where you travel and give presentations? Do you see yourself helping students find careers or mentoring people? Do prefer teaching or listening to others? Of course, none of these are mutually exclusive; they are just questions to ask while you explore your options.

The first step in the decision-making process is identifying whether you are drawn more toward research, clinical practice, or state, federal, or non-profit work. If you find yourself fascinated by the scientific questions behind how the brain works or why people behave the way they do, a research-intensive program like a Ph.D. in psychology, cognitive science, or neuroscience, might be ideal. On the other hand, if you feel called to work directly with individuals in need by providing therapy, diagnostics, or rehabilitation, then a clinical path such as a Psy.D, Ph.D. in clinical psychology, or a master's in counseling, social work, or therapy may better align with your aspirations.

Students should also consider the educational requirements for their desired career pursuit. Doctoral programs often take 5–7 years and emphasize original research, publishing, and teaching. Graduates are then prepared for academic, scientific, or specialized clinical roles. Master's programs, usually 1–3 years in length, are typically more applied and offer quicker entry into the workforce in areas such as school psychology, mental health counseling, or data analysis.

Most importantly, students should reflect on whether they prefer a broader academic exploration (like in developmental or social psychology) or a more specialized applied clinical or technical skill set (such as applied behavior analysis or speech-language pathology). Understanding the degree program structure, time commitment, financial costs, and required licensure can influence your decisions.

Finally, clarify which graduate path aligns with your strengths and values as you gain hands-on experience in research labs, clinical internships, or volunteer work. Informational interviews with current graduate students, professors, or successful professionals provides insight that goes beyond course descriptions or rankings. Trust the process of exploration and allow your academic curiosity and personal experiences guide your path. Remember, there is no single "correct" trajectory; rather, the best path is one that matches your goals, excites your passions, and equips you to make a meaningful contribution to the field.

GRADUATE SCHOOL PATHWAYS

Graduate Path	Focus Area	Additional Information
M.A./M.S. in Psychology	General psychology with flexible specialization	Flexible paths in mental health, HR, or counseling
M.S. in School Psychology	Assessment and support for school-aged children	Practitioners in school systems
M.S. in Speech-Language Pathology	Speech, language, and swallowing disorders	Communications-focused clinical specialists
Master's in Applied Behavior Analysis (ABA)	Behavioral intervention, often with autism spectrum disorders	BCBAs, therapists working in special education
Master's in Biotechnology/ Biomedical Engineering	Medical innovation, devices, neuro tech	R&D, product design, biotech engineers
Master's in Data Science/ Bioinformatics	Data analysis for neuroscience and healthcare	Analysts and machine learning specialists
Master's in Marriage and Family Therapy (MFT)	Couples, marriage, and family therapy practice	Therapists focused on family systems
Master's in Public Health (MPH)	Population health, policy, and disease prevention	Global health leaders or epidemiologists
Master's in Science Communication	Science outreach and public understanding	Writers, educators, science media professionals
Master's in Social Work (MSW)	Clinical practice, case management, mental health advocacy	Clinical social workers, community advocates
Master's/Ph.D. in Neuroscience	Brain-based research intersecting psychology and biology	Researchers in cognitive or behavioral neuroscience
Doctor of Physical Therapy (DPT)	Rehabilitation for injury, stroke, neuro disorders	Hands-on rehab practitioners
Ed.S. in School Psychology	Advanced school psychology practice, often before doctorate	School-based psychologists or specialists
M.D. (Doctor of Medicine)	Clinical diagnosis and treatment of patients	Future neurologists, psychiatrists, clinicians
M.D./Ph.D.	Clinical and research combined (dual degree)	Those seeking to be physician-scientists
Occupational Therapy (OTD or MSOT)	Daily life recovery for physical/ neurological challenges	Rehabilitation and cognitive therapy providers
Ph.D. in Biomedical Sciences	Broad biomedical research including neurobiology	Interdisciplinary researchers
Ph.D. in Clinical Psychology	Diagnosis and treatment of psychological disorders	Licensed psychologists with deep clinical focus
Ph.D. in Cognitive Science	Mind, cognition, AI, and interdisciplinary study	Researchers in mind/brain/ behavior fields
Ph.D. in Computational Neuroscience	Brain modeling, AI, neurotechnology	Engineers, coders, tech-savvy students

Graduate Path	Focus Area	Additional Information
Ph.D. in Counseling Psychology	Therapeutic support, often in university or hospital settings	Therapists or counselors in diverse populations
Ph.D. in Developmental Psychology	Child/adolescent development, education, policy	Developmental researchers or educators
Ph.D. in Industrial-Organizational Psychology	Workplace behavior, performance, and systems	HR professionals, consultants, organizational coaches
Ph.D. in Neuroscience	Brain function, systems, behavior, disease mechanisms	Aspiring researchers or professors
Ph.D. in Psychology	Broad research in cognition, behavior, emotion	Academic or research careers
Ph.D. in Social Psychology	Group behavior, attitudes, and interpersonal dynamics	Academics or consultants in group dynamics
Ph.D. or Psy.D. in Clinical Psychology	Diagnosis and therapy for mental health and behavior	Therapists or mental health specialists
Psy.D. (Doctor of Psychology)	Clinical practice with less emphasis on research	Aspiring clinical practitioners

Ultimately, choosing to study psychology, cognitive science, or neuroscience is more than an academic pursuit. When you reach your junior year, you are truly making a commitment to continued education while learning the very essence of how the mind impacts the body and, in turn, what it means to be human.

Your journey will be fueled by curiosity, compassion, and the desire to uncover the intricate workings of the brain and resulting behaviors. This quest will shape every step of your college experience, challenging you to think critically, ask deeper questions, and approach complex problems from both scientific and humanistic perspectives.

Whether you are decoding neural circuits, exploring the roots of behavior, or helping someone navigate mental health challenges, you can make a difference in peoples' lives. These fields offer a lifelong calling to explore, to heal, to innovate, and to serve. And, in that pursuit, you will not only transform your own understanding, but also contribute to a world that desperately needs insight, empathy, and change.

The brain is the organ of destiny. It holds within its humming mechanism secrets that will determine the future of the human race.

— Wilder Penfield

CHAPTER 11

PREPARATION, NETWORKING & REAL-WORLD SKILLS

"Words have a magical power. They can bring either the greatest happiness or deepest despair; they can transfer knowledge from teacher to student; words enable the orator to sway his audience and dictate its decisions. Words are capable of arousing the strongest emotions and prompting all men's actions."

– Sigmund Freud

S tudying psychology will teach you valuable lessons about health, medicine, and research. As an analytical cog in the wheel of brain science, you will set up studies, follow through with experimental procedures, analyze results, and present findings.

ENGAGE THE INTREPID SPIRIT WITHIN YOU, HUNGRY TO EMERGE.

Your next step is to choose a college where your personality fits into the environment. In college classes, labs, and research, you will receive interactive training while being immersed in the inspiration of fellow classmates. Each project will leave a lasting impression.

In presentations, you can share your inspirations, revelations, and projects with your classmates, professors, and colleagues. Out of school, you will work in clinical and research environments that were never before possible. It is unbelievably thrilling.

Your life will undoubtedly be different and ever-changing since the world around you will evolve from moment to moment. During your lifetime, people may live on the moon; you may be a part of that transition. Over time, whichever area of neuroscience, medicine, policy, or law becomes your focus, you will earn your way to a career of endless possibilities. .

With virtual counseling, social media, and novel therapeutic options, the possibilities are limitless. In school or out of school, you may want to take a few classes on communication dynamics or website editing even though these my not be synonymous with psychology. Additionally, on the leading edge of the Metaverse, you might invent processes that were never before possible.

Psychology is a dynamic, multidimensional field where you will contribute to the ongoing innovations that will transform mental health and save lives. Unfortunately, in some careers, repetitive tasks and uninspiring projects lead employees to loathe their jobs and tick off minutes until their day is done. Psychology, though, offers numerous rewards.

Your life will undoubtedly be different and ever-changing since the world around you will evolve from moment to moment. During your lifetime, people may live on the moon; you may be a part of that transition, considering the impact on space traveler's brains. Over time, whichever area of psychology becomes your focus, you will earn your way to a career of endless possibilities.

So, what big ideas do you have that you want to see come to fruition in your lifetime? Flying into space? Living on the moon? Teleportation? Telepathy? Neurocomputation? Nanomaterials that reduce the size of computers to the size of a credit card and can be inserted into the brain? Natural computer language processing? Quantum computing? A world free of mental health disorders?

Spend time thinking, even though the hours in a day seem short. You may feel as if time slips through your fingers like sand in an hourglass. Resist the temptation to upload your idea before contemplating what you want to express and how you want these to be received. Your electrified contemplations and commitment to school will help you turn your brainstorms into reality.

You will spend more hours than you can imagine in a lab; immerse yourself. While social media opens doors to sites where you can share your ideas, truly magical works are created when time stands still. Today is a precious moment. As you contemplate college choices and tomorrow's future, you will explore your passions. Open doors you never expected and walk inside to discover opportunities that will tantalize and challenge you along the way. As such, you will capture a new, exciting, and eclectic way of life.

Attending a respected school can help you get noticed, although college is truly what you make of it. Your next steps will be aided by professors, classmates, and alumni connections. Networking events open doors for you to find opportunities. Conferences, displays, and contests in school, out of school, in the summer, or through social media can help you get noticed. Bring people into your world. Allow them to feel and interpret your innovative ideas so you can get feedback.

Throughout your varied experiences, you will meet other scientists who may recommend you to employers or inform you about open positions or contract opportunities, even some that are not publicly announced. In addition, many schools have a culminating event like a poster session, panel discussion, or research colloquium where you can put your best foot forward and showcase your work.

Exposure to academic, research, and clinical professionals will open new doors. By interacting with people online or in person you can maintain those connections. Demonstrate competency, produce amazing work, and exhibit work ethic. Despite challenges, put yourself out there.

You could wait for the phone to ring for a clinical or research position. However, you should regularly post ideas, articles, or availability to professional sites. Some individuals pine away by sending in resumes with the hopes of being selected for their ideal position. Remember, graduate school is almost a necessity. On the other hand, students have landed amazing positions by taking the first step. Yet, sometimes taking any position at the start is a steppingstone to your dream life, commitment to service, and opportunity to put your unique mark on society.

BOLD NETWORKING

Networking takes social skills and a bit of moxie. From elevator speeches and professional encounters to interviews and masterclasses, your job is to find a way to get your talent and abilities in front of people and have employers discover your knowledge of scientific research, leadership potential, and willingness to contribute. You have something special and fresh ideas.

Some locations will welcome your dedication, ingenuity, acumen, and impact. How can you be recognized? Meet people. Hand out your resume, give them your business card, ask for their business card, and follow up. Ask if you can call or meet them. Sometimes approaching professionals may seem uncomfortable. They could be too busy, but they might also be willing to give you a few minutes.

Stay in touch with those you meet, even if it is just happenstance or serendipity. Keep a log of each individual's phone, e-mail, and identifying information. Track both the date and location where you met. You never know when you will need it.

If you meet people professionally at a workshop, leadership event, or an academic conference, take the time to get to know something about them. Even if you do not exchange information, you will recognize them at a later date. They may recognize you at a future event too.

Keep training. Seek ways to improve, irrespective of your experience. Lifelong learning improves your ability to maintain up-to-date skills and transition to new ventures. Furthermore, the outside world's perspective changes more quickly when you stay ahead of cutting edge brain science research developments and rapidly expanding artificial intelligence, machine learning, and quantum computing.

Though you should not register for workshops and conferences just for the sake of meeting people, when you attend, be present in your quest to lead, serve, and envision. If your focus is not on learning or professional development, you may appear insincere in your intentions. However, workshops, conferences, and meetings can allow others to see your purpose, vision, and talent.

Big-ticket summer "opportunities" or expensive certificate programs do not always mean better chances or new opportunities. Find time to research specialized programs or graduate schools. Notice changes in the field of psychology. While gathering new thoughts, remember that humility and open-mindedness go a long way. Defer to the wise and listen. There is much you can learn.

STAY IN TOUCH

Do not annoy busy people, but you can keep in touch every couple of months. Communicating more frequently is overwhelming. However, life is long. People who grow with their craft transition fluidly through life's career phases. In brain science, contacts are essential in all phases of your career.

DEVELOP LIFELONG FRIENDSHIPS

Friendships matter. Become lifelong colleagues by finding friends who share mutual interests and offer a sounding board or connections to new opportunities. People tend to stay in touch with "important" people. Note to self: Your contemporaries or peers are important people...although possibly not yet. As you form lists of contacts, you are likely to know these people throughout your career.

Be audacious while also being authentic. Networking can sometimes appear fake or forced as if you are going out on a hunt to find people for your own benefit. Worse, the act of networking can appear like stalking for those who incessantly attempt to connect. The mental image of this type of 'networking' conjures the vision of people congregating around one individual at meetings.

Friendships and the mutual support of allies can be enormously helpful, though 20,000 or even 200,000 followers on your website do not mean you are popular. However, you can have unexpected meaningful exchanges when you get out, meet people, and live life. There are times when deeply moving, casual conversations in non-professional settings could also turn into connections.

Do not lose touch with people or burn bridges along the way. This field is not that big, especially in whatever subspecialty you choose. You will continually see extraordinary talent. You never know. They may contact you to collaborate one day or meet for coffee at an event.

COLLEGE AND CAREER CENTERS

Although psychology and cognitive science departments frequently have internal connections to help you secure an internship or job, you might also speak to someone at your campus career center. They often have interesting and possibly different prospects you might not get elsewhere. In addition, there may be a specific career liaison for graduate psychology and medical programs. Connect with them for help in your search process. Besides, you might want a related job that utilizes your creative, analytical, problem-solving, and presentation skills.

Career center coordinators often have excellent ideas of alternative options you may have never considered. Furthermore, they can assist you with creating a professional resume and cover letters for specific industries that are different from the ones you have for research, clinical opportunities, or industry, especially if you are considering an M.S, MD, DO, PharmD, PsyD, or Ph.D. programs.

Some people you meet may introduce you with past graduates who make excellent connections. Some of them may have completed your program and have been through the ropes, know a few people, and may be able to get you an interview or invite you to an important event in your field. Any contact may help you get your foot in the door or find a job to make money in the meantime.

LINKEDIN

LinkedIn is especially helpful for career search. You can find numerous influential contacts on LinkedIn. After interviews or events, connect with each person you meet on LinkedIn. Keep a contact list of individuals you get to know in your area of interest. Do not constantly try to connect with people you do not really know. However, if you have made the connection, occasionally keep in touch.

While some LinkedIn message boxes may be full and you may not get a reply, you can try. Some people have tens of thousands of LinkedIn followers. I have about 20,000 'contacts', which does not necessitate that I am important. It just means that I have connected with 20,000 people. Remember that a big paycheck or lots of friends does not make you more worthy or successful. Worth and value emanate from within your heart. You have the power to improve your life in any way you choose.

Occasionally on LinkedIn, you hit on a lucky break by making professional connections or create a relationship that turns into a close friend. Some professionals prefer LinkedIn to other methods of communication. While this may seem odd, a few people I have known for decades only communicate with me through LinkedIn. Lastly, I do not have time to communicate with everyone. However, I have connected with some of my most inspiring authors, advisors, academics, and intellectual leaders through LinkedIn.

FINALLY

Most people are willing to help you. Five percent will not. Thus, you have a 19 out of 20 chance of interacting with decent people who have the time and are willing to give you advice. Don't lose faith in humanity just because you run into a few people who are too busy to stop for you or are too self-absorbed that they cannot answer your question. They may be consumed with problems of their own that they cannot yet resolve.

Remember that talent is only the beginning. You need to sell yourself. As you organize your goals and responsibilities, remember to think one step ahead of where you want to be by making a game plan. Since actions speak louder than words, take action without complaining and spread kindness along the way. Burned bridges are tough to reconstruct.

Honesty and trustworthiness are worth more than any accomplishment. Earn this by working hard, being efficient, and telling the truth. As you work in a lab carrying out basic tasks, imagine you are the principal investigator, what would you do? One day you may just be an academic leader and be on the opposite side of this decision-making continuum.

Professionalism in words and deeds is essential. Be productive. Put away all distractions and focus on your tasks. Texts and social media take a surprising amount of time. Get the job done. When you are finished, ask for another project. Do this not because you are brown-nosing, but because you want your group to be successful. Discipline is achieved by creating a goal and making it happen.

A nice note, card, or gift reminds people you are thinking about them, even when you are incredibly busy. Good friends who have your best interest may know doors that are not yet open for you. Keep in touch with them. Remember, every action you take is a steppingstone to your future.

So, go on a walk, meet people, and live fully. Serendipity happens when you live life. However, your education is immensely valuable. The adage goes - success happens when preparation meets opportunity. Thus, preparation is the best way to generate luck. Finally, even the most disciplined person can be lazy or inefficient. Fight this. Stay active. Make your life happen for you.

Here are a few things to remember as you go out to pursue your dreams.

- Work ethic is everything.
- Excellence is expected.
- Learn what you do not know on your own time.
- Come to work prepared.
- Take constructive criticism well.
- Be respectful and courteous.
- Keep your cool under pressure.
- Avoid being timid.
- Stay on task.
- Come early.
- Stay late.
- Take your work seriously.
- Do more than expected.
- Be thoughtful and respectful.
- Read your e-mail/texts after hours in case something is important.
- Ask questions. No question is too stupid.
- Maintain a clean workspace.
- Dress and act professionally.
- Don't gossip or complain.
- Play when you are done.
- Avoid frustrating your phenomenally busy supervisor.
- Be straightforward, and don't beat around the bush.

You've Got This!

4
Regions

87
Programs

COLLEGE
PROFILES AND
REQUIREMENTS

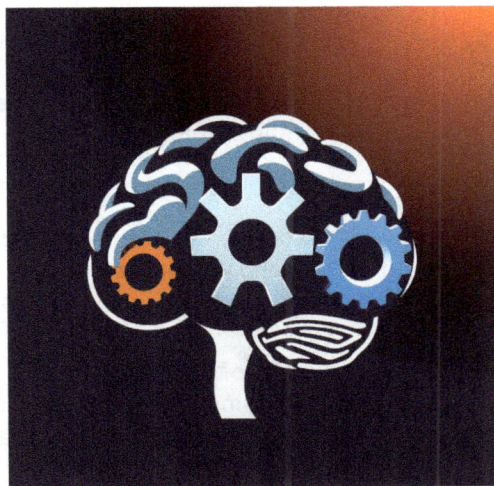

WEST

MIDWEST

NORTHEAST

SOUTH

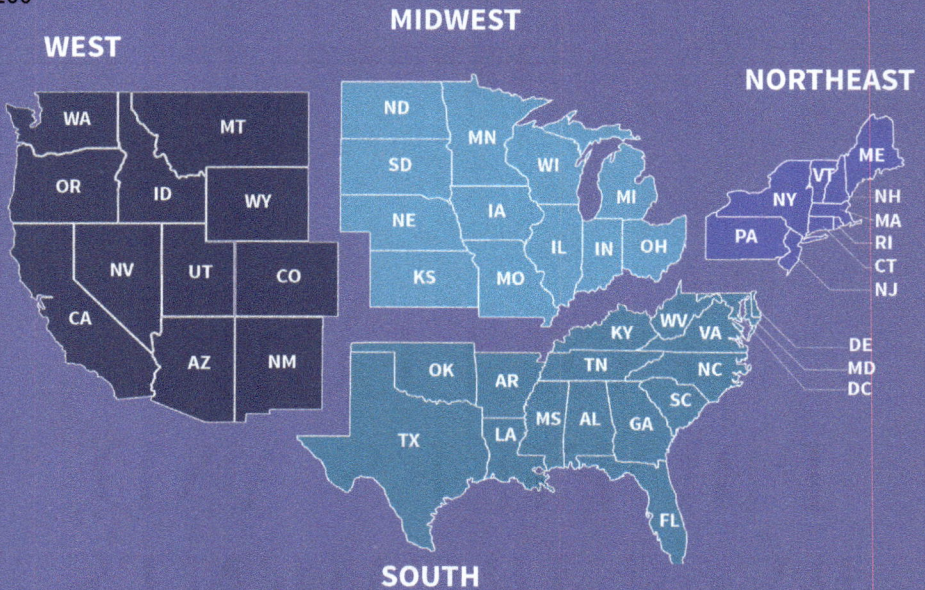

PROGRAMS BY REGION
U.S. CENSUS BUREAU CLASSIFICATIONS

REGION 1 – NORTHEAST

Connecticut, Maine, Massachusetts, New Hampshire, New Jersey, New York, Pennsylvania, Rhode Island, and Vermont

REGION 2 – MIDWEST

Illinois, Indiana, Iowa, Kansas, Michigan, Minnesota, Missouri, Nebraska, North Dakota, Ohio, South Dakota, and Wisconsin

REGION 3 – SOUTH

Alabama, Arkansas, Delaware, District of Columbia, Florida, Georgia, Kentucky, Louisiana, Maryland, Mississippi, North Carolina, Oklahoma, South Carolina, Tennessee, Texas, Virginia, and West Virginia

REGION 4 – WEST

Alaska, Arizona, California, Colorado, Hawaii, Idaho, Montana, Nevada, New Mexico, Oregon, Utah, Washington, and Wyoming

LIST OF PSYCHOLOGY PROGRAMS

The 87 programs listed in the following pages include profiles of solid undergraduate programs in psychology as of April 2025 along with additional programs that offer closely related science/neurosciece degrees. Although many students interested in psychology are frequently also interested in neuroscience, pre-med, biology, chemistry, data science, and biomedical engineering, I published those degree programs in other books.

Studying psychology is not for everyone. Although immensely rewarding, success requires initiative. Some students dual major for greater flexibility. In college, students discover their priorities, commitments, and perseverance. A few choose an alternative path somewhere down the road.

Thus, this book concludes with lists of related programs so you can explore those options. Keep the book handy. Even after you begin college, you may discover helpful summer internships and alternative college programs.

Creating lists is often tedious and cumbersome. These national universities and liberal arts colleges were gathered to help you with this task.

Descriptions of the college programs, tuition, requirements, and deadlines are accurate as of April 2025, though many schools do not publish data and approximations were made to complete the chart. However, the requirements may have changed by the time you purchase this book. Nevertheless, this information is a great place to start!

Note: To simplify the text and fit information into the charts and descriptions, abbreviations were used as well as shortened sentences and acronyms.

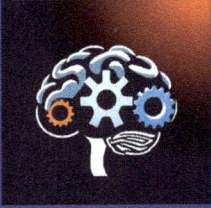

CONNECTICUT

MAINE

MASSACHUSETTS

NEW HAMPSHIRE

NEW JERSEY

NEW YORK

PENNSYLVANIA

RHODE ISLAND

VERMONT

CHAPTER 12

REGION ONE

NORTHEAST

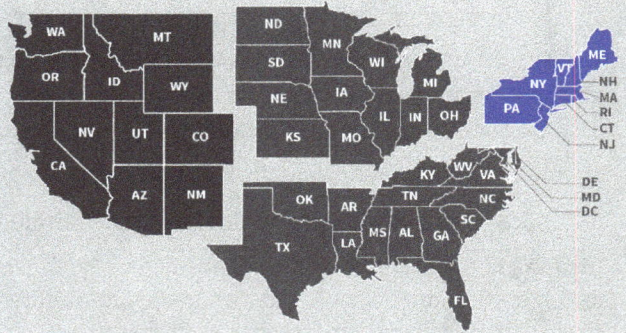

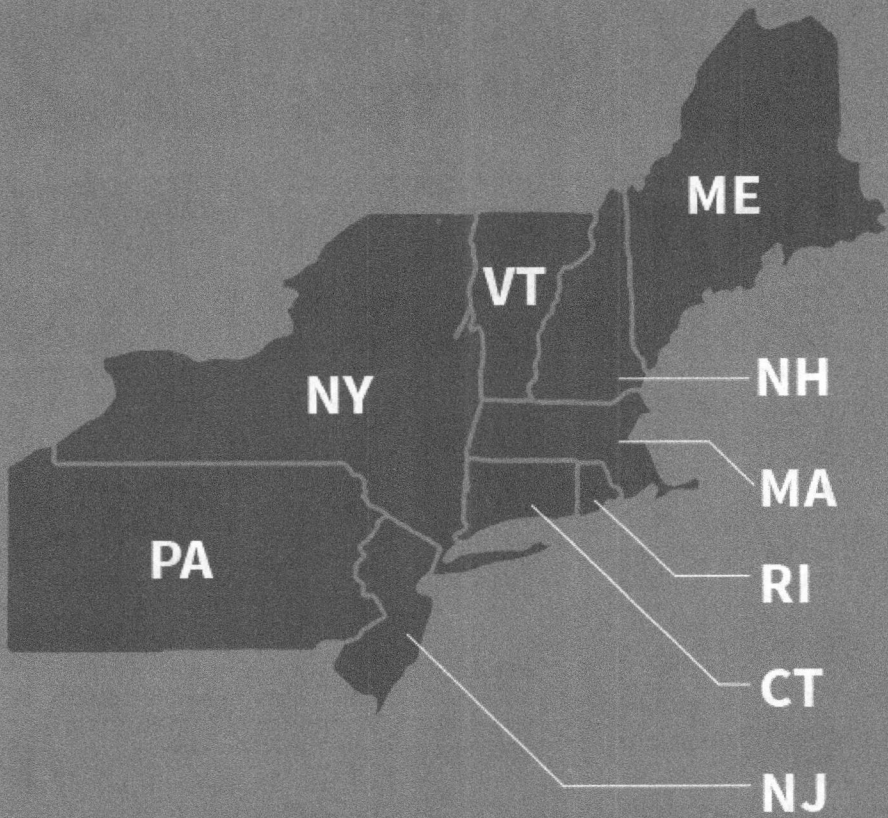

27 *Programs* | **9** *States*

1. *CT – Yale University*
2. *CT – Wesleyan University*
3. *MA - Amherst College*
4. *MA – Boston College*
5. *MA - Boston University*
6. *MA – Brandeis University*
7. *MA – Harvard University*
8. *MA – Massachusetts Institute of Technology*
9. *MA – Northeastern University*
10. *MA - Tufts University*
11. *MA – Wellesley College*
12. *MA – Williams College*
13. *ME – Bowdoin College*
14. *ME – Colby College*
15. *NH - Dartmouth College*
16. *NJ - Princeton University*
17. *NY - Columbia University*
18. *NY – Cornell University*
19. *NY - New York University*
20. *NY – University of Rochester*
21. *PA - Carnegie Mellon University*
22. *PA – Haverford College*
23. *PA – Swarthmore College*
24. *PA - University of Pennsylvania*
25. *PA - University of Pittsburgh*
26. *RI - Brown University*
27. *VT – Middlebury College*

PSYCHOLOGY PROGRAMS

College, Address & Website Public/Private Enrollment	Admit Rate, Average GPA, SAT/ACT, ED/EA	Related Undergrad Majors	Additional Information
Yale University 220 York Street, Room 102, New Haven, CT 06511 yale.edu/ Private UG: ~6,800 Total: ~15,100	Admit Rate: 7% GPA: N/A SAT (ERW): 720-780 SAT (M): 740-800 ACT: 33-35 ED: No, REA: Yes	BS Biology Biomedical Engineering, Chemistry, Cognitive Science, Neuroscience, Physics, Psychology	Yale does not award merit-based financial aid, though families w/incomes below $200,000 receive significant scholarships Neuro/Psych Labs: Brain Imaging Center, Canine Cognition Center, Center for Emotional Intelligence, Center in Child Development & Social Policy, Center for Neuroscience & Regeneration Research, Center for Brain & Mind Health, Child Study Center, Clinical & Affective Neuroscience Lab, Interdiscip. Psychology
Wesleyan University 70 Wyllys Ave Middletown, CT 06459 (860)685-3000 wesleyan.edu Private UG: ~3,100 Total: ~4,011	Admit Rate: ~16% GPA: 3.9 SAT (ERW): 730-770 SAT (M): 750-790 ACT: 33-35 ED: Yes, EA: No	BS Biology, Biochemistry, Chemistry, Integrative Science, Molecular Biology, Neuroscience & Behavior, Psychology	Wesleyan does not offer merit scholarships, only need-based. Students submit the FAFSA & CSS Profile to receive grants & work study. Research: Cognition, Affect, & Psychopathology Studies, Meuroscience & Behavior Program, Reasoning & Decision Making Lab, Schizophrenia Cognition Lab, Summer Research Program; faculty mentored research, seminars, & workshops.
Amherst College 220 South Pleasant Street, Amherst, MA 01002 (413) 542-2328 amherst.edu Private UG: ~1,900	Admit Rate: ~9% GPA: 4.1 SAT (ERW): 740-780 SAT (M): 770–800 ACT: 33-35 ED: Yes, EA: No	BS Biology, Biochemistry, Chemistry, Neuroscience, Psychology, 3-2 & 4-2 dual degree engineering programs	75% of students graduate w/o student loan debt; FAFSA & CSS Profile; Amherst meets 100% need; study away funding State-of-the-art Science Center, a 230,000 sq ft facility; Greenhouse Facility, Science Library, Physiological Psych/Behavioral Neuroscience Lab w/videographic analyses; acute electrophysiological recordings of neuron responses to various stimuli; Cognitive Lab; Social/ Personality Lab The Startup Lab - coordinated by Amherst's venture accelerator.

College, Address & Website Public/Private Enrollment	Admit Rate, Average GPA, SAT/ACT, ED/EA	Related Undergrad Majors	Additional Information
Boston College Devlin Hall 208 140 Commonwealth Avenue Chestnut Hill, MA 02467-3809 *www.bc.edu* Private UG: ~9,654 Total: ~15,234	Admit Rate: 15.9% GPA: 3.8 SAT (ERW): -705-760 SAT (M): 730-780 ACT: 33-34 ED: Yes, EA: No	BS Biology, Biochemistry, Chemistry, Human-Centered Engineering, Neuroscience, Psychology	BC is need-blind and offers merit and need-based scholarships to students, including the Gabelli Presidential Scholars Program. Fifteen students receive a full-tuition merit scholarship regardless of need. Human Neuroscience Lab: researching neural mechanisms underlying human memory, future thinking, creative thinking. Cognitive/Affective Neuroscience Lab: Behavioral/brain imaging; memory/attention & emotion/motivation with fMRI, ERP, polysomnography, & eye-tracking
Boston University 233 Bay State Road, Boston, MA 02215 bu.edu/cas Private UG: ~18,656 Total: ~36,624	Admit Rate: 11% GPA: 3.9 SAT (ERW): 680-740 SAT (M): 710-780 ACT: 32-34 ED: Yes, EA: No	BS Biology Neurobiology, Biochemistry, BME (Neuro focus), Chem, Cognitive & Brain Sciences, Data Science, Neuroscience, Psychology	BU meets 100% financial need. Merit-based scholarships recognize academic, athletic, or artistic achievement regardless of need. Trustee's Scholarship - full-tuition grant AI Research Initiative, Center for Anxiety & Related Disorders, Ctr for Brain Recovery, Center for Memory & Brain, Center for Space Physics, Ctr for Sys Nanoscience, Cognitive Neuroimaging Center, Imaging Systems, Neurophysiology, Data Science & Machine Learning Lab, Robotics Lab, Security Lab
Brandeis University 415 South Street, Waltham, MA 02453 (781) 736-3500 Private UG: ~3,632 Total: ~5,205	Admit Rate: 6% GPA: 3.93 SAT (ERW): 710-770 SAT (M): 740-800 ACT: 32-35 ED: Yes, EA: No	AB Biology (Neurobiology) Biochemistry, Chemistry, Chemical & Biological Engineering, Cognitive Science, Neuroscience, Psychology	Grants/scholarships cover the full cost of tuition for families with household incomes less than $75,000; half the cost for families earning up to $200,000 Research: Behavioral Genetics, Mechanisms of Disease, Biophysics, Cellular & Molecular Neuroscience, Chemical Biology, Learning & Memory, Molecular & Cell Biology, Neural Circuit Dynamics, Neurodegenerative Diseases, Neurogenomics, Sensory Processing, Structural Biology, Synaptic Plasticity

NORTHEAST

PSYCHOLOGY PROGRAMS

College, Address & Website Public/Private Enrollment	Admit Rate, Average GPA, SAT/ACT, ED/EA	Related Undergrad Majors	Additional Information
Harvard University 86 Brattle Street Cambridge, MA 02138 (617) 495-1551 *harvard.edu* Private UG: ~8,527 Total: ~30,391	Admit Rate: 3.5% GPA: 4.22 SAT (ERW): 720-780 SAT (M): 740-800 ACT: 33-35 ED: No, REA: Yes	AB Biology, BME, Chemistry & Physical Biology, Chemistry, Molecular & Cellular Biology, Cognitive Neuroscience, Cognitive Science, Neuroscience, Psychology	Harvard does not award merit aid; average need-based scholarship is over $50,000. Students with family incomes less than $200,000 attend tuition free. Research: AI, Biofilm, Biodiversity, Biomechanics, Biomimetics, Biophysics, Brain Science, Cognitive Science, Cognition, Brain, & Behavior, Computational Neuroscience, Developmental Psychology, Human Performance, Intelligence, Materials Science, Microdevices, Microrobots, Nanoscale Systems, Neuroscience, Physiology, Social Psychology
Massachusetts Institute of Technology 77 Mass Avenue Cambridge, MA 02142 *mit.edu* Private UG: ~4,637 Total: ~11,858	Admit Rate: 4.5% GPA: N/A SAT (ERW): 740-780 SAT (M): 780-800 ACT: 35-36 ED: No, EA: Yes	SB Biology, Biomedical Engineering, Brain & Cognitive Sci, Chemical Eng Chemistry & Biology, Computation & Cognition, Robotics & Autonomous Systems, Transplant Eng	Need-blind; MIT awards families w/full-need (ave scholarship of $45,146), 60% receive aid. Students w/family incomes under $200,000/yr attend MIT tuition-free. Students whose family incomes are below $100,000 will have all expenses covered. Research: Cellular & Molecular Neuroscience, Cognitive Science, Computational Neuroscience, Developmental Psychology, Language/Linguistics, Social Cognition & Moral Psychology, Social Psychology, Systems Neuroscience
Northeastern University 360 Huntington Ave, Boston, MA 02115 *northeastern.edu* Private UG: ~18,498 Total: ~24,078	Admit Rate: 6.7% GPA: N/A SAT (ERW): 710-760 SAT (M): 730-790 ACT: 34-36 ED: Yes, EA: Yes	BS Behavioral Neuroscience, Biochemistry, Biology, Biomedical Engineering Chemistry, Cognitive Science, Psychology	NU meets 100% of need-based aid with 78% of first-year students receiving financial aid. More than $300,000,000 is awarded yearly. Research: Brain ImPACT Lab, Center for Cognitive & Brain Health, Center for Biomedical Computing, Center for Signal Processing, Imaging, Reasoning, & Learning, Cognitive & Brain Sciences, Dev Psychology, EPIC Brain Lab, Health Psych & Behavioral Medicine, Quantitative Psychology, Social & Personality Psych

College, Address & Website Public/Private Enrollment	Admit Rate, Average GPA, SAT/ACT, ED/EA	Related Undergrad Majors	Additional Information
Tufts University 419 Boston Ave, Medford, MA 02155 *northeastern.edu* Private UG: ~6,877 Total: ~13,293	Admit Rate: 11% GPA: N/A SAT (ERW): 710-760 SAT (M): 730-790 ACT: 33-35 ED: Yes, EA: No	BS Biology, Biochemistry, Biomedical Engineering, Biopsychology, Chemistry, Chemical Engineering, Cognitive & Brain Sciences, Psychology	Tufts meets 100% of demonstrated need. Students w/family incomes < $60,000 receive aid w/no student loans. Tufts does not award merit-based financial aid. Consortium for Brain and Cognitive Science, 10 Neuroscience research labs, Tufts' Science & Engineering houses state-of-the-art Advanced Microscopic Imaging Center, Social Cognition Lab, Micro/Nano-Fabrication Facility.
Wellesley College Weaver House, 106 Central Street, Wellesley, MA 02481. *wellesley.edu* Private UG: ~2,417	Admit Rate: 13% GPA: 4.0 SAT (ERW): 730-770 SAT (M): 730-790 ACT: 33-35 ED: Yes, EA: No	BA Biological Sciences, Chemistry, Cognitive & Linguistic Sciences, Neuroscience, Psychology, Pre-Health Track	Wellesley meets 100% of calculated financial need; addl support through Wellesley Students' Aid Society Research: Behavioral Neuroscience, Cellular & Molecular Neuroscience, Clinical Psychology, Cognitive Neuroscience, Cultural Psychology, Developmental Psychology, Social Psychology, Systems & Computational Neuroscience
Williams College Hopkins Hall, 995 Main Street, Williamstown, MA 01267. *williams.edu* Private UG: ~2,100	Admit Rate: 7.5% GPA: 3.9-4.0 SAT (ERW): 730-770 SAT (M): 730-780 ACT: 33-35 ED: Yes, EA: No	BS Biology, Cognitive Science, Computer Science, Psychology, Neuroscience Concentration	Half of Williams students receive aid; families w/incomes <75,000 pay $0, those with incomes <140,000 receive significant aid Research: Behavioral Neuroscience, Cognitive Neuroscience, Computational Models of Cognition, Decision-Making Risk Perception, Developmental Cognitive Neuroscience, Neurobiology of Emotion & Stress, Neuropharmacology, Neuroplasticity, Psychopathology & Brain Function, Visual & Auditory Perception

NORTHEAST

PSYCHOLOGY PROGRAMS

College, Address & Website Public/Private Enrollment	Admit Rate, Average GPA, SAT/ACT, ED/EA	Related Undergrad Majors	Additional Information
Bowdoin College Burton-Little House, 256 Maine St. Brunswick, ME 04011 *bowdoin.edu* Private UG: ~1,950	Admit Rate: 7.7% GPA: 3.9-4.0 SAT (ERW): 710-770 SAT (M): 730-790 ACT: 33-35 ED: Yes, EA: No	BS Biology, Computer Science, Neuroscience, Philosophy, Psychology	Need-blind, meets 100% of demonstrated financial need, if parents earn <$75,000 pay nothing, about 50% receive aid Research: Addiction & Reward Circuits, Behavioral Neuroscience, Cellular & Molecular Neurobiology, Cognitive Neuroscience, Computational Neuroscience & Modeling, Developmental Neuroscience, Emotion & Social Neuroscience, Neuroplasticity & Learning, Psychopathology & Mental Health, Sensory & Motor Systems
Colby College 4800 Mayflower Hill, Waterville, ME 04901 colby.edu Private UG: ~2,300	Admit Rate: 6% GPA: 3.9-4.0 SAT (ERW): 710-760 SAT (M): 720-780 ACT: 33-35 ED: Yes, EA: No	BS Biology, Computer Science, Neuroscience, Philosophy, Psychology	Need-blind, meets 100% of demonstrated financial need, if parents earn <$75,000 pay nothing, about 50% receive aid Research: Addiction, Behavior, & Psychopharmacology, Behavioral Neuroscience, Cognitive Neuroscience, Computational Neuroscience & AI, Emotion & Social Cognition, Mental Health & Clinical Psychology, Molecular & Cellular Neurobiology, Neurodevelopment, Neuroplasticity, Perception & Sensory Systems
Dartmouth College 6016 McNutt Hall, Hanover, NH 03755 *dartmouth.edu/* Private UG: ~4,447 Total: ~6,746	Admit Rate: 5.4% GPA: N/A SAT (ERW): 710-770 SAT (M): 730-790 ACT: 32-35 ED: Yes, EA: No	BS Biology, Biochemistry, Biomedical Engineering, Chemistry, Cognitive Science, Neuroscience, Psychological & Brain Sciences, Psychology	Dartmouth meets 100% demonstrated need; families w/ < $125,000/yr eligible for full tuition scholarships; for families earning <$65,000/year receive tuition, fees, housing, and meals Internships, Study Abroad, 37 Labs, Chemistry Week Events, Neuroscience Center, Consortium for Interacting Minds Research: Cognitive Neuroscience, Computational & Systems Neuroscience Developmental Psychology, Perception & Sensory Processing, Social & Affective Neuroscience

College, Address & Website / Public/Private Enrollment	Admit Rate, Average GPA, SAT/ACT, ED/EA	Related Undergrad Majors	Additional Information
Princeton University Princeton, NJ 08544 *princeton.edu/* Private UG: ~5,604 Total: ~8,829	Admit Rate: 4.6% GPA: 3.93 SAT (ERW): 740-780 SAT (M): 760-800 ACT: 34-35 ED: No, REA: Yes	AB, BSE Biochemistry, Biological Engineering, Biology, Chemical Engineering, Chemistry, Neuroscience, Psychology	Princeton is need-blind. About 62% of undergrads receive aid; average grant of $62,200. Internships, Summer Programs, Co-ops, Study Abroad, Seminar Programs, Corporate Research Partnerships; Summer Undergrad Research Fellows; NSF-Funded Summer REU Program in Biophysics; Artificial Intelligence & Machine Learning Theory, DataDev, DataDebut, Data Science Research and Events
Columbia University 1130 Amsterdam Avenue, New York, NY 10027 *columbia.edu/* Private UG: ~8,832 Total: ~33,776	Admit Rate: 3.8% GPA: N/A SAT (ERW): 740-780 SAT (M): 750-800 ACT: 34-35 ED: Yes, EA: No	BS Biology, Biochemistry, Biomedical Engineering, Chemical Engineering, Chemistry, Neuroscience & Behavior, Psychology	Most students whose families earn less than $150,000 attend Columbia tuition-free. Internships, Summer Programs, Co-ops, Study Abroad, Seminars, Corporate Research Partnerships, DSI Scholars & Collaboratory to enhance data science education, Neuroscience Outreach, Psych/Neuro Senior Thesis Advanced Research, Psychology/Neuro Seminars Institute for Brain Science, Neuroscience of Decision-Making, NeuroTechnology Center, Vision & Graphics Center
Cornell University 430 College Ave., Ithaca, NY 14850 *cornell.edu/* Private UG: ~15,735 Total: ~25,898	Admit Rate: 7.9% GPA: 4.07 SAT (ERW): 710-770 SAT (M): 720-800 ACT: 33-35 ED: Yes, EA: No	BS Biology, Biochemistry, Biological Engineering, BME, Chemical Engineering, Chemistry, Cognitive Science, Neuroscience, Psychology	Most students w/family incomes less than $150,000 attend tuition-free. Internships, Summer Programs, Co-ops, Study Abroad, Seminar Programs, State-of-the-Art Facilities, Corporate Partnerships Brain & Behavior Research Group, Computational & Psychology Lab, Institute for Developmental Psychobiology, Institute of Psychology & Neuroscience, Nano- & Micro-Scale Eng

NORTHEAST

PSYCHOLOGY PROGRAMS

College, Address & Website Public/Private Enrollment	Admit Rate, Average GPA, SAT/ACT, ED/EA	Related Undergrad Majors	Additional Information
New York University 27 West 4th Street, New York, NY 10014 cas.nyu.edu/ Private UG: ~29,401 Total: ~59,144	Admit Rate: 8% GPA: 3.71 SAT (ERW): 690-760 SAT (M): 700-800 ACT: 31-34 ED: Yes, EA: No	BS Biology, Biochemistry, Biomedical Engineering,, Biomolecular Eng, Chemical Engineering, Chemistry, Cognitive Science, Neuroscience, Psychology	NYU meets 100% of applicant's financial need - $37,000 average scholarship; $2.7 million in research scholarships 10-week immersive neuroscience summer research program; SURP, NYU Access Grads, equipment - histology, microscopy, digital imaging, eye movement recording, magnetoencephalography, fMRI, EEG AI, Big Data, Clinical Psych, Cognition, Cognitive Neuroscience, Computer Vision, Perception, Personality Psych, Social Psych
University of Rochester 300 Wilson Boulevard, Rochester, NY 14627 rochester.edu Private UG: ~6,521 Total: ~11,741	Admit Rate: 35% GPA: N/A SAT (ERW): : 650-720 SAT (M): 680-790 ACT: 30-34 ED: Yes, EA: No	BS Biology, Biochemistry, Biomedical Engineering, Brain & Cognitive Science, Chemical Engineering, Chemistry, Neuroscience, Psychology	Merit, Need-Based, & International Student Scholarships; Study Abroad/Research Funds Research: Adolescence, Cell Signaling & Comm, Comp Modeling, Developmental Psychopathology, Language Processing & Acquisition, Learning, Memory, & Adaptive Plasticity, Motivation, Neurobiology of Disease, Perception & Action BCS & Neuroscience Undergrad Council, Cognitive Science Interest Gp, Mindfulness & Meditation Club, Neurodiversity Club, Neuroscience Undergrad Council, Psych Undergraduate Council, Society of Undergraduate Psychology Students
Carnegie Mellon University 5000 Forbes Avenue, Pittsburgh, PA 15213 cmu.edu Private UG: ~7,509 Total: ~16,779	Admit Rate: 11.5% GPA: 3.9 SAT (ERW): 720-770 SAT (M):770-800 ACT: 34-35 ED: Yes, EA: No	BS Biological Sciences, Biomedical Engineering, Chemical Engineering, Chemistry, Cognitive Science, Neuroscience, Psychology	CMU offers need-based grants & endowed scholarships. Current students can win design, sustainability, research, and engagement scholarships - $75,000/year Research: Cognitive Neuroscience, Comp Neuroscience, Development & Education Psychology, Cryptography, Cybersecurity, Human-Computer Interaction, Natural & Artificial Intelligence, Neural Engineering & Technology, Neurobiology of Disease, Perception & Action, Robotics, Social & Health Psychology, Systems Neuroscience

College, Address & Website Public/Private Enrollment	Admit Rate, Average GPA, SAT/ACT, ED/EA	Related Undergrad Majors	Additional Information
Haverford College 370 Lancaster Ave, Haverford, PA 19041 *haverford.edu* Private UG: ~1,479	Admit Rate: 12.4% GPA: N/A SAT (ERW): 720-770 SAT (M):740-780 ACT: 33-35 ED: Yes, EA: No	BS Biology, Chemistry, Neuroscience, Psychology Concentration: Biochemistry Minors: Neuroscience, Psychology	Haverford does not provide merit-based aid for students, but does meet 100% need. Special Programs w/Bryn Mawr: Bi-College Interdisciplinary Neuroscience Program Research: Biological Psychology, Cognitive Psychology, Social/Personality Psychology, Cultural Psychology Labs: Behavioral Neuroscience, Dev Psych, Human Cognitive Neuroscience Lab, Personality/Social Psychology Lab, Cognition Lab, Stress Physiology Lab
Swarthmore College Parrish Hall, 2nd Floor, 500 College Avenue Swarthmore, PA 19081 *swarthmore.edu* Private UG: ~1,644	Admit Rate: 7.5% GPA: 4.1 SAT (ERW): 720-770 SAT (M): 770-790 ACT: 34-35 ED: Yes, EA: No	BS Biology, Biochemistry, Chemistry, Cognitive Science, Neuroscience, Psychology	Swarthmore meets 100% of students' demonstrated financial need with an average award of about $63,000. Research: Behavioral & Cognition, Neuroscience, Biochemistry, Cognitive Development, Cognitive Science, Computational Memory, Developmental/ Molecular Biology, Neurobiology, Perception & Action, Physiological Psychology, Psycholinguistics, Social Psychology
University of Pennsylvania 3535 Market St. Suite 850 Philadelphia, PA 19104 *upenn.edu* Private UG: ~10,106 Total: ~22,432	Admit Rate: 5.4% GPA: N/A SAT (ERW): 740-770 SAT (M): 770-790 ACT: 34-36 ED: Yes, EA: No	BS Biology, Biochemistry, Biomedical Engineering, Chemical Engineering, Chemistry, Cognitive Science, Neuroscience, Psychology	Penn meets 100% of demonstrated need w/grants/work-study; students graduate debt-free. Families w/ incomes up to $200,000 are eligible for full-tuition scholarships. Psych/Neuro Lab: Abramson Cancer Center, Brain Behavior Lab, Center for Brain Injury & Repair, Center for Cognitive Neurosci, Center for Neurodegenerative Disease Research, Ctr for Neurobiology & Behavior, Center for Sleep & Circadian Neurobiology, Institute for Diabetes, Obesity, & Metabolism, Institute for Immunology, Institute for Neuroscience

NORTHEAST

PSYCHOLOGY PROGRAMS

College, Address & Website Public/Private Enrollment	Admit Rate, Average GPA, SAT/ACT, ED/EA	Related Undergrad Majors	Additional Information
University of Pittsburgh 4227 Fifth Avenue, Alumni Hall, Pittsburgh, PA 15260 *pitt.edu* Public UG: ~19,980 Total: ~29,238	Admit Rate: 67% GPA: 4.1 SAT (ERW): 630-720 SAT (M): 620-750 ACT: 28-33 ED: No, EA: No Rolling: Yes	BS Biological Sciences Biochemistry, Bioengineering, Chemical Engineering, Chemistry, Neuroscience, Psychology	Pitt offers the Pitt Pell Plus Program which doubles the federal grant to the maximum. Pitt also offers merit-based scholarships based on academic achievement (Dec 1). Psych/Neuro Labs: Brain Institute, Center for the Neural Basis of Cognition, Center for Neuroanatomy w/Neurotropic Viruses, & Alzheimer Disease Research Center, Center for Neuroscience, Clinical Psychology Center, Learning Research & Development Center Research: Behavioral, Systems, Cognitive, Cellular, Developmental & Molecular Neuroscience
Brown University 198 Dyer Street, Providence, RI 02903 *brown.edu* Private UG: ~6,792 Total: ~9,948	Admit Rate: 8% GPA: N/A SAT (ERW): 710-770 SAT (M): 730-790 ACT: 33-35 ED: Yes, EA: No	AB Biology, Biochemistry, Biomedical Engineering, Chemical Engineering, Chemistry, Cognitive Science, Neuroscience, Psychology	About 44% of students receive aid of ~$56,000/yr. Brown covers tuition for families earning < $125,000. For families earning < $60,000, Brown covers tuition, room, board, books, & an additional scholarship Research: Brain Science, Biomedical Eng, Computational & Experimental Res in Mathematics, Health, Data Science, Environment, Global Health Initiative, Innovation Institute, Molecular & Nanoscale Innovation
Middlebury College Emma Willard House, 131 S. Main Street Middlebury, VT 05753 *middlebury.edu.* Private UG: ~2,774	Admit Rate: 12% GPA: 4.04 SAT (ERW): 700-770 SAT (M): 740-780 ACT: 33-34 ED: Yes, EA: No	BS Biology, Chemistry, Neuroscience, Psychology	Middlebury does not offer merit-based scholarships, but does commit to meeting 100% need. Research: Behavioral Genetics, Behavioral Neuroendocrinology, Behavioral Neurophysiology, Clinical Psychophysiology, Cognitive Psychology, Neurodevelopment, Psychobiology of Sex Differences,, Psychopharmacology, Social Neuroscience

CHAPTER 13

REGION TWO

MIDWEST

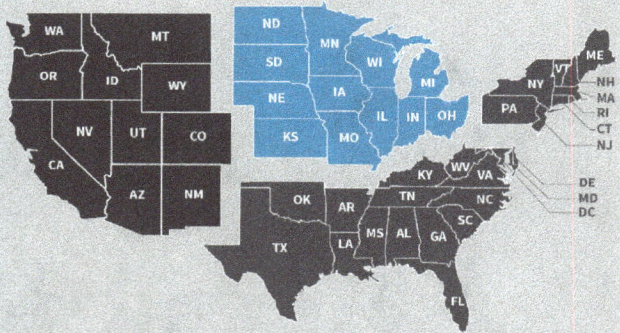

18 Programs | 12 States

1. IA – University of Iowa
2. IL – DePaul University
3. IL - Northwestern University
4. IL - University of Chicago
5. IL – University of Illinois at Chicago
6. IL – University of Illinois, Urbana-Champaign
7. IN – Purdue University
8. IN – University of Indiana, Bloomington
9. IN - University of Notre Dame
10. KS – University of Kansas
11. MI – Michigan State University
12. MI - University of Michigan
13. MN – University of Minnesota
14. MO – University of Missouri
15. MO - Washington University in St. Louis
16. OH – Oberlin College
17. OH – The Ohio State University
18. WI – University of Wisconsin

PSYCHOLOGY PROGRAMS

College, Address & Website Public/Private Enrollment	Admit Rate, Average GPA, SAT/ACT, ED/EA	Related Undergrad Majors	Additional Information
University of Iowa 2900 University Capitol Centre 201 S. Clinton Street, Iowa City, IA 52242 *www.uiowa.edu/* Public UG: ~22,738 Total: ~30,779	Admit Rate: 84% GPA: 3.83 SAT (ERW): 570-670 SAT (M): 560-660 ACT: 22-28 ED: No, EA: Yes, Rolling: Yes	BA, BS Biology, Biomedical Sciences, Biomedical Engineering, Biochemistry & Molecular Biology, Chemical Engineering, Chemistry, Neuroscience, Psychology	Iowa awards scholarships recognizing outstanding academic achievements and other accomplishments. Other awards include: Iowa Scholars, National Scholars, & Iowa Flagship Research: Attention, Behavioral Neuroscience, Brain Imaging, Cognitive Neuroscience, Developmental Psychopathology, Emotion, Executive Function, Health Psychology, Learning & Memory, Visual Perception
DePaul University 2400 N Sheffield. Avenue, Chicago, IL 60614 *depaul.edu.* Private UG: ~14,188 Total: ~21,210	Admit Rate: 74% GPA: 3.8 SAT (ERW): 530-640 SAT (M): 570-650 ACT: 24-30 ED: No, EA: Yes	BS Biochemistry, Biological Sciences, Chemical Engineering, Chemistry, Neuroscience, Psychology	DePaul awards more than $57 million in scholarships to incoming freshman students/yr along w/over $11 million in need-based donation-based aid. DePaul Scholarship Application, College-Specific Scholarships Research: Alzheimer's Disease, Brain & Language Processing, Chronic Illness, Cognitive Neuroscience, Community Psychology, Computational Neuroscience, Data Analysis & Visualization, Medical Imaging, Neuroethics, Social Development
Northwestern University 633 Clark St, Evanston, IL 60208 *northwestern.edu/* Private UG: ~8,846 Total: ~22,801	Admit Rate: 7% GPA: 4.1 SAT (ERW): 730-770 SAT (M): 760-800 ACT: 33-35 ED: Yes, EA: No	BS Biological Sciences, Biomedical Engineering, Chemical Engineering, Chemistry, Cognitive Science, Neuroscience, Psychology	Most families w/incomes under $150,000 receive ~$50,000; NU Scholarship, NU Endowed Sch., Good Neighbor, Great U, Questbridge, Founder's Scholar, Karr Achievement Award, Chicago Star Scholarship Brain-Machine Interfaces, Cellular & Molecular Neuroscience, Clinical Psychology, Cognitive & Perceptual Psychology, Developmental Psychology, Health Psychology, Human-Robot Interaction, Neuropsychology, Predictive Analytics, Social Psychology

College, Address & Website Public/Private Enrollment	Admit Rate, Average GPA, SAT/ACT, ED/EA	Related Undergrad Majors	Additional Information
University of Chicago 915 E 60th St., Chicago, IL 60637 *uchicago.edu/* Private UG: ~7,011 Total: ~18,452	Admit Rate: 4.7% GPA: N/A SAT (ERW): 730-770 SAT (M): 770-800 ACT: 34-35 ED: Yes, EA: Yes	BA, BA Biological Chemistry, Biology Sciences (Cancer Biology, Cell & Molecular Bio), Chemistry, Genetics, Immunology, Microbiology, Medical Chem, Neuroscience, Psychology	Merit scholarships auto considered for outstanding students w/o consideration of need. UChicago Empower Initiative guarantees free tuition for families w/incomes <$125,000/year tuition, room, board, for families earning < $60,000/year Research: Cognition & Behavior, Comp. Neuroscience, Dev Psychology, Neurodevelopment & Plasticity, Neuroscience Institute, Social Psych, Translational & Clinical Neuroscience
University of Illinois at Chicago 1200 W Harrison St. Chicago, IL 60607 *uic.edu* Public UG: ~22,495 Total: ~33,906	Admit Rate: 75% GPA: 3.5-3.7 SAT (ERW): 560-660 SAT (M): 540-690 ACT: 24-30 ED: No, EA: Yes	BS Biochemistry, Biological Sciences, Biomedical Engineering, Chemical Engineering, Chemistry, Neuroscience, Psychology	About 56% of UIC students receive need based aid. UIC offers several merit-based scholarships for incoming first-year students: Chancellor's Fellows, President's Award, Merit Tuition Research: Addiction, Brain Trauma, Development, Genetics, Imaging, Learning & Plasticity, Motor System, Neurodegeneration, Psychiatric Disorders, Sensory Neuroscience
University of Illinois, Urbana-Champaign 901 West Illinois Street, Urbana, IL 61801 *illinois.edu* Public UG: ~35,120 Total: ~56,916	Admit Rate: 42.4% GPA: 3.85 SAT (ERW): 660-740 SAT (M): 680-790 ACT: 29-34 ED: No, EA: Yes	BS Biochemistry, Bioengineering, Brain & Cognitive Science, Chemical & Biomolecular Engineering, Integrative Biology, Molecular & Cellular Biology, Psychology	Applicants are automatically considered for merit-based scholarships. 70% of UIUC undergrad receive aid. Supplemental form for need-based scholarships. AI, Attention & Perception, Behavioral Neuroscience, Brain Plasticity, Clinical-Community Psychology, Cognitive Neuroscience, Cognitive Psychology, Developmental Psychology, Human-Centered Data, Machine Learning, Molecular & Cellular Neuroscience, Social-Personality Psychology

MIDWEST

College, Address & Website Public/Private Enrollment	Admit Rate, Average GPA, SAT/ACT, ED/EA	Related Undergrad Majors	Additional Information
Purdue University Purdue University, West Lafayette, IN 47907 *purdue.edu/* Public UG: ~44,170 Total: ~58,009	Admit Rate: 53% GPA: 3.67 SAT (ERW): 590-710 SAT (M): 610-760 ACT: 27-34 ED: No, EA: Yes	BS Biology (Conc Cell, Molec & Developmental, Genetics, Health & Disease, Microbio, Neurobiology & Physiology), Biochemistry, Biomedical Eng, Brain & Beh Sci, Chemical Eng, Chemistry, Chemical Bio, Psychological Sci	Purdue offers need/merit based funds & scholarships; 15% of applicants receive merit awards each year. Some dept scholarships require the Purdue Supplemental Scholarship Application, which considers both need and merit. Research: Aging & Neurodegeneration, Devt, Genetics, & Neuropharmacology, Diversity & Inclusion, Behavior, Learning & Memory, Maladaptive Behavior, Neuroengineering, Neurotrauma & Neuropathology, Perception & Performance
University of Indiana, Bloomington 940 E. Seventh St. Bloomington, IN 47405 *indiana.edu/* Public UG: ~37,000 Total: ~48,424	Admit Rate: 80.4% GPA: 3.98 SAT (ERW): 600-710 SAT (M): 630-720 ACT: 28-33 ED: No, EA: Yes	BA, BS Biology, Chemistry, Cognitive Science, Human Biology, Intelligent Systems Engineering, Neuroscience, Psychology	IU awards millions of dollars in financial aid and scholarships each year, encompassing merit- and need-based scholarships, donor-funded scholarships, and department-specific awards. Research: Behavioral Neuroscience, Clinical & Translational Neuroscience, Cognitive/Computational Neuroscience, Developmental Psychology, Molecular & Cellular Neuroscience, Neuroimaging & Brain Mapping, Neuropsychology, Sensory & Perception Neuroscience, Social Neuroscience, Systems Neuroscience
University of Notre Dame Notre Dame, IN 46556 *nd.edu/* Private UG: ~8,874 Total: ~12,809	Admit Rate: 11.1% GPA: N/A SAT (ERW): 690-760 SAT (M): 710-790 ACT: 32-35 ED: No, REA: Yes	BS Biochemistry, Biological Sciences, Biology, Chemical Engineering, Chemistry, Neuroscience & Behavior, Psychology	ND offers first-year students, need-based scholarship/grant of ~$55,045; ~70% receive some financial aid. About 3% of students receive merit money. Research: Clinical Science, Cognition, Brain, & Behavior, Computational Neuroscience, Developmental Psych, Evolution of Nervous Systems, Hormonal Influence on Behavior, Neurodegenerative & Neuropathology, Neuroendocrinology, Quantitative Psychology, Visual Cognition

College, Address & Website Public/Private Enrollment	Admit Rate, Average GPA, SAT/ACT, ED/EA	Related Undergrad Majors	Additional Information
University of Kansas 1266 Oread Ave. Lawrence, KS 66045 *ku.edu* Public UG: ~22,250 Total: ~30,770	Admit Rate: 88% GPA: 3.68 SAT (ERW): 530-650 SAT (M): 520-640 ACT: 21-27 ED: No, EA: No Rolling: Yes	BA, BS Behavioral Neuroscience, Biology, Chemical Engineering, Chemistry, Human Biology, Psychology	About 20% of KU students receive Pell Grants. Merit Scholarships include: Freshman & Transfer, Kansas Comprehensive Grant, Kansas Education Opportunity Scholarship Research: Behavioral Psych, Cognitive Neuroscience & Cognitive Science, Cultural Psych, Develop. Science, Health Psych, Learning, Quantitative & Computational Method, Sleep Research, Social Neuroscience
Michigan State University 426 Auditorium Road, Room 250, East Lansing, MI 48824 *msu.edu/* Public UG: ~41,234 Total: ~52,089	Admit Rate: 88% GPA: 3.5-4.0 SAT (ERW): 540-650 SAT (M): 570-670 ACT: 24-30 ED: No, EA: Yes, Rolling	BS Biology, Biomedical Engineering, Chemical Engineering, Chemistry, Genomics & Molecular Genetics, Neuroscience, Psychology	Submit FAFSA to access need-based grants, loans, & work study. MSU offers grants for High-Achievement, Criteria-Specific, Michigan & Non-Resident President's, Provost's & Dean's Scholarship Research: Behavioral Neuroscience, Cognition & Cognitive Neuroscience, Ecological/Community Psychology, Organizational Psychology, Social/ Personality Psychology
University of Michigan 500 S. State St., Ann Arbor, MI 48109 *umich.edu/* Public UG: ~34,454 Total: ~52,855	Admit Rate: 18% GPA: 3.87 SAT (ERW): 660-740 SAT (M): 690-790 ACT (C): 31-34 ED: No, EA: Yes	BS Biochemistry, Biology, Biomedical Eng Biopsychology (BCN), Chemical Engineering, Chemistry, Cognitive Science, Neuroscience, Psychology	Intl Student Scholarships, Merit, Need-Based, & Study Abroad ~70% of UMich students receive some aid; Ph.D. students receive full funding - tuition waiver, monthly living stipend, & health insurance Research: Brain Science, Center for Computational Medicine & Bioinformatics, Cognition & Cognitive Neuroscience, Center for Human Growth & Devt, Molecular & Cellular Biology, Neural Engineering Lab

MIDWEST

PSYCHOLOGY PROGRAMS

College, Address & Website Public/Private Enrollment	Admit Rate, Average GPA, SAT/ACT, ED/EA	Related Undergrad Majors	Additional Information
University of Minnesota 240 Williamson Hall, 231 Pillsbury Dr SE Minneapolis, MN 55455 *umn.edu/* Public UG: ~39,556 Total: ~57,000	Admit Rate: 73% GPA: 3.57-3.96 SAT (ERW): 660-720 SAT (M): 680-770 ACT (C): 27-32 ED: No, EA: Yes	BS Biochemistry, Biology, Biomedical Eng Chemical Eng, Chemistry, Genetics, Cell Biology, & Development, Microbiology, Neuroscience, Psychology	UMinn awards $50+ million academic scholarships to freshman/yr. Applic. automatically considered Research: Clinical Science. Cognition, Drug Abuse/Addiction, Neuroimaging, Neuropharm/ & Neurooncology, Neuropsychiatric Disease, Auditory & Vestibular Systems, Optogenetics, Regenerative Medicine for Neural Systems, Psychopathology, Synaptic Plasticity & Learning
University of Missouri 230 Jesse Hall Columbia, MO 65211 *missouri.edu/* Public UG: ~24,449 Total: ~31,543	Admit Rate: 77% GPA: N/A SAT (ERW): 550-650 SAT (M): 600-680 ACT: 23-29 ED: No, EA: Yes	BA, BS Biological Sciences (Medical Science & Human Biology), Biochemistry, Biological Eng, Biomedical Eng, Chemical Eng, Chemistry, Psychology	Missouri Land Grant covering 100% of unmet need for tuition/fees for Pell Grant-eligible Missouri residents. Merit scholarships include: Curators Scholars, Chancellor's Award, Excellence Award, & Provost's Award Research: Addiction, Aging, Autism, Decision Making, Depression, Memory, Perception, Psychopathology, Reward Systems
Washington University in St. Louis 1 Brookings Dr, St. Louis, MO 63130 *wustl.edu* Private UG: ~8,267 Total: ~16,399	Admit Rate: 12% GPA: 4.21 SAT (ERW): 720-760 SAT (M): 760-800 ACT: 33-35 ED: Yes, EA: No	BS Biochemistry, Biology, Biomedical Engineering, Chemical Engineering, Chemistry, Cognitive Neuroscience, Psychology, Minors: Quantum Engineering, Robotics	Wash U offers need and merit money to help students fund college. Average need-based package is $72,252 w/ about 42% of students. Academic, Scholar, & Division Scholarships Available. Research: Aging & Development, Behavior, Brain, & Cognition, Clinical Psychology, Neurodegeneration, Neuroengineering, Neurogenomics, Neuroimmunology, Pain & Addiction, Sleep Research, Social & Personality Psychology

College, Address & Website / Public/Private Enrollment	Admit Rate, Average GPA, SAT/ACT, ED/EA	Related Undergrad Majors	Additional Information
Oberlin College 38 E. College St, Oberlin, OH 44074 oberlin.edu/ Private UG: ~2,886	Admit Rate: 34.3% GPA: N/A SAT (ERW): 710-760 SAT (M): 690-780 ACT: 32-35 ED: Yes, EA: No	BS Biochemistry, Biology, Chemistry, Cognitive Science, Neuroscience, Psychology 3-2 Engineering Program	Grants, scholarships, loans, and on-campus jobs to meet 100% of need. Admitted students are automatically considered for merit-based money. Research: Behavioral Analysis, Cell Culture Studies, Chemogenetics, Cognitive Science, Computational Modeling, Human EEG Studies, Neural Basis of Behavior, Optogenetics, Perception, Physiological Reactivity
The Ohio State University 281 W. Lane Ave. Columbus, OH 43210 *osu.edu* Public UG: ~52,269 Total: ~66,901	Admit Rate: 57% GPA: N/A SAT (ERW): 590-690 SAT (M): 620-740 ACT: 26-32 ED: No, EA: Yes	BS Biochemistry, Biology, Biomedical Engineering, Chemical Engineering, Chemistry, Cognitive Science, Neuroscience, Psychology	About 80% of first-year students receive financial aid. OSU-Funded Merit Scholarships, Eminence Fellows Program & Scholarship, Special Eligibility Scholarships Research: Behavioral Neuroscience, Clinical Psychology, Cognitive Neuroscience Decision Psych, Devt Psychology, Neurodevelopment & Regeneration, Neuroimaging & Brain Mapping, Psychoneuroimmunology, Social Neuroscience
University of Wisconsin 702 West Johnson Street, Madison, WI 53715 *wisc.edu* Public UG: ~37,230 Total: ~49,886	Admit Rate: 43% GPA: 3.87 SAT (ERW): 650-720 SAT (M): 700-790 ACT: 28-33 ED: No, EA: Yes	BS Biochemistry, Biology, Biomedical Engineering, Chemical Engineering, Chemistry, Neuroscience, Psychology	Freshman Award, Dept Scholarships, LEED Scholars Prog, Scholarships for Cont Students, STAR Scholarship Half of the freshman class receives an average aid package of about $16,000. Research: Artificial Intelligence, Big Data Analysis, Cognition & Cognitive Neuroscience, Computer Vision, Drug Action & Development, Molecular & Cellular Pharmacology, Neural Mechanisms, Neurobiology, Robotics Translational Neuroengineering

MIDWEST

CHAPTER 14

REGION THREE

SOUTH

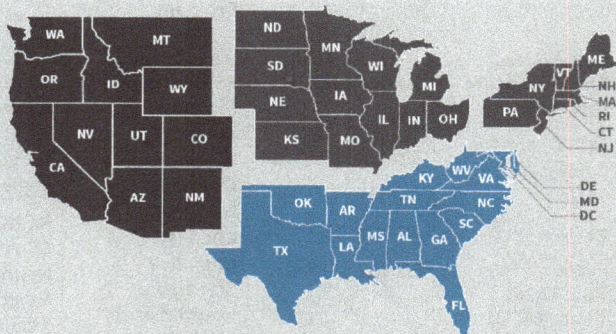

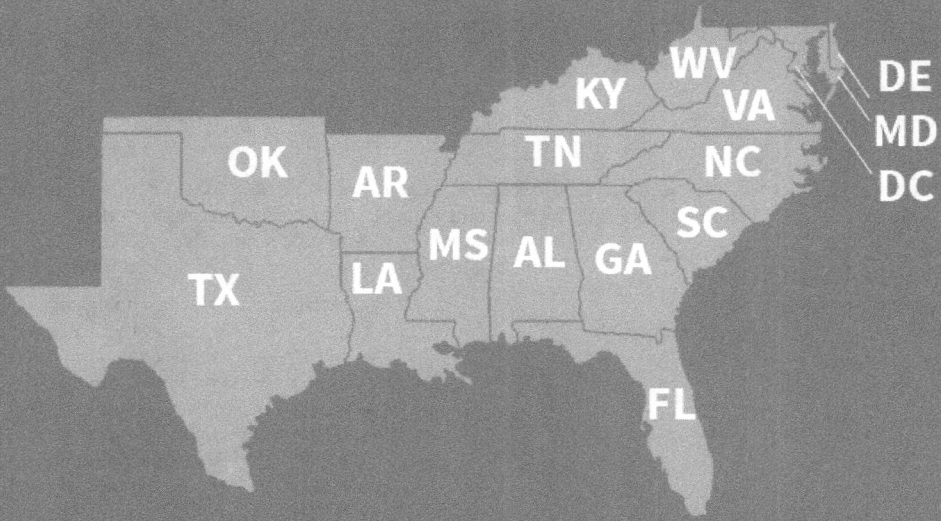

18 *Programs* | **16** *States*

1. AL – Auburn University
2. AL – University of Alabama, Birmingham
3. DC - Georgetown University
4. FL – Florida State University
5. FL - University of Florida
6. FL – University of Miami
7. GA - Emory University
8. GA – University of Georgia
9. LA – Tulane University
10. MD - Johns Hopkins University
11. NC - Duke University
12. NC - University of North Carolina, Chapel Hill
13. NC – Wake Forest University
14. TN - Vanderbilt University
15. TX - Rice University
16. TX – Southern Methodist University
17. TX - University of Texas at Austin
18. VA - University of Virginia

PSYCHOLOGY PROGRAMS

College, Address & Website Public/Private Enrollment	Admit Rate, Average GPA, SAT/ACT, ED/EA	Related Undergrad Majors	Additional Information
Auburn University The Quad Center Auburn Univ, AL 36849 *auburn.edu/* Public UG: ~26,874 Total: ~34,195	Admit Rate: 46% GPA: 4.1 SAT (ERW): 590-670 SAT (M): 620-700 ACT: 25-30 ED: No, EA: Yes	BA, BS Biology Biochemistry, Biomedical Eng, Chemical Eng, Chemistry, Neuroscience, Psychology (Conc. Cognitive & Behavioral Neuroscience)	Auburn offers numerous in-state & out-of-state scholarships (GPA & ACT) & National Merit stipend (merit & need) Research Labs: Auburn Psychological Services Ctr, MRI Research Ctr; Siemens 7T MAGNETOM, 3T Verio scanners w/ adv stimulus pres equipment, MR eye tracking, EEG; Cognitive & Affective Neuro Lab; Neural & Physiological Underpinnings of Emotional & Cognitive Processes. Labs feature a behavioral psychophysiology setup.
University of Alabama, Birmingham 1729 2nd Ave S. Birmingham, AL 35294 *uab.edu/* Public UG: ~32,500 Total: ~45,000	Admit Rate: 87% GPA: 3.8 SAT (ERW): 570-660 SAT (M): 600-710 ACT: 22-30 ED: No, EA: No Rolling: Yes	BS Biology, Biochemistry, Biomedical Engineering, Chemical Engineering, Chemistry, Cognitive Science, Neuroscience, PreMedical Track, Psychology	UAB offers merit-based scholarships to in-state & out-of-state students, based on SA/ACT and high school GPA. Research Labs: Brain Institute, Psych Labs Comprehensive Neuroscience Center Research: Epigenetic Mechanisms; Pain, Cognition; Neurodegeneration; Stress, Behavioral Neurobio; Health Disparities, Neural Structure & Function, Obesity & Eating Neuromodulation, Behavior, Psychophysiology, Rehabilitation; Interdisciplinary Research, Clinical Care, & Education in Neuroscience.
Georgetown University White-Gravenor Hall Room 103 37th & O St. NW Washington, DC 20057 *georgetown.edu* Private UG: ~8,000 Total: ~21,000	Admit Rate: 12% GPA: 4.2-4.6 SAT (ERW): 730-770 SAT (M): 730-790 ACT: 32-35 ED: No, REA: Yes	BS Biochemistry, Biology, Chemistry, Global Health, Neuroscience, Psychology	Georgetown offers need-based financial aid & not merit-based scholarships except athletic & donor awards. Research: Affective, Behavioral, Cognitive, & Developmental Neuroscience, Learning & Memory, Neuroplasticity, Perception & Sensory Systems, Psychopathology & Clinical Psychology, Social & Cultural Psychology/Neuroscience, Decision Science & Cognitive Control

College, Address & Website / Public/Private Enrollment	Admit Rate, Average GPA, SAT/ACT, ED/EA	Related Undergrad Majors	Additional Information
Florida State University A2500 Univ Ctr 282 Champions Tallahassee, FL 32306 *fsu.edu* Public UG: ~32,500 Total: ~44,000	Admit Rate: 23% GPA: 4.2-4.6 SAT (ERW): 630-700 SAT (M): 610-690 ACT: 27-31 ED: No, EA: Yes, Rolling: Yes	BS Behavioral Neuroscience, Biochemistry, Biomedical Engineering, Cell/ Bioprocess Eng, Biomaterials & Biopolymers Eng Cell & Molecular Neuroscience, Chemical Eng, Chemistry, Neuroscience, Psychology	FSU offers need & merit-based money, out-of-state tuition waivers, & honors program opportunities (GPA/test scores) Research Labs: Neuroscience Facility, Cognitive Neuroscience of Human Memory Lab; Brain-Gut Circuit Lab; fMRI, EEG, motion tracking, memory Research: Biophysics, Electrophysiology of Excitable Cells, Neurotransmitter Action, development & plasticity, circadian Rhythms, Feeding & Regulatory Processes; Genetic & Molecular Bases of Behavior.
University of Florida 201 Criser Hall Gainesville, FL 32611 *ufl.edu/* Public UG: ~34,924 Total: ~54,814	Admit Rate: 23% GPA: 4.5-4.7 SAT (ERW): 670-740 SAT (M): 690-760 ACT: 30-34 ED: No, EA: Yes	BA, BS Biology, Biochemistry & Molecular Bio, Biomedical Eng, Chemical Eng, Chemistry, PreMed Track, Neuroscience, Psychology	Presidential Gold & Platinum Scholars' Florida Bright Futures; FL Academic & FL Medallion Scholars; Alumni, Sunshine, CLAS, & Gator Nation Scholarships Research Ctrs & Inst: Brain Institute, Ctr for Cognitive Aging & Memory; Cognitive Neuroscience Lab; Genetics Institute Research: Neural Systems, Behavioral & Cognitive Neuroscience, Cognition & Memory, Brain Aging, Neurodegenerative Diseases
University of Miami 1306 Stanford Dr Suite 1210 Coral Gables, FL 33146 *miami.edu/* Private UG: ~12,883 Total: ~19,400	Admit Rate: 19% GPA: 3.8-4.0 SAT (ERW): 660-730 SAT (M): 700-760 ACT (C): 26-32 ED: Yes, EA: Yes	BA, BS Biology, Biochemistry & Molecular Bio, Biomedical Eng (Biomaterials & Tissue, Electrical Mechanical, PreMed), Chemical Engineering, Chemistry, Pre-Med Track, Psychology	UM automatically considers applicants for merit awards, including full cost of attendance; transfer scholarships also Psych/Neuro Labs: Neuroimaging Facility, Brain Connectivity & Cognition Lab, Memory & Mindfulness Lab, Cognitive & Beh Neuroscience Lab Research: Cognitive Neuroscience, Brain Connectivity & Cognition, Neurodevelopmental Disorders ASD; Brain Imaging, Behavioral Mechanisms, Learning, Decision-Making, Thoughts

SOUTH

PSYCHOLOGY PROGRAMS

College, Address & Website Public/Private Enrollment	Admit Rate, Average GPA, SAT/ACT, ED/EA	Related Undergrad Majors	Additional Information
Emory University 1390 Oxford Rd. NE, Atlanta, GA 30322 *emory.edu/* Private UG: ~8,332 Total: ~16,019	Admit Rate: 10% GPA: 3.9 SAT (ERW): 730-770 SAT (M): 760-800 ACT: 31-34 ED: Yes, EA: No	BS Anthropology & Human Biology, Biology, Biophysics, Chemistry, Global Health, Neuroethics, Neuroscience & Behavioral Bio, Nursing, Nutrition, Psychology	Emory meets 100% need; 61% receive financial aid; CSS, FAFSA, Work Study Robert W. Woodruff Dean's Achievement Scholarship, George W. Jenkins Scholarship, Liberal Arts Scholarship, Oxford Scholars Program, Lettie Pate Whitehead Scholarships Internships, Co-Ops; Science Seminars, Multiple state-of-the-art lab. The Center for Disease Control is adjacent to the Emory campus.
University of Georgia 210 S Jackson St. Athens, GA 30602 *uga.edu* Public UG: ~31,513 Total: ~42,400	Admit Rate: 37% GPA: 4.03-4.33 SAT (ERW): 620-730 SAT (M): 660-740 ACT: 29-34 ED: No, EA: Yes	BS Biochemistry & Molecular Bio, Biology, Biochemical Engineering, Biological Eng, Biomedical Eng, Chemistry, Cognitive Science, Neuroscience, Psychology	UGA awards merit-based scholarships. Recently, UGA offered $35.2+ million in grants, scholarships, & awards to 14% of first-year students based on GPA/tests Neuro/Psych Labs: Clinical Affective Neuroscience Lab, (fMRI, EEG, ECG, EDA) Regenerative Bioscience Center Research: Alzheimer's & Parkinson's, Brain Injury, Imaging, Nervous System, Neurodegenerative Conditions, Novel Treatments, Regenerative Medicine
Tulane University Gibson Hall 210 6823 St Charles Ave. New Orleans, LA 70118 *tulane.edu/* Private UG: ~8,549 Total: ~14,472	Admit Rate: 13% GPA: 4.3 SAT (ERW): 690-760 SAT (M): 700-780 ACT: 31-35 ED: Yes, EA: Yes	BS, BSE Biology, Biological Chemistry, Biomedical Eng, Cell & Molecular Biology, Chemical Eng, Chemistry, Cognitive Science, Neuroscience, Psychology	Merit & Need-Based Scholarships from $1,000 to full tuition; separate appl, essay, or project required for some. Psych/Neuro Labs: Tulane Brain Inst, Clinical Neuroscience Research Center; extensive computer facilities & lab spaces dedicated to psych research. Research: Neurodegenerative Diseases, Cognitive Neuroscience, Brain Devt, Novel Therapies for Stroke, Dementia, & Traumatic Brain Injury

College, Address & Website Public/Private Enrollment	Admit Rate, Average GPA, SAT/ACT, ED/EA	Related Undergrad Majors	Additional Information
Johns Hopkins University 3400 N. Charles St., Mason Hall, Baltimore, MD 21218-2683 *jhu.edu* Private UG: ~6,161 Total: ~29,786	Admit Rate: 5.7% GPA: 4.0-4.4 SAT (ERW): 720-760 SAT (M): 760-800 ACT: 34-36 ED: Yes, EA: No	BS Biology, Biomedical Engineering, Chemical Engineering, Chemistry, Cognitive Science, Molecular & Cellular Biology Neuroscience, Psychology	JHU meets 100% need; grants: the Clark Scholarship & Hodson Gilliam Success Scholarship; merit-based awards: The Hodson Trust Scholarship, Charles R. Westgate Scholarship in Eng, National Fellowships Program, ROTC Research: Biopsychology, Cognitive Psychology, Developmental Psychology, Cellular & Molecular Neuroscience, Devt Neuroscience, Systems, Cognitive, & Computational Neuroscience, Neurobiology of Disease, Neural Circuits
Duke University Office of Admissions, 2138 Campus Drive, Box 90588 Durham, NC 27708 *duke.edu/* Private UG: ~6,523 Total: ~17,499	Admit Rate: 5.4% GPA: 4.17 SAT (ERW): 740-760 SAT (M): 750-800 ACT: 34-35 ED: Yes, EA: No	BS Biology, Biochemistry, Biomedical Engineering, Chemistry, Neuroscience, PreMed Track, Psychology, Minors: Machine Learning & Artifi cial Intelligence	21% of first-year students attend tuition-free. Duke meets 100% need. Other expenses include study away, summer study, and equipment. Merit scholarships are offerred. Duke Institute for Brain Sciences Research: Attention, Clinical Psych, Cognition & the Brain, Developmental Psych, Emotion, Executive Function, Language, Social Psych, Systems & Integrative Neuroscience; Memory, Morality, Motor Control, Perception
University of North Carolina Jackson Hall, 174 Country Club Rd, Chapel Hill, NC 27514 *unc.edu/* Public UG: ~20,681 Total: ~32,234	Admit Rate: 15% GPA: 3.9 SAT (ERW): 640-730 SAT (M): 630-750 ACT: 29-33 ED: No, EA: Yes	BA, BS Biochemistry, Biology, Chemistry, Neuroscience, Psychology	60% graduate w/no loan debt; stipends for faculty-guided research, Scholarships include Carolina Covenant, Chancellor's Science & Abrams, and Division Grants Research: Behavioral & Integrative Neuroscience, Clinical Psych, Cognitive Psychology, Developmental Psychology, Quantitative Psych, Social Psychology UNC advances psychology & neuroscience; interdisciplinary collaboration & innovative research

SOUTH

PSYCHOLOGY PROGRAMS

College, Address & Website Public/Private Enrollment	Admit Rate, Average GPA, SAT/ACT, ED/EA	Related Undergrad Majors	Additional Information
Wake Forest University 1533 S Main St, Winston-Salem, NC 27127 wfu.edu/ Private UG: ~5,471 Total: ~9,121	Admit Rate: 21% GPA: 4.1 SAT (ERW): 680-740 SAT (M): 690-760 ACT: 31-35 ED: Yes, EA: No	BS Biology, Biochemistry & Molecular Biology, Biomedical Eng, Materials Science & Eng, Chemical Engineering, Chemistry, Neuroscience, Psychology	WFU meets 100% of financial need; Nearly half of all undergrads receive financial assistance in the form of loans, grants, or both. Merit-aid awards also. Behavioral Neuroscience, Brain-Body. Clinical Neuroscience, Clinical Psych, Cognitive Psych, Developmental Psych, Memory. Movement Disorder Research, Neuroanatomy, Neurobio & Behavior, Neuropharmacology, Personality & Social Psych, Quantitative Psych, Self-Regulation & Well-Being, Stroke Research
Vanderbilt University 2305 West End Avenue, Nashville, TN 37203 admissions.vanderbilt.edu/ Private UG: ~7,175 Total: ~13,640	Admit Rate: 5.1% GPA: 4.2 SAT (ERW): 720-770 SAT (M): 740-790 ACT: 33-35 ED: Yes, EA: No	BS Biochemistry, Biological Sciences, Chemical Biology, Chemistry, Chemical & Biomolecular Engineering, Cognitive Studies, Neuroscience, Psychology	250 Merit-Based Scholarship Winners: Apply after submitting app, full tuition; Freshman Mentor Program, Cancer Center, Chemistry Colloquium Series, Internships, Study Abroad, Vanderbilt Brain Institute Research: Addiction, Anxiety, Clinical Science, Cognition & Cognitive Neuroscience, Cognition in Context, Devel. Neuroscience, Memory, Motor Functions, Neuroendocrine Signaling, Neuroengineering, Quantitative Methods, Sensory Functions, Sleep
Rice University 6100 Main Street, Houston, TX 77005 admission.rice.edu/ Private UG: ~4,800 Total: ~8,800	Admit Rate: 8% GPA: 4.2 SAT (ERW): 750-770 SAT (M): 760-790 ACT: 34-35 ED: Yes, EA: No	BS Biochemistry, Biology, Biomedical Eng, Cell Biology, Chemical Eng, Chemistry, Genetics, Integrative Biology, Neuroscience, Psychology	Incomes below $75,000 receive aid covering full tuition, fees, room/board; $75,000-$140,000 receive aid covering full tuition; 140,000-$200,000 receive grants covering half of their tuition. Rice has 11 self-governing residential colleges w/living, dining, & activities. A faculty member serves as a liaison. Traditions, school spirit, gardens, involvement, honor code, races, events

PSYCHOLOGY PROGRAMS

College, Address & Website Public/Private Enrollment	Admit Rate, Average GPA, SAT/ACT, ED/EA	Related Undergrad Majors	Additional Information
Southern Methodist University 6425 Boaz Lane, Dallas, TX 75205 *www.smu.edu* Private UG: ~7,285 Total: ~12,116	Admit Rate: 61% GPA: 3.75 SAT (ERW): 660-730 SAT (M): 660-750 ACT: 30-34 ED: Yes, EA: Yes	BA, BS Biochemistry, Biological Sciences, Biomedical/ Mechanical Eng, Chemical Eng, Chemistry, Neuroscience, Psychology	SMU offers need & merit scholarships; average aid pkg ~$56,000; President's Scholar Award, Hunt Leadership Prog, Distinguished Scholarship, Second Century Scholarship, National Merit, IB Scholars, Departmental Scholarships Research: Aging, Biological Bases of Beh, Clinical & Cognitive Psychology, Comp. Neuroscience, Developmental Psych, Health Psych, Neuroendocrinology, Neuroeng, Neuropharmacology, Neurophys, Personality, Social Psych
University of Texas at Austin 101 East 21st St Austin, TX 78712 *utexas.edu* Public UG: ~42,444 Total: ~51,913	Admit Rate: 11% GPA: 3.8 (unwt) SAT (ERW): 610-730 SAT (M): 620-750 ACT: 29-34 ED: No, EA: Yes	BS Biochemistry, Biology, Biomedical Engineering, Chemical Eng, Chemistry, Neuroscience, Psychology	UT offers over 3,000 scholarships to incoming and current students. Neuro/Psych Labs: Machine Learning Lab, Artificial Intelligence Lab, Texas Robotics, Texas Quantum Institute Research: Addiction, AI (computer vision, haptics, robotics, natural language processing), Brain & Behavior, Cell/ Molecular Neuroscience, Clinical Psychology, Cognition, Brain, & Behavior, Learning & Memory, Sensory/Motor Systems, Social Personality Psychology
University of Virginia 190 McCormick Rd, Peabody Hall Charlottesville, VA 22904 *virginia.edu/* Public UG: ~17,618 Total: ~25,944	Admit Rate: 16.4% GPA: 4.31 SAT (ERW): 700-760 SAT (M): 710-780 ACT: 32-35 ED: Yes, EA: Yes	BS Behavioral Neuroscience, Biology, Biochemistry Biomedical Engineering, Chemical Eng, Chemistry, Cognitive Science, Psychology	UVA has endowed need-based & merit scholarships; automatic consideration. Scholarships for current students & hardship scholarships available. Research: Cellular & Computational. Neuroscience, Clinical Treatments, Lifespan Development, Human Neuroscience, Neuronal Circuits, & Behavior, Neurodegeneration & Aging, Neurogenomics, Neurotechnology & Therapeutics, Plasticity, Social Determinants of Health, Social Psychology, Systems Neuroscience

SOUTH

CHAPTER 15

REGION FOUR

WEST

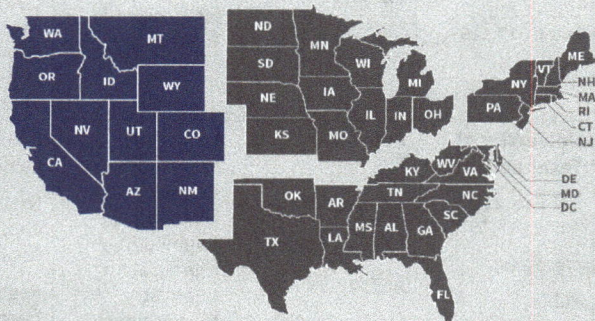

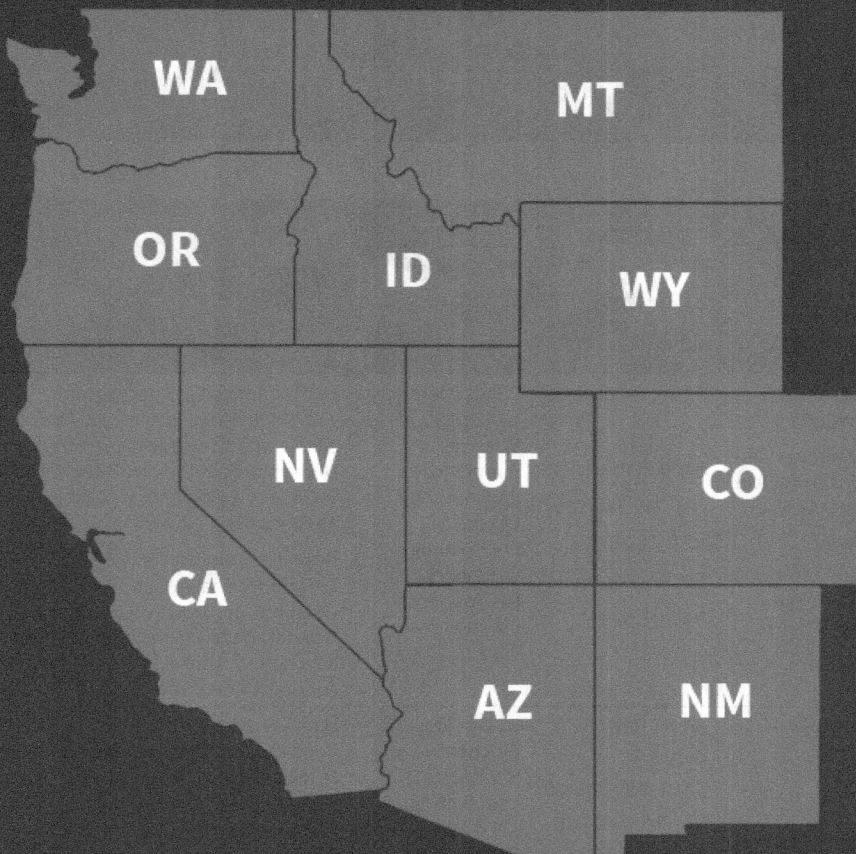

24 Programs | **13** States

PSYCHOLOGY PROGRAMS

College, Address & Website Public/Private Enrollment	Admit Rate, Average GPA, SAT/ACT, ED/EA	Related Undergrad Majors	Additional Information
Arizona State University Student Services 1151 S Forest Ave Tempe, AZ 85281 *asu.edu* Public UG: ~114,484 Total: ~145,655	Admit Rate: 88% GPA: 3.5 SAT (ERW): 540-680 SAT (M): 580-700 ACT: 21-28 ED: No, EA: No Rolling: Yes	BS Biochemistry, Biological Sciences, Biomedical Engineering, Chemical Engineering, Chemistry, Neuroscience, Psychology	ASU's financial aid package is ~$17,000; ~ 51% receive aid. Merit scholarships include: New American University Scholarship, National Merit, President's, Provost's, & Dean's Awards as well as 20 Finn Awards Research: Adolescent Stress & Emotion, Behavioral Neuroscience, Cognitive Sci, Decision Neuroscience, Developmental Psychology, Health Psychology, Learning & Devt, Memory & Aging, Perception, Social Psychology
University of Arizona 1200 E. University Blvd, Tucson, AZ 85721 *arizona.edu/ admissions* Public UG: ~45,025 Total: ~56,544	Admit Rate: 86% GPA: 3.5 SAT (ERW): 570-680 SAT (M): 570-690 ACT: 21-28 ED: No, Rolling: Yes	BS Biology, Biochemistry, Biomedical Engineering, Chemical Engineering, Chemistry, Neuroscience & Cognitive Science, Psychological Science	U of A ensures affordability by offering need & merit scholarships. About 83% receive aid w/75% receiving an ave of $10,415. Merit awards include: Wildcat Tuition Awards, AZ Tuition Awards, National Scholars Tuition Awards Neuro/Psych Labs: Neurology Core Lab, Stem Cell Lab, Psychophysiology Lab, Cognition & Neuroimaging Lab Research: Aging, Behavior, Cognition, Computational Modeling, Drug Development, Emotion, Language, Learning, Memory, Neurodegeneration, Sensory Processing
Claremont McKenna College Kravis Center 888 Columbia Ave. Claremont, CA 91711 *cmc.edu/* Private UG: ~1,388	Admit Rate: 9.6% GPA: 4.0+ SAT (ERW): 720-750 SAT (M): 750-780 ACT: 33-35 ED: Yes, EA: No	BS Biology, Biochemistry, Chemistry, Neuroscience, Psychological Sciences, and a 3+2 Engineering Program	CMC meets 100% of the demonstrated financial need w/average $65,837. About 48% received financial aid. Merit aid includes $15,000 McKenna Scholars, & full-tuition Seaver Scholars Research: Applied Psychology, Autism, Cognitive Neuroscience, Cultural Influence on Mental Health, Decision Neuroscience, Developmental Psychology, Human Learning & Memory, Leadership & Organizational Psychology, Neuroeconomics, Social Psychology

College, Address & Website	Admit Rate, Average GPA, SAT/ACT, ED/EA	Related Undergrad Majors	Additional Information
Occidental College Collins House 1600 Campus Rd. L.A., CA 90041 *oxy.edu/* Private UG: ~2,000	Admit Rate: 44% GPA: 3.65 (unwt) SAT (ERW): 690-750 SAT (M): 690-770 ACT: 31-34 ED: Yes, EA: No	BS Biochemistry, Biology, Chemistry, Cognitive Science, Neuroscience, Psychology	Oxy meets 100% need w/ave award of $51,951, also Community Impact, Honors, Trustee, President's & Leadership Awards Research: Clinical Psychology & Mental Health, Computational Neuroscience & Machine Learning, Conceptual Devt & Cognitive Psychology, Health-Risk Behaviors in Adolescents & Young Adults, Multisensory Perception & Cognition, Neurobiology & Neural Development, Psychology of Art and Aesthetics, Social Perception & Intergroup Relations
Pepperdine University 24255 PCH Malibu, CA 90263 *pepperdine.edu* Private UG: ~3,533 Total: ~8,976	Admit Rate: 49% GPA: 3.68-3.89 SAT (ERW): 670-770 SAT (M): 680-770 ACT: 30-33 ED: No, EA: Yes	BS, BS Biology, Biochemistry, Chemistry, Nursing, Psychology, 3/2 Engineering Program	Pepperdine's average financial aid package is about $49,123 and 85-90% receive aid. Merit Aid includes: George Pepperdine Achievement Award & Departmental Scholarships Neuro/Psych Labs: ARC Center for Positive Psychology, Couples, Family, and Children, & Forensic Psychology, Culture & Trauma Research Lab, Social Brain Research Init, Neuropsychology Research Group (neurochemistry, brain activity, & cognition in humans)
Pomona College 333 N. College Way, Claremont, CA 91711 *pomona.edu/ admissions-aid* Private UG: ~1,761	Admit Rate: 6.8% GPA: N/A SAT (ERW): 730-770 SAT (M): 750-800 ACT: 33-35 ED: Yes, EA: No	BS Biology, Chemistry, Cognitive Science, Molecular Biology, Neuroscience, Psychological Science, 3/2 Engineering Program	Pomona College offers need-based aid & does not offer merit-based scholarships for academic or athletic achievements. About 54% receive an average award of ~$71,000. Neuro/Psych Labs: MIC Lab (fMRI & fNIRS), Culture, Race, & Brain Lab, & the Neuroscience & Psychology Computer Labs Research: Aging, Behavior, Brain, Bilingualism, Cell Science, Cognition, Emotion, Language, Memory, Neuropharmacology, Social Behavior & Interaction, Systems Neuroscience

WEST

PSYCHOLOGY PROGRAMS

College, Address & Website	Admit Rate, Average GPA, SAT/ACT, ED/EA	Related Undergrad Majors	Additional Information
San Diego State University 5500 Campanile Dr San Diego, CA 92182 sdsu.edu Public UG: ~32,896 Total: ~38,000	Admit Rate: 32% GPA: 3.73 SAT/ACT: Not Considered ED: No, EA: No	BA, BS Biology, Chemistry (Emphasis in Biochemistry), Nursing, Psychology (Emphasis in Neuroscience) Minor: Cognitive & Behavioral Neuroscience	SDSU's ave aid pkg is ~$14,000; ~53% receiving aid; net price $13,000. SDSU Merit Scholarship, Axtec Scholarship Neuro/Psych Labs: Brain Development Imaging Lab, Center for Clinical & Cognitive Neuroscience, Translational Emotion Neuroscience & Development Lab, Lab for Language & Cognitive Neuroscience Research: Aging, Alcohol, Behavior, Cognition, Developmental Psychology, Experimental Psychopathology, Health Psychology, Neuropsychology, Social Psychology
Santa Clara University 500 El Camino Real Santa Clara, CA 95053 scu.edu Private UG: ~6,115 Total: ~9,178	Admit Rate: 47% GPA: 3.73 SAT (ERW): 670-730 SAT (M): 680-750 ACT: 30-33 ED: No, EA: Yes	BS Biochemistry, Biology, Bioengineering, Chemistry, Neuroscience, Psychology, PreHealth Pathway	SCU meets 100% need from Cal Grant applicants, as well as the Presidential (full tuition) Scholarship, Provost, Dean's & Johnson Scholars Award Neuro/Psych: Applied Spirituality Inst, Neural Circuits, Systems, & Behavior Lab, Sobrato Campus for Discovery & Innovation Research: Addiction, Anxiety, Neural Mechanisms of Behavior along with advanced labs for neuroscience research
Stanford University 355 Galvez Street, Stanford, CA 94305 *stanford.edu/* Private UG: ~7,554 Total: ~17,469	Admit Rate: 4% GPA: 3.96 SAT (ERW): 750-780 SAT (M): 750-800 ACT: 34-35 ED: No, REA: Yes	BS Biochemistry, Biology, Bioengineering, Chemical Engineering, Chemistry, Neuroscience, Psychology, Symbolic Systems	Families with incomes of $150,000 or less attend college tuition free. Stanford does not offer merit scholarships, 58% receive aid The France-Stanford Ctr for Interdiscip Studies partners w/French Ministry of Foreign Affairs for Humanities & STEM Neuro/Psych Labs: Cognitive & Systems Neuroscience Lab, Center for Interdisciplinary Brain Sciences Research, Media & Personality Lab, Mind & Body Lab, NeuroAI Lab, Neurosciences Inst, Psychophysiology Lab, Social Learning Lab, Social Neuroscience Lab, Well-Being Lab

College, Address & Website	Admit Rate, Average GPA, SAT/ACT, ED/EA	Related Undergrad Majors	Additional Information
University of California, Berkeley Berkeley, CA 94720 *berkeley.edu/* Public UG: ~33,078 Total: ~45,699	Admit Rate: 11% GPA: 4.31-4.65 SAT/ACT Not Considered ED: No, EA: No	BA Bioeng, Chemical Bio, Chemical Eng, Chemistry, Cognitive Science, Integrative Bio, Molecular & Cell Biology, Neurobiology, Psychology	Berkeley, Fiat Lux, & Middle-Class Scholarships - no additional app required. Complete the FAFSA or CA Dream Act Application. Regents & Chancellor's - $2,500 for scholars w/o financial need. Neuro/Psych Labs: Brain Imaging Center, Neuroscience Institute, Institute of Cognitive & Brain Sciences, Center for Theoretical Neuroscience
University of California, Davis One Shields Avenue, Davis, CA 95616 *ucdavis.edu/ admissions* Public UG: ~32,200 Total: ~41,239	Admit Rate: 42.1% GPA: 4.0-4.26 SAT/ACT Not Considered ED: No, EA: No	BA, BS Biol Sci Biochemistry & Molecular Biology, Biomedical Eng, Cell Biology, Chemical Eng, Chemistry, Cognitive Sci, Neurobiology, Physiology & Behavior, Psychology	$4 million scholarships ($100 - $14,000). Merit scholarships include academics, activities, career interests, geographic origin, & talent Psych/Neuro Labs: Center for Mind & Brain, Center for Neuroscience, MIND Institute, Cognitive Neuroscience of Language Laboratory Research: ADHD, Autism, Cognition, Human Brain Mapping, Imaging, Language, and Perception
University of California, Irvine 4000 Mesa Rd., Irvine, CA 92697 *uci.edu* Public UG: ~29,303 Total: ~37,350	Admit Rate: 28.8% GPA: 4.07-4.28 SAT/ACT Not Considered ED: No, EA: No	BS Biochem & Molecular Bio, Biological Sci, Biomedical Eng, Chemical Eng, Chemistry, Developmental & Cell Biology, Genetics, Human Bio, Microbiology & Immunology, Nursing, Psychological Science	Scholarships; Henry Samueli Endowed Scholarships; Regents, Chancellor's Excellence, Director's Scholarship – No additional application necessary Research: Autism, Cognitive & Behavioral Neuroscience, Cognitive Psychology, Developmental Psych, Human Cognition, Neurodegenerative Disease, Neuroimaging & Brain Mapping, Social Psychology, Stem Cell Research in Neuroscience

WEST

PSYCHOLOGY PROGRAMS

College, Address & Website	Admit Rate, Average GPA, SAT/ACT, ED/EA	Related Undergrad Majors	Additional Information
University of California, Los Angeles 405 Hilgard Ave Los Angeles, CA 90095 *ucla.edu/* Public UG: ~33,040 Total: ~46,678	Admit Rate: 8.8% GPA: 4.20-4.31 SAT/ACT Not Considered ED: No, EA: No	BS Biochem, Bio, Bioeng, Chemical Eng, Chemistry, Cognitive Science, Human Biology & Society, Microbiology, Immunology & Molec. Genetics, Molecular, Cell, & Dev Biology, Neuroscience, Nursing, Physiological Sci, Psychobiology, Psychology	Need-based scholarships, complete an online "UCLA Scholarship Application" available through MyUCLA & submit a FAFSA or Dream Act application by the March 2 priority deadline every year. Adv Equipment: Electrophysiology, Eye-Tracking, Neuroimaging (fMRI, PET, Psychophysiology Recording) Optogenetics Research: Behavioral & Cognitive Neuroscience, Clinical Psych, Cognitive Psych, Develop. Psych, Health Psych, Neurogenetics, Neuroimaging & Brain Mapping, Quantitative Psych, Social Psychology, Psychology of Addiction
University of California, San Diego 9500 Gilman Drive, La Jolla, CA 92093 *ucsd.edu/* Public UG: ~34,955 Total: ~45,273	Admit Rate: 26.8% GPA: 4.11-4.29 SAT/ACT Not Considered ED: No, EA: No	BS Biochemistry, Bioengineering Bioinformatics, Biosystems, Biotechnology, Chemical Eng, Chemistry, Cognitive, Human Biology, Microbiology, Molec. & Cell Bio, Neurobiology, Psychology	Regents & Chancellor's Scholarships offer money w/o financial need; Ellen & Roger Revelle Scholarship. Complete qs in portal & submit a FAFSA or Dream Act apply by March 2 priority deadline yearly Research: Cognitive & Behavioral Neuroscience, Cognitive Psychology, Developmental Psychology, Autism, Neurodegenerative Disease & Disorder Research, Neuroimaging & Brain Maps, Social Psychology, Stem Cell Research in Neuroscience, Human Cognition
University of San Diego 5998 Alcala Park, San Diego, CA 92110 *sandiefo.edu/* Private UG: ~5,800 Total: ~9,100	Admit Rate: 50% GPA: 4.02 SAT (ERW): 600-680 SAT (M): 590-690 ACT: 26-31 ED: No, EA: No	BS Behavioral Neuroscience, Biology, Chemistry, Cognitive Science, Nursing, Psychological Sciences	About 200 million was awarded to students w/an average of ~$40,000; about 2/3 comes directly from USD. Merit scholarships are about $20,000-$30,000. Research: Behavioral Medicine, Behavioral Neuroscience, Clinical Psychology, Developmental Psychology, Health Psychology, Neuroscience, Cognition, & Behavior, Sleep Research, Social Psychology, Social Psychology,

College, Address & Website	Admit Rate, Average GPA, SAT/ACT, ED/EA	Related Undergrad Majors	Additional Information
University of San Francisco 2800 Turk Blvd, San Francisco, CA 94118 *www.usf.edu* Private UG: ~6,000 Total: ~7,500	Admit Rate: 51% GPA: 3.61 SAT (ERW): 610-670 SAT (M): 630-700 ACT: 26-31 ED: No, EA: Yes	BS Biochemistry, Biology, Chemistry, Engineering, Neuroscience, Nursing, Psychology	USF provides both merit-based and need-based scholarships for undergraduates. Undergraduate Merit Scholarships ($18,000-$31,000), Comprehensive Package Psych/Neuro Labs: AI Lab & Clinical Neuroinformatics Lab Research: AI, Cognitive Science, Data Science, Neuroinformatics, Neuroscience, Human Motor Learning, & Science Communication.
University of Southern California Univ Park Campus Los Angeles, CA 90089 *admission.usc.edu/* Private UG: ~21,000 Total: ~47,000	Admit Rate: 9.2% GPA: 3.83 SAT (ERW): 720-760 SAT (M): 730-780 ACT: 32-35 ED: No, EA: Yes	BS Biochemistry, Biology, Biomedical Eng, Chemical Engineering, Chemistry, Cognitive Science, Molecular & Cellular Eng, Neuroscience, Psychology	Merit scholarships for academic, art, or athletic talent. Internships, research, fellowships, summer programs; Global Summit, Grand Challenges; Ctrs, Inst, Competitions & Entrepreneurship Research: Affective/Decision Neurosci, Behavioral & Cognitive Neuroscience, Clinical Science, Computational Neuroimaging, Health Psychology, Language & Literacy Development, Neuroscience, Developmental Psychology, Social Psychology
University of Colorado, Boulder Regent Admin Center 125, Boulder, 552 UCB CO 80309 *colorado.edu* Public UG: ~31,960 Total: ~38,428	Admit Rate: 81% GPA: 3.67 SAT (ERW): 580-690 SAT (M): 600-690 ACT: 25-31 ED: No, EA: Yes	BA, BS Biology, Biochemistry, Biomedical Engineering, Chemical Engineering, Chemistry, Neuroscience, Psychology	CUB scholarship application opens Nov 1 - closes Feb 1 or March 1 Equipment: fMRI (high-res), EEG, Computational Modeling, Eye-Tracking Research: Behavioral & Cognitive Neuroscience, Circadian Neurobiology, Clinical Psychology, Computational Neuroscience, Develop. Psychology, Neurobiology of Social Behavior & Stress, Neural Mechanisms of Motivated Behavior & Substance Abuse, Social Psychology

WEST

PSYCHOLOGY PROGRAMS

College, Address & Website	Admit Rate, Average GPA, SAT/ACT, ED/EA	Related Undergrad Majors	Additional Information
University of Hawaii at Manoa 2600 Campus Rd Honolulu, HI 96822 *hawaii.edu* Public UG: ~15,000 Total: ~19,500	Admit Rate: 80% GPA: N/A SAT (ERW): 530-640 SAT (M): 540-650 ACT: 20-27 ED: No, EA: No Rolling: Yes	BA, BS Biology, Biochemistry, Biomedical Engineering, Chemical Engineering, Chemistry, Nursing, Psychology	UH Need & Merit Money, Academic Merit Scholarships, Kuaana Tuition Waiver, Higher Education Scholarship Program, Yamamura Scholarship Psych/Neuro Labs: Brain & Behavior Lab, Cognition, Neuroscience, & Social Proram, Intergroup Social Perception Lab Brain Imaging, EEG, fMRI, tDCS, Behavioral Neuroscience Facilities, Cutting Edge Resources
University of New Mexico 1155 Univ. Blvd, SE Albuquerque, NM 87106 *unm.edu* Public UG: ~19,500 Total: ~26,000	Admit Rate: 78% GPA: 3.4 SAT (ERW): 480-590 SAT (M): 440-570 ACT: 19-26 ED: No, EA: No Rolling: Yes	BS Biology, Biochemistry, Biomedical Engineering, Chemical Engineering, Chemistry, Nursing, Psychology	NM Residents & Non-Resident Grants: Scholarships (Regents & Presidential Scholarships); Amigo Scholarship, Transfer & Departmental Scholarships Psych/Neuro Labs: Clinical Neuroscience Core, Psychology Clinical Neuroscience Center, Mind Research Network, Center for Brain Recovery & Repair, TMS, MRI Research: Neural basis of intelligence, cognitive/affective psychopathology
University of Nevada, Reno 1664 N. Virginia St. Reno, NV 89557 *unr.edu* Public UG: ~18,000 Total: ~20,000	Admit Rate: 85% GPA: 3.44 SAT (ERW): 540-660 SAT (M): 530-650 ACT: 20-26 ED: No, EA: Yes	BS Biochemistry, Biology, Biomedical Engineering, Chemical Engineering, Chemistry, Nursing, Psychology	Financial aid for eligible students, Department of Psychology Scholarships, Dean's Scholarship, Continuing Scholarships Psych/Neuro Labs: Neuroimaging Core (MRI, EEG, 3T Scanners, NIRS Systems), Center for Integrative Neuroscience, Cognitive & Brain Sciences Program Research: Attention, Behavior, Cognitive, Neuroscience, Memory, Neuropsychology. Perception, Psychophysics, Social Psychology

College, Address & Website	Admit Rate, Average GPA, SAT/ACT, ED/EA	Related Undergrad Majors	Additional Information
University of Oregon 1217 U of Oregon Eugene, OR 97403 *www.uoregon.edu* Public UG: ~20,626 Total: ~24,462	Admit Rate: 85% GPA: 3.46-4.06 SAT (ERW): 560-660 SAT (M): 540-650 ACT (C): 22-28 ED: No, EA: Yes	BA, BS Biology, Biochemistry, Biomedical Engineering, Chemical Engineering, Chemistry, Neuroscience, Psychology	UO aids students in access & affordability Department of Psychology Scholarships, University-Wide Scholarships Psych/Neuro Labs: Institute of Neuroscience, Lab of Cognitive Neuroscience, Brain & Memory Lab, Developmental Social Neuroscience Lab, Interdisciplinary Cognitive Sciences, Oregon Memory Group, Human Cognition, Neural Systems
University of Utah 201 S 1460 E, Salt Lake City, UT 84112 *utah.edu/* Public UG: ~28,064 Total: ~36,881	Admit Rate: 87% GPA: 3.68 SAT (ERW): 590-700 SAT (M): 590-700 ACT (C): 22-29 ED: No, EA: Yes Rolling: Yes	BS, BS Biology, Biochemistry, Biomedical Engineering, Chemical Engineering, Chemistry, Nursing, Psychology	UU scholarships; departmental scholarships, & alumni association scholarships. Equipment: fMRI, PET, EEG, Eye-Tracking, Scanners, Two-Way Mirrors, Animal Modeling, Adv Microscopy Research: Behavioral & Cognitive Neuroscience,Cellular Neuroscience, Clinical Psych, Develop. Psychology, Neurobiology of Disease, Social Psych
University of Washington 1400 NE Campus Parkway, Seattle, WA, 98195 *washington.edu* Public UG: ~45,097 Total: ~62,763	Admit Rate: 42.5% GPA: 3.74-3.98 SAT (ERW): 640-740 SAT (M): 640-750 ACT: 30-34 ED: No, EA: No	BS Biochemistry, Biology, Bioengineering, Chemical Engineering, Chemistry, Neuroscience, Nursing, Psychology	About 600 students rec scholarships; UW About 100 undergrad Academic Excellence Awards. Non-Resident Purple & Gold Scholarships; Honors Program funds; Washington NASA Space Grant; Dept & UW Scholarships. Research: Adult/Child Clinical Psychology, Cognition & Perception, Computational Neuroscience, Developmental Psychology, Neural Systems & Behavior, Neurology, Quantitative Psychology, Social & Personality

WEST

CHAPTER 16

ALPHABETICAL LIST OF PROFILED PROGRAMS

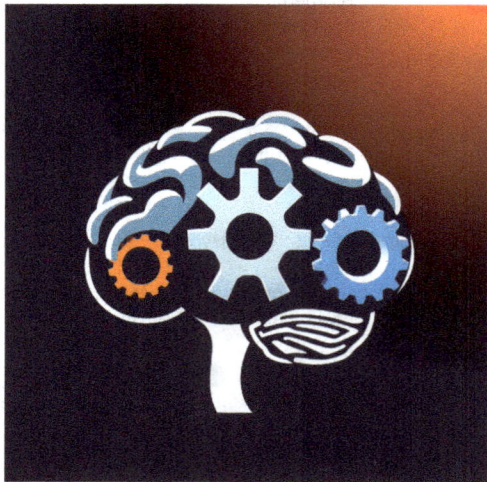

School
Amherst College
Boston College
Boston University
Brandeis University
Brown University
Cal Tech
Carnegie Mellon University
Case Western Reserve University
Columbia University
Cornell University
Dartmouth College
Duke University
Emory University
Harvard University
Johns Hopkins University
Lehigh University
Massachusetts Institute of Technology
New York University
Northeastern University
Northwestern University
Princeton University
Rice University
Stanford University
Swarthmore College

School
Tufts University
University of Arizona
University of California, Berkeley
University of California, Davis
University of California, Irvine
University of California, Los Angeles
University of California, San Diego
University of Chicago
University of Colorado, Boulder
University of Illinois (UIUC)
University of Michigan
University of North Carolina, Chapel Hill
University of Notre Dame
University of Pennsylvania
University of Rochester
University of Southern California
University of Texas at Austin
University of Utah
University of Virginia
University of Washington
University of Wisconsin
Vanderbilt University
Washington University in St. Louis
Yale University

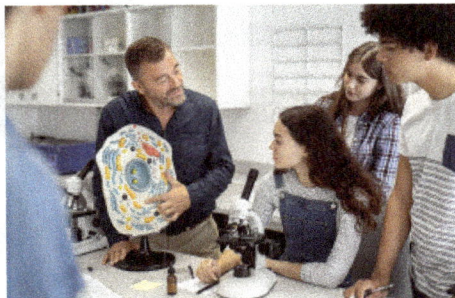

CHAPTER 17

SELECTED U.S. COLLEGES FOR PSYCHOLOGY

	School			School
1	Stanford University		39	Boston College
2	Harvard University		40	Emory University
3	Yale University		41	UC Davis
4	Princeton University		42	University of Georgia
5	UC Berkeley		43	Claremont McKenna College
6	University of Pennsylvania		44	Northeastern University
7	UCLA		45	Tufts University
8	Vanderbilt University		46	Wake Forest University
9	Duke University		47	University of Minnesota
10	Rice University		48	Barnard College
11	Columbia University		49	San Diego State University (SDSU)
12	Cornell University		50	University of South Florida
13	Northwestern University		51	University of Central Florida
14	MIT		52	Williams College
15	Dartmouth University		53	Texas A&M University
16	University of Michigan		54	Tulane University
17	University of Illinois (UIUC)		55	Amherst College
18	NYU		56	Wesleyan University
19	University of Southern California		57	University of Alabama
20	Brown University		58	The College of William & Mary
21	Washington University in St. Louis		59	University of Pittsburgh (Pitt)
22	Boston University		60	Swarthmore College
23	Georgetown University		61	Wellesley College
25	University of Chicago		62	John Jay College
25	University of Florida		63	Bryn Mawr College
26	UC San Diego (UCSD)		64	Indiana University Bloomington
27	Carnegie Mellon University		65	Purdue University
28	UNC Chapel Hill		66	Villanova University
29	Cornell University		67	Clemson University
30	UC Irvine		68	University of Richmond
31	University of Virginia		69	Occidental College
32	Johns Hopkins University		70	Washington & Lee University
33	University of Texas at Austin		71	Haverford College
34	University of Notre Dame		72	Bowdoin College
35	University of Miami		73	Southern Methodist University
36	Florida International University		74	University of Houston
37	Pomona College		75	Davidson College
38	University of Washington			

CHAPTER 18

SELECTED PROGRAMS FOR SPORT PSYCHOLOGY

SELECTED COLLEGES OFFERING SPORTS PSYCHOLOGY

	School
A–C	☐ Adams State University – BA and minor in Sport Psychology
	☐ Arizona State University – BS in Counseling and Applied Psychological Science with a concentration in Sports and Performance Counseling
	☐ Ball State University – Minor in Sport and Exercise Psychology
	☐ Barry University – BS in Applied Sport and Exercise Sciences with a concentration in Sport, Exercise, and Performance Psychology
	☐ California Baptist University – BS in Sport and Performance Psychology (available in-person and online)
	☐ California State University, Fresno – Sport psychology coursework as part of Kinesiology
	☐ California State University, Long Beach – BS in Kinesiology with an option in Sport Psychology
	☐ California State University, Sacramento – MS in Kinesiology with coursework in Sport Psychology
	☐ California State University, San Bernardino – MA in Psychological Science with emphasis on performance psychology research
	☐ California State University, San Marcos – BA in Kinesiology with courses in sport and exercise psychology
	☐ Cornell College – BA in Kinesiology with a concentration in Exercise Science and emphasis in Sport, Exercise, and Performance Psychology
D–I	☐ Ithaca College – Minor in Sport and Exercise Psychology
K–M	☐ Keene State College – Minor in Sport and Exercise Psychology
	☐ Kent State University – BS and minor in Sport, Exercise, and Performance Psychology
	☐ Lock Haven University – Minor in Sport and Performance Psychology

	School
	☐ Michigan State University – MS in Kinesiology with a concentration in Psychological Aspects of Sport and Physical Activity
	☐ Miami University (Ohio) – Courses available in sport psychology through Kinesiology and Health
N–R	☐ National University – BA in Sport Psychology (with CMPC-preparatory coursework)
	☐ Pacific Lutheran University – Minor in Exercise and Sport Psychology
	☐ Robert Morris University – BS in Psychology with a concentration in Sport Psychology
	☐ Rowan University – Minor in Psychology of Sport and Exercise
S	☐ Southern Illinois University Edwardsville – Minor in Exercise and Sport Psychology
	☐ Springfield College – MS and M.Ed. in Sport and Exercise Psychology; PhD in Sport and Exercise Psychology
T–U	☐ Texas A&M University – Master's in Kinesiology with concentration in Performance Psychology
	☐ Texas A&M University – Kingsville – BS in Kinesiology with a concentration in Exercise Science/Performance Psychology; Minor in Performance Psychology
	☐ Texas State University – Minor in Sport Psychology
	☐ University of Denver – BA in Kinesiology and Sport Studies, MA in Sport and Performance Psychology
	☐ University of Florida – MS in Applied Physiology and Kinesiology with emphasis in High-Performance Coaching (Sport Psychology emphasis)
	☐ University of Georgia – BS in Exercise and Sport Science, MS in Kinesiology w/concentration in Exercise Psychology
	☐ University of Illinois (UIUC) – BS in Kinesiology w/ specialization in Exercise Psychology & Health Behavior
	☐ University of Iowa – Minor in Sport Studies w/topic related to sport psychology

School	
☐	University of Maryland – BS in Kinesiology w/courses in The Psychology of Sports and Exercise
☐	University of Michigan – BS in Sport Management
☐	University of Minnesota – MS & PhD in Kinesiology w/ emphasis in Sport and Exercise Psychology
☐	University of Montana – Minor in Sport Psychology
☐	University of North Carolina at Greensboro – MS & PhD in Kinesiology with a concentration in Sport and Exercise Psychology
☐	University of North Texas – PhD in Counseling Psychology with an elective cluster in Sport Psychology
☐	University of Olivet – BA and minor in Sports Psychology
☐	University of Tennessee, Knoxville – PhD in Counseling Psychology with sport psychology electives
☐	University of Texas at Austin – BS in Kinesiology w/courses in sport psychology and Exercise & Sport Psychology Laboratory
☐	University of West Florida – Minor in Sport and Exercise Psychology
☐	University of Western States – MS and PsyD programs in Sport and Performance Psychology
☐	University of Wisconsin – MS in Kinesiology w/focus on Exercise Psychology
W ☐	West Texas A&M University – Minor in Sport Psychology
☐	West Virginia University – BS and minor in Sport and Exercise Psychology; PhD in Kinesiology with a concentration in Sport and Exercise Psychology

CHAPTER 19

SELECTED U.S. COLLEGES FOR NEUROSCIENCE

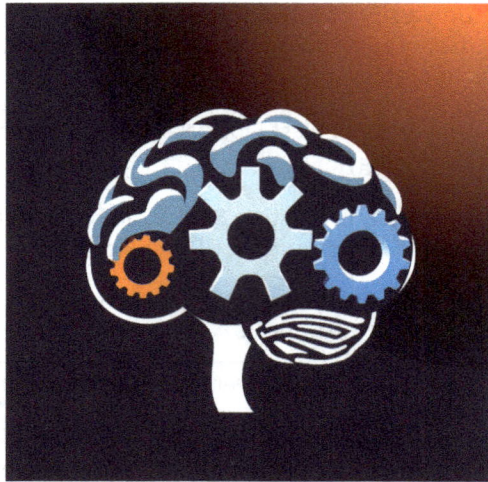

S/N	School	S/N	School
1	MIT	40	University of Minnesota
2	Harvard University	41	University of Florida
3	Stanford University	42	Indiana University, Bloomington
4	Johns Hopkins University	43	University of Texas at Austin
5	Yale University	44	University of Miami
6	Columbia University	45	University of Rochester
7	Dartmouth College	46	Davidson College
8	Brown University	47	Barnard College
9	Rice University	48	Washington & Lee University
10	Vanderbilt University	49	Bowdoin College
11	Princeton University	50	Boston College
12	University of Pennsylvania	51	Wellesley College
13	Duke University	52	Middlebury College
14	Georgetown University	53	Amherst College
15	Washington University in St. Louis	54	Florida State University
16	UC San Diego (UCSD)	55	UC Davis
17	UCLA	56	Hamilton College
18	Pomona College	57	University of Wisconsin
19	Northwestern University	58	Lehigh University
20	Carnegie Mellon University	59	Texas A&M University
21	CalTech	60	Auburn University
22	Johns Hopkins University	61	Ohio State University
23	New York University	62	Case Western Reserve
25	University of Michigan	63	Ohio State University
25	University of Washington	64	University of Maryland
26	Claremont McKenna College	65	Purdue University
27	University of Chicago	66	Tulane University
28	University of Notre Dame	67	University of Alabama
29	University of Southern California	68	University of Virginia
30	Georgia Tech	69	Yeshiva University
31	UC Berkeley	70	Haverford College
32	UC Irvine (UCI)	71	Virginia Tech
33	Boston University	72	Colgate University
34	Swarthmore College	73	Bates College
35	University of Pittsburgh	74	The College of William & Mary
36	Emory University	75	Vassar College
37	UNC Chapel Hill	76	Trinity University
38	Northeastern University	77	Macalester College
39	Cornell University	78	Colby College

CHAPTER 20

ABET ACCREDITED UNIVERSITIES FOR BIOMEDICAL ENGINEERING

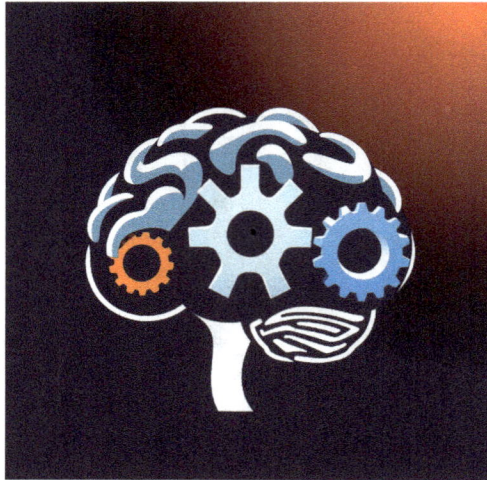

School	Year Accredited
Arizona State University, Tempe, AZ	Oct 1, 1986
Boston University, Boston, MA	Oct 1, 1983
Brown University, Providence, RI	Oct 1, 1973 – Sep 30, 2000, Oct 1, 2004
Bucknell University, Lewisburg, PA	Oct 1, 2007
California Baptist University, Riverside, CA	Oct 1, 2015
California Polytechnic State University, SLO, San Luis Obispo, CA	Oct 1, 2012
Case Western Reserve University, Cleveland, OH	Oct 1, 1977
Catholic University of America, Washington, DC	Oct 1, 1988
City University of New York, City College, New York, NY	Oct 1, 2009
College of New Jersey, Ewing, NJ	Oct 1, 2011
Colorado State University, Fort Collins, CO	Oct 1, 2014
Columbia University, New York, NY	Oct 1, 2005
Drexel University, Philadelphia, PA	Oct 1, 2000
Duke University, Durham, NC	Oct 1, 1972
Duquesne University, Pittsburgh, PA	Oct 1, 2018
Fairfield University, Fairfield, CT	Oct 1, 2017
Florida Institute of Technology, Melbourne, FL	Oct 1, 2014
Florida International University, Miami, FL	Oct 1, 2004
Gannon University, Erie, PA	Oct 1, 2012
The George Washington University, Washington, DC	Oct 1, 2006
Georgia Institute of Technology, Atlanta, GA	Oct 1, 2003
Grand Canyon University, Phoenix, AZ	Oct 1, 2018
Harding University, Searcy, AR	Oct 1, 2014
Illinois Institute of Technology, Chicago, IL	Oct 1, 2007
Indiana Institute of Technology, Fort Wayne, IN	Oct 1, 2010
Indiana University, Indianapolis, IN	Oct 1, 2008
Johns Hopkins University, Baltimore, MD	Oct 1, 1983
Lawrence Technological University, Southfield, MI	May 1, 2011
Louisiana Tech University, Ruston, LA	Oct 1, 1978
Marquette University, Milwaukee, WI	Oct 1, 1983
Marshall University, Huntington, WV	Oct 1, 2020
Miami University, Oxford, OH	Oct 1, 2012
Michigan Technological University, Houghton, MI	Oct 1, 2003
Milwaukee School of Engineering, Milwaukee, WI	Oct 1, 1988
Mississippi State University, Mississippi State, MS	Oct 1, 2017
New Jersey Institute of Technology, Newark, NJ	Oct 1, 2005

School	Year Accredited
North Carolina State University at Raleigh, Raleigh, NC	Oct 1, 2002
Northwestern University, Evanston, IL	Oct 1, 1982
The Ohio State University, Columbus, OH	Oct 1, 2010
Saint Louis University, Saint Louis, MO	May 1, 2005
Pennsylvania State University, University Park, PA	Oct 1, 2007
Polytechnic University of Puerto Rico, San Juan, Puerto Rico	Oct 1, 2018
Purdue University at West Lafayette, West Lafayette, IN	Oct 1, 2006
Rensselaer Polytechnic Institute, Troy, NY	Oct 1, 1972
Rochester Institute of Technology, Rochester, NY	Oct 1, 2014
Rose-Hulman Institute of Technology, Terre Haute, IN	Oct 1, 2005
Rowan University, Glassboro, NJ	Oct 1, 2017
Rutgers University, New Brunswick, NJ	Oct 1, 2005
San Jose State University, San Jose, CA	Oct 1, 2014
Stevens Institute of Technology, Hoboken, NJ	Oct 1, 2008
Stony Brook University, New York, NY	Oct 1, 2004
SUNY Binghamton, Vestal, NY	Oct 1, 2006
SUNY Buffalo, Buffalo, NY	Oct 1, 2013
Texas A&M University, College Station, TX	Oct 1, 1977
Trine University, Angola, IN	Oct 1, 2016
Tufts University, Medford, MA	Oct 1, 2010
Tulane University, New Orleans, LA	Oct 1, 1981
Union College, Schenectady, NY	Oct 1, 2010
University of Akron, Akron, OH	Oct 1, 2000
University of Alabama at Birmingham, Birmingham, AL	Oct 1, 2005
University of Arizona, Tucson, AR	Oct 1, 2014
University of Arkansas, Fayetteville, AR	Oct 1, 2012
University of California, Davis, Davis, CA	Oct 1, 2011
University of California, Irvine, Irvine, CA	Oct 1, 2006
University of Central Oklahoma, Edmond, OK	Oct 1, 2007
University of Cincinnati, Cincinnati, OH	Oct 1, 2003
University of Connecticut, Storrs, CT	Oct 1, 2005
University of Delaware, Newark, DE	Oct 1, 2013
University of the District of Columbia, Washington, DC	Oct 1, 2019
University of Florida, Gainesville, FL	Oct 1, 2016
University of Hartford, West Hartford, CT	Oct 1, 2002
University of Houston, Houston, TX	Oct 1, 2012
University of Iowa, Iowa City, IA	Oct 1, 1984

School	Year Accredited
University of Maine, Orono, ME	Oct 1, 2012
University of Memphis, Memphis, TN	Oct 1, 2008
University of Miami, Coral Gables, FL	Oct 1, 1995
University of Michigan, Ann Arbor, MI	Oct 1, 2004
University of Minnesota - Twin Cities, Minneapolis, MN	Oct 1, 2002
University of Nevada, Reno, Reno, NV	Oct 1, 2018
University of North Texas, Denton, TX	Oct 1, 2017
University of Oklahoma, Norman, OK	Oct 1, 2018
University of Rhode Island, Kingston, RI	Oct 1, 2011
University of Rochester, Rochester, NY	Oct 1, 2002
University of South Carolina, Columbia, SC	May 1, 2010
University of South Florida, Tampa, FL	Oct 1, 2019
University of Southern California, Los Angeles, CA	Oct 1, 2008
University of Tennessee at Knoxville, Knoxville, TN	Oct 1, 2001
University of Texas at Arlington, Arlington, TX	May 1, 2016
University of Texas at Austin, Austin, TX	Oct 1, 2005
University of Texas at Dallas, Richardson, TX	Oct 1, 2014
University of Texas at San Antonio, San Antonio, TX	Oct 1, 2014
University of Utah, Salt Lake City, UT	Oct 1, 2008
University of Vermont, Burlington, VT	Oct 1, 2018
University of Virginia, Charlottesville, VA	Oct 1, 2006
University of Wisconsin - Madison, Madison, WI	Jun 1, 2003
University of Wisconsin - Milwaukee, Milwaukee, WI	Oct 1, 2019
Vanderbilt University, Nashville, TN	Oct 1, 1990
Virginia Commonwealth University, Richmond, VA	Oct 1, 2002
Washington University, Saint Louis, MO	Oct 1, 2004
Wayne State University, Detroit, MI	Oct 1, 2013
Wentworth Institute of Technology, Boston, MA	Oct 1, 2014
West Virginia University, Morgantown, WV	Oct 1, 2016
Western New England University, Springfield, MA	Oct 1, 2004
Wichita State University, Wichita, KS	Oct 1, 2012
Widener University, Chester, PA	Oct 1, 2014
Worcester Polytechnic Institute, Worcester, MA	Oct 1, 2001
Wright State University, Dayton, OH	Oct 1, 1988

CHAPTER 21

ABET ACCREDITED CHEMICAL ENGINEERING PROGRAMS

School	Year Accredited
Akron, University of, Akron, OH	1970
Alabama, University of, Tuscaloosa, AL	1950
Alabama, University of, Huntsville, AL	1986
Arizona, University of, Tucson, AZ	1963
Arizona State University, Tempe, AZ	1966
Arkansas, University of, Fayetteville, AR	1952
Auburn University, Auburn, AL	1950
Brigham Young University, Provo, UT	1961
Brown University, Providence, RI	1985
Bucknell University, Lewisburg, PA	1942
California, University of, Berkeley, CA	1952
California, University of, Davis, CA	1966
California, University of, Irvine, CA	1994
California, University of, Los Angeles, CA	1983
California, University of, Riverside, CA	1995
California, University of, San Diego, CA	1985
California, University of, Santa Barbara, CA	1968
California Institute of Technology, Pasadena, CA	1926
California State Polytechnic University, Pomona, CA	1972
California State University, Long Beach, CA	1980
Carnegie Mellon University, Pittsburgh, PA	1925
Case Western Reserve University, Cleveland, OH	1925
Christian Brothers University, Memphis, TN	1985
Cincinnati, University of, Cincinnati, OH	1925
Clarkson University, Potsdam, NY	1938
Clemson University, Clemson, SC	1959
Cleveland State University, Cleveland, OH	1954 1963 1966
Colorado, University of, Boulder, CO	1950
Colorado School of Mines, Golden, CO (Chemical and Pet. Ref. Eng.)	1956
Colorado State University, Ft. Collins, CO	1981
Columbia University, New York, NY	1925
Connecticut, University of, Storrs, CT	1964
Cooper Union, New York, NY	1941
Cornell University, Ithaca, NY	1936
Dayton, University of, Dayton, OH	1969
Delaware, University of, Newark, DE	1941
Detroit Mercy, University of, Detroit, MI	1940 1949 1951

School	Year Accredited
Drexel University, Philadelphia, PA	1936 1947 1949
Florida A&M University/Florida State University, Tallahassee, FL	1987
Florida Institute of Technology, Melbourne, FL	1983
Florida, University of, Gainesville, FL	1942
Georgia Institute of Technology, Atlanta, GA	1938
Hampton University, Hampton, VA	1992
Houston, University of, Houston, TX	1957
Howard University, Washington, DC	1977
Idaho, University of, Moscow, ID	1950
Illinois, University of, Urbana, IL	1933
Illinois at Chicago, University of, Chicago, IL	1976
Illinois Institute of Technology, Chicago, IL	1925
Iowa, University of, Iowa City, IA	1926 1950 1953
Iowa State University, Ames, IA	1925
Johns Hopkins University, Baltimore, MD	1940 1968 1983
Kansas, University of, Lawrence, KS	1949
Kansas State University, Manhattan, KS	1951
Kentucky, University of, Lexington, KY	1969
Lafayette College, Easton, PA	1956
Lamar University, Beaumont, TX	1958
Lehigh University, Bethlehem, PA	1932 1951 1953
Louisiana State University, Baton Rouge, LA	1939
Louisiana Tech University, Ruston, LA	1956
Louisville, University of, Louisville, KY (5 year master's degree)	1935
Maine, University of, Orono, ME	1950
Manhattan College, Riverdale, NY	1964
Maryland, University of, College Park, MD & Baltimore County, MD (1987)	1942
Massachusetts, University of, Amherst, MA	1958
Massachusetts, University of, Lowell, MA	1971
Massachusetts Institute of Technology, Cambridge, MA	1925
Michigan, University of, Ann Arbor, MI	1925
Michigan State University, East Lansing, MI	1954
Michigan Technological University, Houghton, MI	1947
Minnesota, University of, Minneapolis, MN	1925
Minnesota, University of, Duluth, MN	1990
Mississippi, University of, University, MS	1954
Mississippi State University, Mississippi State, MS	1964

School	Year Accredited
Missouri, University of, Columbia, MO	1940
Missouri, University of, Rolla, MO	1951
Montana State University, Bozeman, MT	1948
Nebraska, University of, Lincoln, NE	1954
Nevada, University of, Reno, NV	1987
New Hampshire, University of, Durham, NH	1964
New Haven, University of, New Haven, CT	1995
New Jersey Institute of Technology, Newark, NJ	1950
New Mexico, University of, Albuquerque, NM	1976
New Mexico Institute of Mining and Technology, Socorro, NM	1999
New Mexico State University, Las Cruces, NM	1967
New York, City College of the City University of, New York, NY	1953
New York, State University of, Buffalo, NY	1966
North Carolina Agricultural & Technical State University, Greensboro, NC	1991
North Carolina State University, Raleigh, NC	1948
North Dakota, University of, Grand Forks, ND	1939 1942 1951
Northeastern University, Boston, MA	1942
Northwestern University, Evanston, IL	1947
Notre Dame, University of, Notre Dame, IN	1949
Ohio State University, Columbus, OH	1925
Ohio University, Athens, OH	1963
Oklahoma, University of, Norman, OK	1940
Oklahoma State University, Stillwater, OK	1950 1976 (master's program 1976 1986) 1983
Oregon State University, Corvallis, OR	1942
Pennsylvania, University of, Philadelphia, PA	1936
Pennsylvania State University, University Park, PA	1936
Pittsburgh, University of, Pittsburgh, PA	1931 1965, 1967
Polytechnic University, Brooklyn, NY	1925
Prairie View A&M University, Prairie View, TX	1994
Princeton University, Princeton, NJ	1934
Puerto Rico, University of, Mayaguez, PR (5 year program)	1970
Purdue University, West Lafayette, IN	1933
Rensselaer Polytechnic Institute, Troy, NY	1925
Rhode Island, University of, Kingston, RI	1954
Rice University, Houston, TX	1941
Rochester, University of, Rochester, NY	1941

School	Year Accredited
Rose Hulman Institute of Technology, Terre Haute, IN	1950
Rutgers The State University of New Jersey, New Brunswick, NJ	1971
San Jose State University, San Jose, CA	1966
South Alabama, University of, Mobile, AL	1985
South Carolina, University of, Columbia, SC	1956
South Dakota School of Mines and Technology, Rapid City, SD	1960
South Florida, University of, Tampa, FL	1976
Southern California, University of, Los Angeles, CA	1950 1952, 1960
Southwestern Louisiana, University of, Lafayette, LA	1956 1963, 1967
Stevens Institute of Technology, Hoboken, NJ	1986
Syracuse University, Syracuse, NY	1940
Tennessee, University of, Knoxville, TN	1939
Tennessee Technological University, Cookeville, TN	1970
Texas, University of, Austin, TX	1943
Texas A&M University, College Station, TX	1946
Texas A&M University Kingsville, Kingsville, TX	1978
Texas Tech University, Lubbock, TX	1965
Toledo, University of, Toledo, OH	1964
Tri State University, Angola, IN	1979 1989, 1990
Tufts University, Medford, MA	1952
Tulane University, New Orleans, LA	1954
Tulsa, University of, Tulsa, OK	1958
Tuskegee University, Tuskegee, AL	1984
Utah, University of, Salt Lake City, UT	1952
Vanderbilt University, Nashville, TN	1949
Villanova University, Villanova, PA	1951
Virginia Commonwealth University, Richmond, VA	2001
Virginia Polytechnic Institute and State University, Blacksburg, VA	1938
Virginia, University of, Charlottesville, VA	1943
Washington, University of, Seattle, WA	1926
Washington State University, Pullman, WA	1951
Washington University, St. Louis, MO	1948
Wayne State University, Detroit, MI	1950
West Virginia Institute of Technology, Montgomery, WV	1972
West Virginia University, Morgantown, WV	1948
Widener University, Chester, PA	1985
Wisconsin Madison, University of, Madison, WI	1925

School	Year Accredited
Worcester Polytechnic Institute, Worcester, MA	1942
Wyoming, University of, Laramie, WY	1974
Yale University, New Haven, CT	1982
Youngstown State University, Youngstown, OH	1974

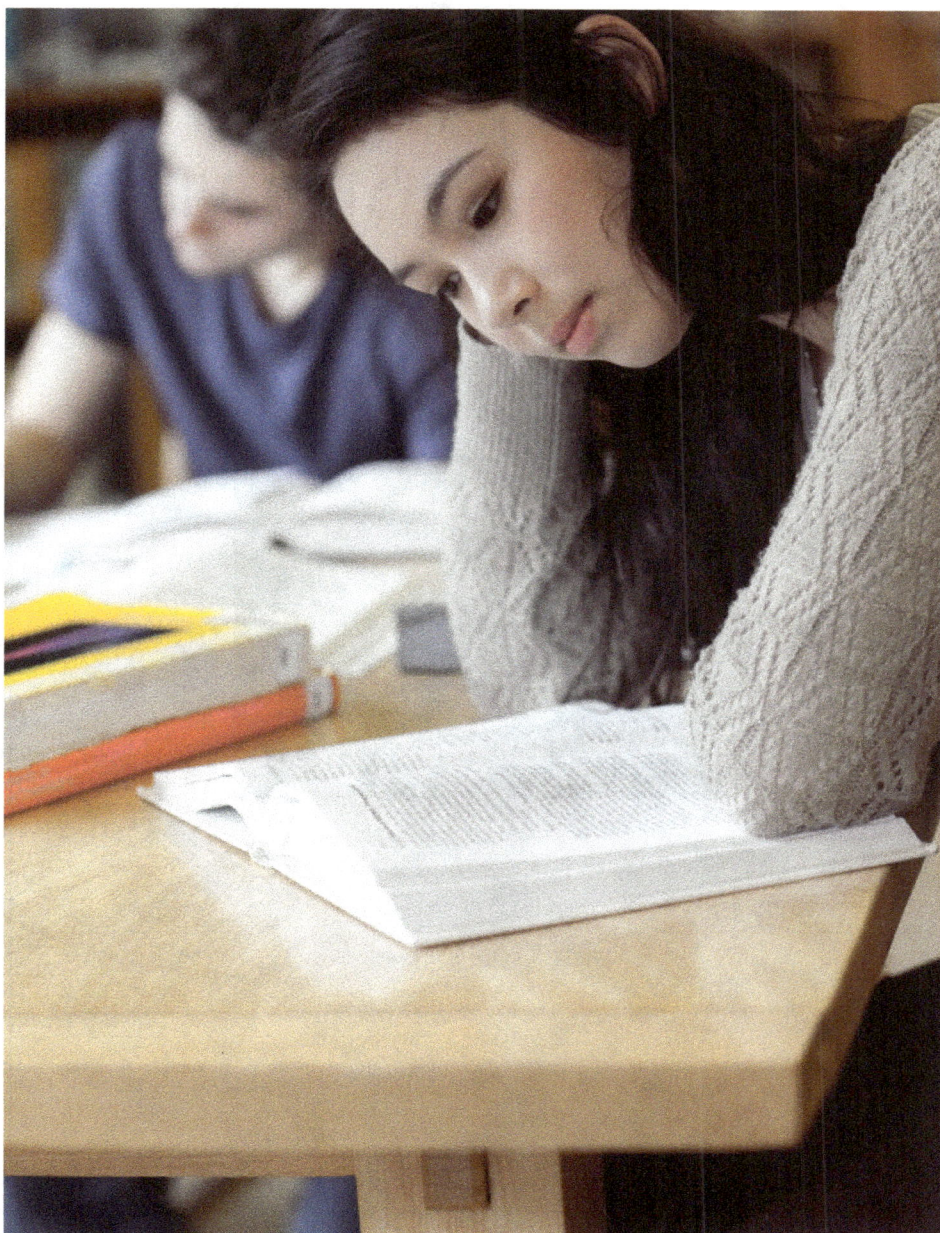

CHAPTER 22

COMBINED BA/MD, BS/MD PROGRAMS BY STATE

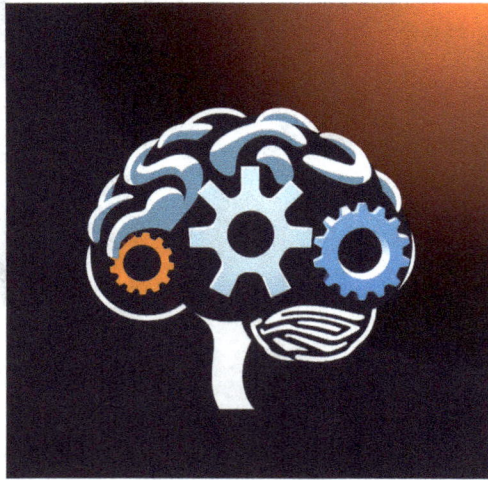

BA/MD, BS/MD PROGRAMS BY STATE

Note: Check for Program Revisions or Deletions

School
ALABAMA
University of Alabama at Birmingham School of Medicine
COLORADO
University of Colorado School of Medicine
CONNECTICUT
University of Connecticut School of Medicine
DISTRICT OF COLUMBIA
The George Washington University School of Medicine and Health Sciences
Howard University College of Medicine
FLORIDA
Florida Atlantic University College of Medicine
University of Central Florida College of Medicine
University of Florida College of Medicine
University of Miami School of Medicine
University of South Florida College of Medicine
GEORGIA
Augusta University - Medical College of Georgia
ILLINOIS
Northwestern School of Medicine (Discontinued)
University of Chicago School of Medicine
University of Illinois College of Medicine
LOUISIANA
Tulane University School of Medicine
MASSACHUSETTS
Boston University School of Medicine
MICHIGAN
Wayne State University School of Medicine
MINNESOTA
University of Minnesota Medical School

School
MISSOURI
Saint Louis University School of Medicine
University of Missouri - Kansas City School of Medicine
NEVADA
University of Nevada, Reno, School of Medicine (Suspended)
NEW JERSEY
Rowan University Cooper Medical School
Rutgers - New Jersey Medical School
Rutgers Medical School
NEW MEXICO
University of New Mexico School of Medicine
NEW YORK
Albany Medical College
CUNY School of Medicine
Hofstra/Northwell School of Medicine
Stony Brook University - Renaissance School of Medicine
SUNY Downstate Medical Center College of Medicine
SUNY Upstate Medical University College of Medicine
University of Rochester School of Medicine and Dentistry
OHIO
Case Western Reserve University School of Medicine
University of Toledo College of Medicine and Life Sciences
University of Cincinnati College of Medicine
PENNSYLVANIA
Drexel University College of Medicine
Temple University School of Medicine
Thomas Jefferson University Medical College
University of Pittsburgh School of Medicine
PUERTO RICO
Ponce Health Sciences University School of Medicine
RHODE ISLAND
Brown University Medical School

School
SOUTH CAROLINA
University of South Carolina School of Medicine - Columbia
TENNESSEE
Meharry Medical College
TEXAS
Baylor College of Medicine
Rice University (Discontinued)
VIRGINIA
Virginia Commonwealth University School of Medicine
WEST VIRGINIA
Marshall University School of Medicine

CHAPTER 23

COMBINED BA/MD, BS/MD PROGRAMS BY PROGRAM LENGTH

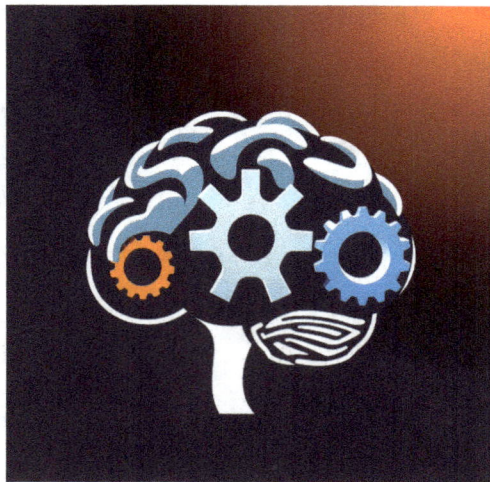

BA/MD, BS/MD PROGRAMS BY PROGRAM LENGTH

Note: Check for Program Revisions or Deletions

Length	School
6 YEARS	Howard University College of Medicine
	University of Missouri - Kansas City School of Medicine
7 YEARS	Albany Medical College
	Augusta University Medical College of Georgia
	Cooper Medical School of Rowan University
	CUNY School of Medicine
	Florida Atlantic University College of Medicine
	The George Washington University School of Medicine and Health Sciences
	Marshall University School of Medicine
	Meharry Medical College
	Northwestern University School of Medicine
	Ponce Health Sciences University School of Medicine
	Rowan University (See Cooper Medical School)
	Rutgers - New Jersey Medical School
	Rutgers - Johnson Medical School
	Temple University School of Medicine
	Thomas Jefferson University Medical College
	University of Chicago School of Medicine
	University of Florida College of Medicine
	University of Miami School of Medicine
	University of South Carolina School of Medicine - Columbia
	University of South Florida College of Medicine
8 YEARS	Albany Medical College
	Augusta University Medical College of Georgia
	Baylor College of Medicine
	Boston University School of Medicine
	Brown University Medical School
	Case Western Reserve University School of Medicine
	Drexel University College of Medicine
	Florida Atlantic University College of Medicine
	Hofstra/Northwell School of Medicine
	Rutgers - Medical School
	Saint Louis University School of Medicine
	SUNY Downstate Medical Center College of Medicine

School	Year Accredited
8 YEARS	SUNY Upstate Medical University College of Medicine
	Stony Brook University - Renaissance School of Medicine
	Temple University School of Medicine
	Tulane University School of Medicine
	University of Alabama at Birmingham School of Medicine
	University of Cincinnati College of Medicine
	University of Colorado School of Medicine
	University of Connecticut School of Medicine
	University of Illinois College of Medicine
	University of Miami School of Medicine
	University of Minnesota Medical School
	University of New Mexico School of Medicine
	University of Pittsburgh School of Medicine
	University of Rochester School of Medicine and Dentistry
	University of Toledo College of Medicine and Life Sciences
	Virginia Commonwealth University School of Medicine
	Wayne State University School of Medicine

CHAPTER 24

COMBINED BA/DO, BS/DO PROGRAMS BY STATE

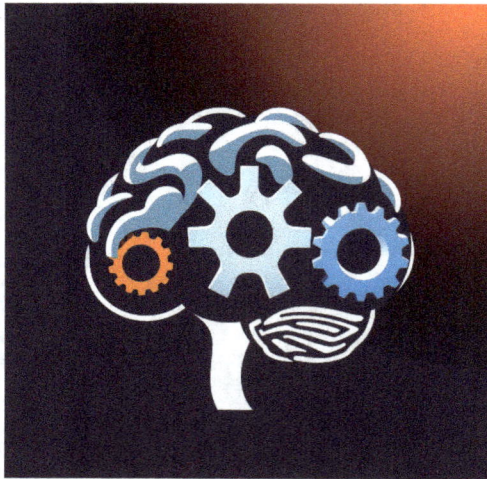

COMBINED BA/BS – DO PROGRAMS BY STATE

Note: Check for Program Revisions or Deletions

School
Arizona
A.T. Still University of Health Sciences Kirksville College of Osteopathic Medicine – 8-year program associated with the Massachusetts College of Pharmacy and Health Sciences
California
Western University of Health Sciences College of Osteopathic Medicine of the Pacific (Western U/COMP) – 8-year program with CSUs and 7-year program associated with Pitzer College
Florida
Nova Southeastern University Dr. Kiran C. Patel College of Osteopathic Medicine (NSU-KPCOM) – 7 or 8 year program
Illinois
Chicago College of Osteopathic Medicine of Midwestern University (CCOM) – 8-year program – 4+4 with Illinois Tech
Maine
University of New England College of Osteopathic Medicine (UNE-COM) – Associated with University of Hartford, Utica College, etc.
Michigan
Michigan State University College of Osteopathic Medicine (MSU-COM) – Associated with Michigan State University – 7- year program with Lyman Briggs College

School
Missouri
Kansas City University College of Osteopathic Medicine (KCUMB-COM) – 8-year program associated with Wayne State, Univ of Missouri, St. Louis, and Rockhurst University, etc.
New Jersey
Rowan University College of Osteopathic Medicine – 7-year program affiliated with Rutgers University – Camden – BS/MD or BS/DO
New York
New York Institute of Technology College of Osteopathic Medicine (NYIT-COM) – 8-year program associated with Adelphi University
Oklahoma
Oklahoma State University Center for Health Sciences College of Osteopathic Medicine, Tulsa – 7-year – undergrad at one of 7 OK colleges
Pennsylvania
Lake Erie College of Osteopathic Medicine (LECOM) – 7 – 8-year program associated with Seton Hill Univ, etc
Philadelphia College of Osteopathic Medicine (PCOM) – 8-year program associated with Adelphi University, Gannon University or the Univ of the Sciences in Philadelphia
Texas
Texas College of Osteopathic Medicine (TCOM) – Part of the Texas Joint Admissions Medical Program (JAMP)

CHAPTER 25

COMBINED BA/DO, BS/DO PROGRAMS BY PROGRAM LENGTH

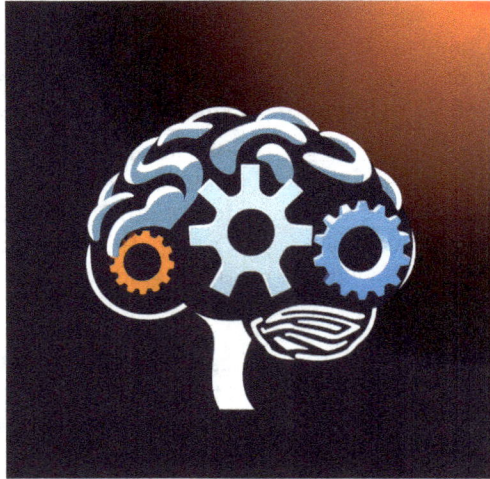

COMBINED BA/BS – DO PROGRAMS BY PROGRAM LENGTH

Note: Check for Program Revisions or Deletions

Length	School
7-Year	Lake Erie College of Osteopathic Medicine (LECOM)
	Michigan State University College of Osteopathic Medicine (MSU-COM)
	Nova Southeastern University Dr. Kiran C. Patel College of Osteopathic Medicine (NSU-KPCOM)
	Oklahoma State University Center for Health Sciences College of Osteopathic Medicine
	Rowan University College of Osteopathic Medicine
8-Year	A.T. Still University of Health Sciences Kirksville College of Osteopathic Medicine
	Chicago College of Osteopathic Medicine of Midwestern University (CCOM)
	Kansas City University College of Osteopathic Medicine (KCUMB-COM)
	Lake Erie College of Osteopathic Medicine (LECOM)
	New York Institute of Technology College of Osteopathic Medicine (NYIT-COM)
	Nova Southeastern University Dr. Kiran C. Patel College of Osteopathic Medicine (NSU-KPCOM)
	Philadelphia College of Osteopathic Medicine (PCOM)
	Texas College of Osteopathic Medicine (TCOM) 8 years
	University of New England College of Osteopathic Medicine (UNE-COM) 7 or 8 years
	Western University of Health Sciences College of Osteopathic Medicine of the Pacific (Western U/COMP) – 8 years

CHAPTER 26

COMBINED BA/BS – DDS/DMD PROGRAMS BY STATE

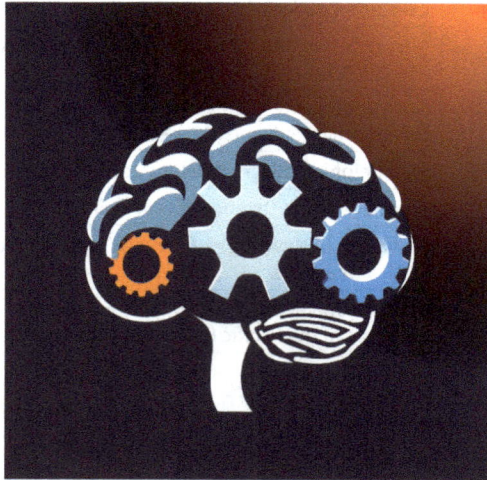

COMBINED BA/BS – DDS/DMD PROGRAMS BY STATE

Note: Check for Program Revisions or Deletions

School	School
California University of the Pacific Pre-Dental Advantage Program	**Missouri** University of Missouri Kansas City (UMKC) DDS Reserved Admission Program
Colorado University of Colorado Denver BA/BS-DDS Program (Colorado Residents Only)	**Nevada** University of Nevada BS-DMD Program (Nevada Residents Only)
Connecticut University of Connecticut Special Program in Dental Medicine	**New Jersey** Rutgers School of Dental Medicine (RSDM) Early Assurance Program (EAP)
District of Columbia Howard University BS/DDS Combined Education Program	**New York** New York University BS/DDS Program Stony Brook University Scholars for Dental Medicine (SFDM)
Florida Nova Southeastern Univ. Dual Admission Dental Medicine Program University of Florida Early Assurance Program	**Ohio** Case Western Reserve University Pre-Professional Scholars Program (PPSP)
Georgia Augusta U. BS-DMD Professional Scholars Program	**Pennsylvania** LECOM (Lake Erie College of Osteopathic Medicine) Early Acceptance Dental Medicine Program (EAP) Temple University 3+4 Accelerated BA + DMD University of Pennsylvania Bio-Dental Program University of Pittsburgh Dental Medicine Guaranteed Admission Program (GAP)
Kentucky University of Louisville Early Admission to Dentistry Program (ULEAD)	
Illinois Southern Illinois University Combined Arts & Sciences Dental Curriculum (BS-DMD Honors Program)	
Massachusetts Boston University – Modular Medical/Dental Integrated Curriculum (MMEDIC) – Early Assurance Pro-gram Tufts University Eight-Year Early Assurance	**Texas** University of Texas Dental Early Acceptance Program (DEAP - Texas Residents)
	Virginia Virginia Commonwealth University Guaranteed Admission Program for Dentistry
Michigan University of Detroit Mercy Seven-Year Dental Program	**Wisconsin** Marquette University Pre-Dental Scholars Program

CHAPTER 27

COMBINED BA/BS – DDS/DMD PROGRAMS BY PROGRAM LENGTH

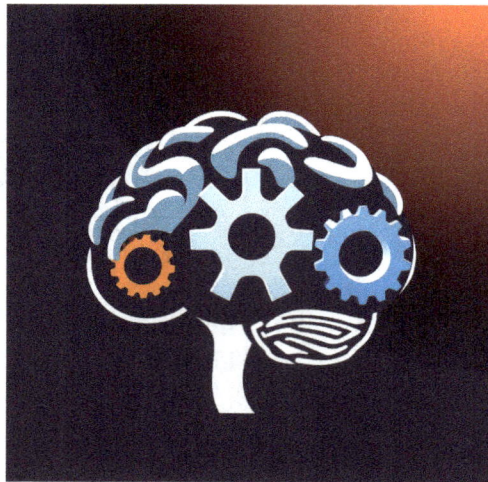

COMBINED BA/BS – DDS/DMD PROGRAMS BY STATE BY PROGRAM LENGTH

Note: Check for Program Revisions or Deletions

Length	School
5 Years	University of the Pacific Pre-Dental Advantage Program
6 Years	Howard University BS/DDS Combined Education Program
	University of the Pacific Pre-Dental Advantage Program
7 Years	Augusta U. BS-DMD Professional Scholars Program
	Case Western Reserve University Pre-Professional Scholars Program (PPSP)
	Marquette University Pre-Dental Scholars Program
	New York University BS/DDS Program
	Nova Southeastern Univ. Dual Admission Dental Medicine Program
	Southern Illinois University Combined Arts & Sciences Dental Curriculum (BS-DMD Honors Program)
	Temple University 3+4 Accelerated BA + DMD
	University of Detroit Mercy Seven-Year Dental Program
	University of Florida Early Assurance Program
	University of Nevada BS-DMD Program (Nevada Residents Only)
	University of the Pacific Pre-Dental Advantage Program
	University of Pennsylvania Bio-Dental Program
	University of Texas Dental Early Acceptance Program (DEAP - Texas Residents)
8 Years	Augusta U. BS-DMD Professional Scholars Program
	Boston University – Modular Medical/Dental Integrated Curriculum (MMEDIC) – Early Assurance Program
	LECOM (Lake Erie College of Osteopathic Medicine) Early Acceptance Dental Medicine Program (EAP)
	Nova Southeastern Univ. Dual Admission Dental Medicine Program
	Rutgers School of Dental Medicine (RSDM) Early Assurance Program (EAP)
	Stony Brook University Scholars for Dental Medicine (SFDM)
	Tufts University Eight-Year Early Assurance
	University of Colorado Denver BA/BS-DDS Program (Colorado Residents Only)
	University of Connecticut Special Program in Dental Medicine
	University of Louisville Early Admission to Dentistry Program (ULEAD)
8 Years	University of Missouri Kansas City (UMKC) DDS Reserved Admission Program
	University of Pittsburgh Dental Medicine Guaranteed Admission Program (GAP)
	Virginia Commonwealth University Guaranteed Admission Program for Dentistry

CHAPTER 28

ACT & SAT CONCORDANCE TABLE

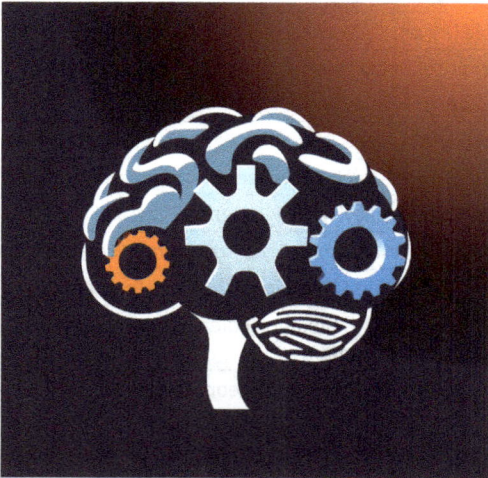

ACT	SAT	SAT Range
36	1590	1570–1600
35	1540	1530–1560
34	1500	1490–1520
33	1460	1450–1480
32	1430	1420–1440
31	1400	1390–1410
30	1370	1360–1380
29	1340	1330–1350
28	1310	1300–1320
27	1280	1260–1290
26	1240	1230–1250
25	1210	1200–1220
24	1180	1160–1190
23	1140	1130–1150
22	1110	1100–1120
21	1080	1060–1090
20	1040	1030–1050
19	1010	990–1020
18	970	960–980
17	930	920–950
16	890	880–910
15	850	830–870
14	800	780–820
13	760	730–770
12	710	690–720
11	670	650–680
10	630	620–640
9	590	590–610

https://www.act.org/content/dam/act/unsecured/documents/ACT-SAT-Concordance-Information.pdf

Live your dreams today remembering that discipline is the
bridge between dreams and achievement!

"We believe in the American Dream that all people rich or poor can
go as far in life as their talents and persistence will take them."
– Lizard Publishing Vision

At Lizard, we help you make your dreams come true.

CONTACT INFORMATION

Phone: 949-753-2888
E-mail: collegeguide@yahoo.com
Website: collegelizard.com and Lizard-publishing.com

YOU MAY PURCHASE AVAILABLE BOOKS ON THE FOLLOWING PAGES AT:

https://www.amazon.com/stores/author/B01N5II43V

Email: collegeguide@yahoo.com
Website: collegelizard.com

LIZARD

JOURNEY TO ART, DANCE, MUSIC, THEATRE, FILM, AND FASHION SERIES

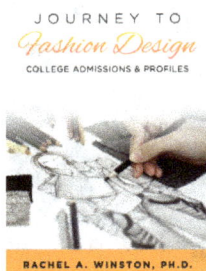

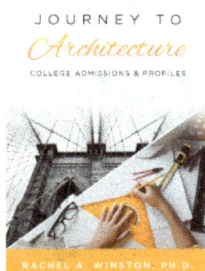

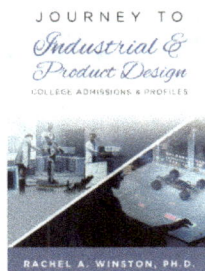

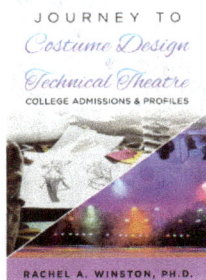

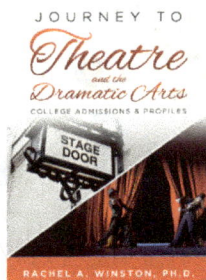

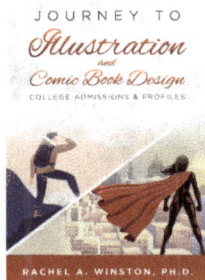

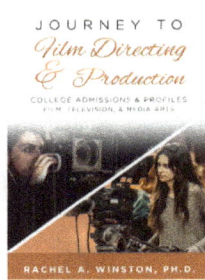

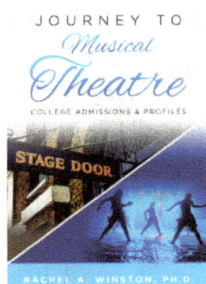

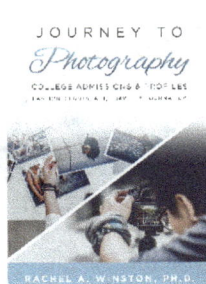

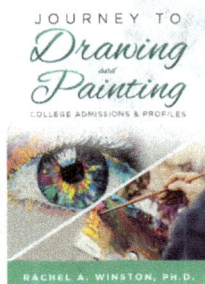

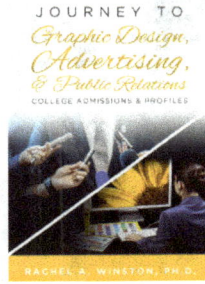

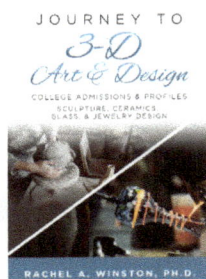

JOURNEY TO
Fashion Design
COLLEGE ADMISSIONS & PROFILES
RACHEL A. WINSTON, PH.D.

JOURNEY TO
Fashion Merchandising
COLLEGE ADMISSIONS & PROFILES
RACHEL A. WINSTON, PH.D.

JOURNEY TO
Architecture
COLLEGE ADMISSIONS & PROFILES
RACHEL A. WINSTON, PH.D.

JOURNEY TO
Industrial & Product Design
COLLEGE ADMISSIONS & PROFILES
RACHEL A. WINSTON, PH.D.

JOURNEY TO
Costume Design & Technical Theatre
COLLEGE ADMISSIONS & PROFILES
RACHEL A. WINSTON, PH.D.

JOURNEY TO
Theatre and the Dramatic Arts
COLLEGE ADMISSIONS & PROFILES
RACHEL A. WINSTON, PH.D.

JOURNEY TO
Illustration and Comic Book Design
COLLEGE ADMISSIONS & PROFILES
RACHEL A. WINSTON, PH.D.

JOURNEY TO
Film Directing & Production
COLLEGE ADMISSIONS & PROFILES
FILM, TELEVISION, & MEDIA ARTS
RACHEL A. WINSTON, PH.D.

JOURNEY TO
Musical Theatre
COLLEGE ADMISSIONS & PROFILES
RACHEL A. WINSTON, PH.D

JOURNEY TO
Photography
COLLEGE ADMISSIONS & PROFILES
RACHEL A. WINSTON, PH.D.

JOURNEY TO
Drawing and Painting
COLLEGE ADMISSIONS & PROFILES
RACHEL A. WINSTON, PH.D.

JOURNEY TO
Graphic Design, Advertising, & Public Relations
COLLEGE ADMISSIONS & PROFILES
RACHEL A. WINSTON, PH.D.

JOURNEY TO
3-D Art & Design
COLLEGE ADMISSIONS & PROFILES
SCULPTURE, CERAMICS
GLASS, & JEWELRY DESIGN
RACHEL A. WINSTON, PH.D.

COMPREHENSIVE HEALTH CARE SERIES

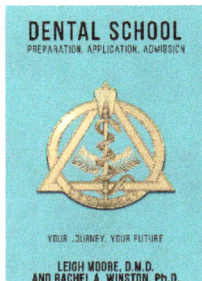

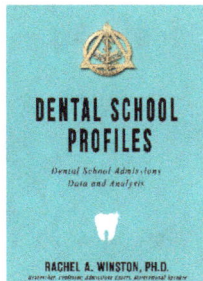

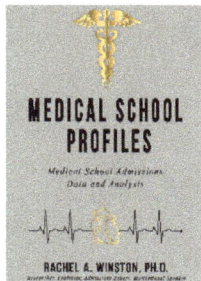

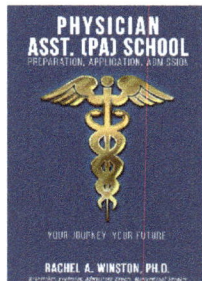

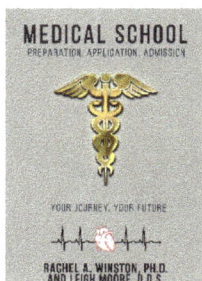

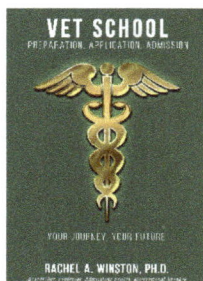

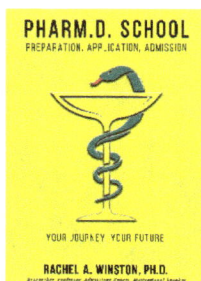

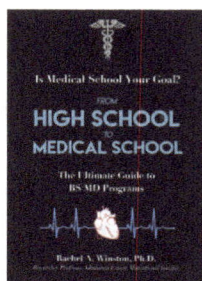

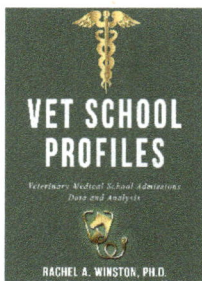

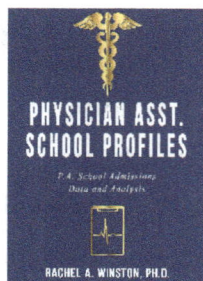

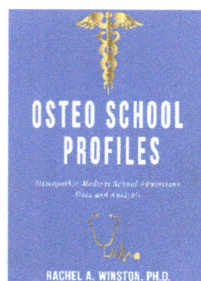

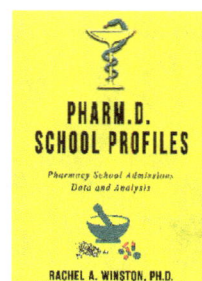

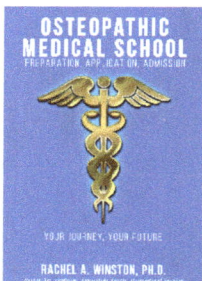

COMPREHENSIVE ENGINEERING SERIES

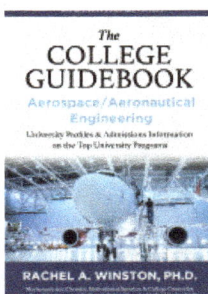

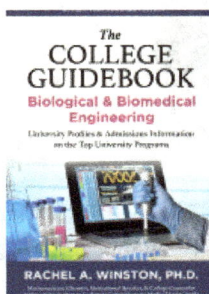

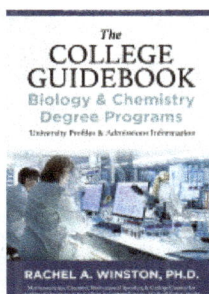

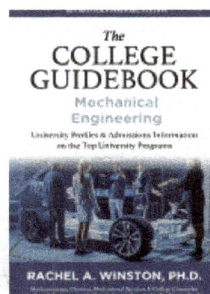

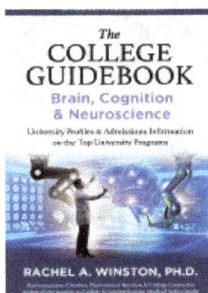

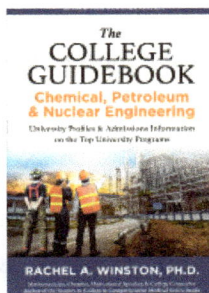

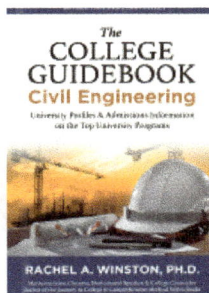

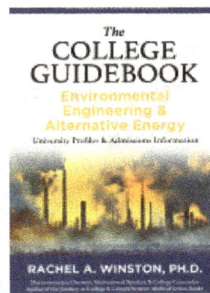

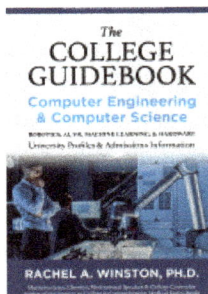

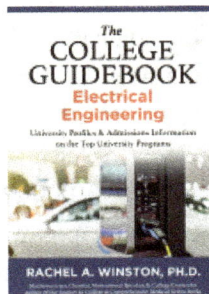

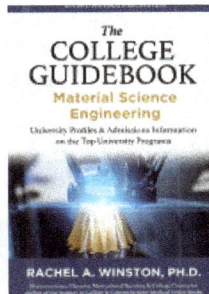

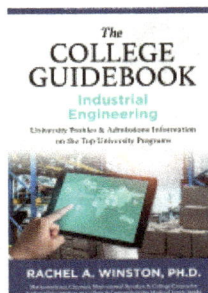

The
COLLEGE GUIDEBOOK
Aerospace/Aeronautical Engineering
University Profiles & Admissions Information on the Top University Programs

RACHEL A. WINSTON, PH.D.

The
COLLEGE GUIDEBOOK
Biological & Biomedical Engineering
University Profiles & Admissions Information on the Top University Programs

RACHEL A. WINSTON, PH.D.

The
COLLEGE GUIDEBOOK
Biology & Chemistry Degree Programs
University Profiles & Admissions Information

RACHEL A. WINSTON, PH.D.

The
COLLEGE GUIDEBOOK
Mechanical Engineering
University Profiles & Admissions Information on the Top University Programs

RACHEL A. WINSTON, PH.D.

The
COLLEGE GUIDEBOOK
Brain, Cognition & Neuroscience
University Profiles & Admissions Information on the Top University Programs

RACHEL A. WINSTON, PH.D.

The
COLLEGE GUIDEBOOK
Chemical, Petroleum & Nuclear Engineering
University Profiles & Admissions Information on the Top University Programs

RACHEL A. WINSTON, PH.D.

The
COLLEGE GUIDEBOOK
Civil Engineering
University Profiles & Admissions Information on the Top University Programs

RACHEL A. WINSTON, PH.D.

The
COLLEGE GUIDEBOOK
Environmental Engineering & Alternative Energy
University Profiles & Admissions Information

RACHEL A. WINSTON, PH.D.

The
COLLEGE GUIDEBOOK
Computer Engineering & Computer Science
ROBOTICS, AI, ML, MACHINE LEARNING, & HARDWARE
University Profiles & Admissions Information

RACHEL A. WINSTON, PH.D.

The
COLLEGE GUIDEBOOK
Electrical Engineering
University Profiles & Admissions Information on the Top University Programs

RACHEL A. WINSTON, PH.D.

The
COLLEGE GUIDEBOOK
Material Science Engineering
University Profiles & Admissions Information on the Top University Programs

RACHEL A. WINSTON, PH.D.

The
COLLEGE GUIDEBOOK
Information & Data Science
University Profiles & Admissions Information on the Top University Programs

RACHEL A. WINSTON, PH.D.

The
COLLEGE GUIDEBOOK
Industrial Engineering
University Profiles & Admissions Information on the Top University Programs

RACHEL A. WINSTON, PH.D.

INDEX

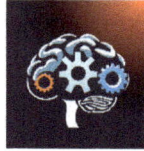

www.ingramcontent.com/pod-product-compliance
Lightning Source LLC
Chambersburg PA
CBHW051954270326
41929CB00015B/2651